INFO WE TRUST

INFO WE TRUST

How to Inspire the World with Data

written and illustrated by

R J A N D R E W S

WILEY

Names: Andrews, RJ, (Digital storyteller), author.
Title: Info we trust : how to inspire the world with data / written and illustrated by RJ Andrews.
Description: Hoboken, New Jersey : John Wiley & Sons, 2019. | Includes bibliographical references and index. |
Identifiers: LCCN 2018048217 (print) | LCCN 2018056994 (ebook)
| ISBN 978-1-119-48390-8 (ePub) | ISBN 978-1-119-48389-2 (hardcover) | ISBN 978-1-119-48391-5 (ePDF)
Subjects: LCSH: Information visualization. | Digital storytelling.
Classification: LCC QA76.9.I52 (ebook) | LCC QA76.9.I52 .A54 2019 (print) |
    DDC 001.4/226—dc23
LC record available at https://lccn.loc.gov/2018048217

V10006984_121818

For Kelly,
my North Star

Of course the first thing to do was to make a grand survey of the country she was going to travel through. 'It's something very like learning geography,' thought Alice, as she stood on tiptoe in hopes of being able to see a little further.

LEWIS CARROLL

THROUGH THE LOOKING-GLASS, AND WHAT ALICE FOUND THERE

ONWARD

SENSATIONAL

METAPHORICAL

MATHEMAGICAL

ORIGIN

CONTENTS

ANCIENT ROOTS

Dreu is an ancient word that means tree. It is sometimes written as *dóru* or *deru*. It is a word so old that we can no longer read it directly. We intuit its prehistoric existence by the long shadow it casts across language. Many more recent words share a similar sound and similar meaning. The Sanskrit word *dru* (tree or wood) is one example of an old descendant of dreu. Today, dreu's shadow persists in words like *druid* (tree seer) and *dryad* (wood nymph).

Over time, *dreu* evolved to embody the functional qualities of wood: solid, firm, strong. These qualities traveled with its sound into Europe, where it became the Ancient Greek *droón* (strong, mighty), Latin *durus* (hard, rough), and the Old Norse *trausta* (strong). The corresponding Old Norse *traust* conveyed a type of social strength: help, confidence, protection and assistant support. This social bond evolved into the Old High German word *trost* (fidelity), from which we can most clearly identify the modern word *trust*.

Trust is a firm belief in the strength or reliability of something or someone. It is a precious thing, not easily gained, and often in short supply. Trust conveys a confidence in the signals the world is delivering to you: They must be true, or at least in some sort of harmony with facts and reality. Trust is forever tied linguistically to *truth*, from the Old English *treowian* (to believe) and *treowe* (faithful). Both also stem from the ancient word *dreu*. They are almost indistinguishable from *treow*, the Old English word for tree.

The word *information* also has a social origin story. Today, information is defined as facts provided or learned. Information is what is represented and conveyed by a particular arrangement. The spirit of information lies in its transmission. The word stems from the Latin verb *informare:* to shape or fashion. Its roots combine for a dynamic picture: *in* (into), *forma* (a form), and *ation* (something resulting of an action). Information is putting things into a particular form. Information is action.

In an epic way, information and trust, knowledge and trees, have been associated for a long time. Trees provide us with shelter, protection, food, medicine, fire, energy, weapons, tools, and construction materials. Stretching against gravity, from beneath the earth to the heavens above, trees are powerful symbols of growth, decay, and resurrection. Across history, trees were revered around the world. Ancient Assyrians, Akkadians, and Egyptians all had sacred trees. Gautama Buddha's scene of enlightenment occurs under the holy Bodhi tree. Isaac Newton watched an apple fall in his mother's garden, and the secrets of gravity began to unfold. The Mayan tree of life provided an axis onto which the universe clings. The Norse *Yggdrasil* tree provides a similar skeleton that connects the underworld, middle earth, and heavens.

These revered trees are all expressions of the *axis mundi,* the cosmic world axis. It appears throughout world beliefs and philosophies as the pole at the center of the world. The axis mundi is visually suggested in nature by a tree, mountain, vine, column of smoke, stalk of grain, and sometimes the upright human form itself. The axis mundi is reflected in human design too. Picture a tower, ladder, flagpole, cross, steeple, minaret, totem pole, pillar, obelisk, rocket, or skyscraper. The axis mundi symbol may originate with our own evolutionary ancestors, who lived in trees. Back then, the tree was at the center of their world. Its trunk was the axis connecting the dangers of the forest floor to the energy of the sun.

The Bible's legendary tree is the Garden of Eden's tree of knowledge. The wisdom it gave forecasts our own human mortality.

The Garden teaches that the world of our personal experience is not the limit to what is possible. We are all able to imagine a better world. We have the agency to help step toward our visions during the short time we get to be here. We are motivated to transcend our own day-to-day historic condition through the search for better worlds and more eternal truths. Mircea Eliade described this ambition of humanity as a *nostalgia for paradise*. It is the deep desire to become more authentic and more complete through better knowing the heart of reality.

Conveying information we trust is what this book is all about. It seeks dynamic action that puts things into forms for us that are strong and true. Pre-data archetypal images of trees, strength, social bonds, and *hope for what might be* are some of the visions that guided me through this book's construction. I believe that if we work hard to understand, together we can realize a better world. We need one another, because individually we do not know very much. I am excited to share with you what I have learned, so far.

THE GOAL OF OUR CRAFT

This art takes as given that sight is there, but not rightly turned nor looking at what it ought to look at...

THE ALLEGORY OF THE CAVE

PLATO'S REPUBLIC, c. 380 BC

Once upon a time, the tree was our home. Snakes and big cats were our enemies. Detecting one would send us into high alert.

I once got to witness this kind of predator-induced chaos, standing on the muddy banks of the Mara River in Kenya. Across the water, a distant herd of wildebeests approached. Perhaps they will attempt a river crossing? Then, we spotted the back of a juvenile lion in the grass, halfway between us and the herd. The cat was on the hunt, moving toward the wildebeests. We could see the lion's trap, but we were not the only ones watching.

Suddenly, a shriek rang out across the savanna. A treetop baboon had spotted the lion too. Baboons hate lions. They keep watch and alert their troop with a distinctive howl that warns: *Beware! Lions!* The wildebeests heard the baboon's message. They stopped, abandoned the crossing, and retreated back up the ridge.

Safaris introduced me to a dizzying diversity of life. Some of the animal names—kudu, duiker, colobus—were as unfamiliar as the names of the national parks—Elgon, Nakuru, Baringo. How many species are there? Where did they live? Which ones are common? Which ones are endangered? How did they all relate? I was adrift. A question that launches a search reminds me of a scientist who wishes to test a hypothesis. Something fantastic might result from our hunch, if only we had the data that could help us see.

I dove into learning about African wildlife, beginning with a dusty field guide. It introduced me to the nuances of taxonomy and threatened species status. Then, I discovered an international organization that studies and works to conserve biodiversity. I paired its data on hundreds of large African mammals with maps and illustrations to show myself, and eventually the world, a new view. A portion of this interactive project, titled *Endangered Safari*, is drawn below. It helped orient me to the wildlife I encountered.

CRITICAL or
ENDANGERED
VULNERABLE

Facing shows
population size:
→ STABLE
← DECLINE

Other kinds of data adventures have more exploratory origins.

I first heard about author Mason Currey listening to the radio driving down a North Carolina highway. He was promoting his 2013 book, *Daily Rituals*. It chronicles how 161 painters, scientists, and other creative people spent their productive days. Before the radio segment was over, I already knew I wanted to map its contents. There was no motivating question or expectation. There was only eagerness to see what was going on inside the world that Currey had assembled. That was excitement enough.

It took only a few days to get Currey's book, catalog different types of activities, and arrange sixteen of its rituals into 24-hour cycles. A poster, called *Creative Routines*, soon materialized. Mozart's routine from 1781 is adapted above. Immersing yourself in a new world to get a sense of it all, reminds me of ethnography. Its field-work embeds ethnographers within a culture. There, they record observations for later synthesis and interpretation. You can see the originals of both projects, safari and routines, at InfoWeTrust.com. Sometimes a question leads us to data. Sometimes data makes us question. These are only two of the many ways ideas take shape.

We will soon submerge into the practical mechanics of how it all works. Writing this book gave me the opportunity to develop new data stories, which I am excited to share with you. But first, I want to equip you with a mythic perspective that empowers the creative. I will also attempt to answer some questions you might have. For example, what is "info we trust?"

Data Stories

Conveying information we trust is a dynamic activity that puts our world into forms that are strong and true. Absolute truth is a tricky thing. At our outset, we are most concerned with truth's pursuit, as an arrow shot straight toward its target is an arrow shot *true*. As a creator, I consider the making of information to be a craft. It is a rational and optimistic way to grow our knowledge and elevate our ability to take action.

Our craft is often referred to by its artifacts: charts, maps, diagrams, and so on. The lively exchanges these items produce is what makes them meaningful. We see the map, *a noun*, but *the verb* of seeing is what matters most. Meaning is attained while making and perceiving. Without our action, the map is stale. It has no life.

Meaningful information is often made with data. Data is like water. With effort, both data and water are captured from the environment, pooled in reservoirs, and delivered to where they are needed. The same water could irrigate a farm, spout from a palace fountain, or mix concrete for a new building. Likewise, we use data to revive, entertain, and build. Data may be a frozen snapshot, like an Antarctic ice core sample, but it may also be a dynamic stream, always rushing past.

Early peoples had a serious regard for large bodies of water, and for good reason. The sea's depths were impenetrable and storms arrive from the sea; to venture out to sea is daring. Many storied sea monsters turned out to be real. An entire class of ancient creation myths told that the universe emerged from a watery chaos that was dark, formless, and void-like.

Today, this watery vision reminds me of the cosmic soup that appeared immediately after our universe's Big Bang. Mysterious, and sometimes foreboding, water is also the symbol of hope and rebirth. From chaos springs creation and life. The chaos of the cosmos, water, and data are each formless and full of potential. The power of water anchors our conception of data as a wellspring of creation that deserves respect. We thirst for water, but too much drowns.

The world of myth is threatened from the deep. The epic poem of Beowulf faces the title hero with *writhing sea-dragons, wolfish swimmers,* and a *bewildering horde of sea-beasts* found at *the heaving depths.* Undeterred, Beowulf confronts the threat. *Beowulf got ready, donned his war-gear, indifferent to death; his mighty, hand-forged, fine-webbed mail would soon meet with the menace underwater.*

The watery dragons of chaos represent all that threatens to overwhelm us. We do not know the real world. How could we? Our capacity to understand is minuscule compared to the vast complexity of reality. Despite our limited capabilities, we do not drown. We have thrived. Our perceptions and explanations of what is going on carry us through the chaos that is really out there. Across our journey through reality, we must depend on one another. We cannot each grasp it all, so we trust in the knowledge of others. We sense that this knowledge, our ability to help one another navigate, can always be improved.

The hero is the one who confronts the unknown, learns how to better navigate the chaos of reality, and shares the lesson with all. Imagine a monster invades your community. If you are strong and clever, you confront the brute, win the encounter, and deliver everyone out of danger. If you are lucky, you learn how to navigate that kind of threat. By facing the unknown, you gain some knowledge that will be useful in future encounters, and share the lesson. Everyone learns and advances by virtue of your heroic action.

This book's blue margins are packed with quotes, explanations, and diagrams. Dance between the black and blue text across your first read, or just focus on the central narrative and save the marginalia for later.

The monsters of the abyss reappear in a number of traditions: the Heroes, the Initiates, go down into the depths of the abyss to confront marine monsters; this is a typical ordeal of initiation. Variants indeed abound: sometimes a dragon mounts guard over a "treasure"—a sensible image of the sacred, of absolute reality.
MIRCEA ELIADE, 1952

Our willingness to distinguish good and evil may be one of our most enhancing attributes, it is important to realize "good" and "bad" are categories we impose on the world—they are not of the world itself.
ZANDER AND ZANDER, 2000

The heroes who dive into chaos to grapple with reality can gain great rewards. The mythical dragon is often portrayed as guarding gold or pearls. In mythology, the individual hero wins the treasure, is celebrated by the people, then parents future generations. Rescuing fair maidens is a dated trope, but we can still get the message: Across our evolution, those who figured out how to better manage reality are the ones who thrived. More importantly, the real treasure is not what is lavished upon the triumphant hero. The boon is the learning that the hero delivered to people. True heroes expand our collective body of knowledge.

Dark and mysterious, but full of potential, data is the primordial soup of our age. It is the pool we must dive into, just as Beowulf dove underwater. Ancient heroes benefited from having brute strength and clever wits. Today, we have even more abilities to encounter and wrangle new understanding from chaos. But, like old mythology, for our gains to have meaning, they must be shared.

There is a superficial contradiction between the archetypal images of *data* and *story*. Data evokes cinematic binary code falling down a computer screen. Story kindles memories of wisdom shared around the campfire. Story is easily understood as entertaining anecdotes. The word evokes predictable narrative arcs, the kind used in serial fiction to attract and hold attention. The same clichéd story is the sugar that makes lessons palatable. At its worst, the word puts objective rationalists on alert. We know story can be used to manipulate emotions and deceive. This conception of story is not incorrect, but it is incomplete. Story has a lot more to teach us about conveying information than mere conflict, climax, and resolution. We call narrative discourse "story," but it is really only an input to the real story playing inside our heads. Our experience of time, and our ability to identify what

matters, are two extraordinary aspects of our lived experience. On a timescale too short for us to discern, we perceive the world in sequence, and infuse it with significance. Story is how we make sense of these stimuli to our self: We perceive the world in the ordered moments that our senses detect and we assign meaning as we go. A coherent personal reality emerges and we act in relation to this inner monologue. Story is our believed truth. Without this reality-generating story, we would drown in the chaos of sensory overload.

On a timescale too large for us to survive, story is also how we transmit knowledge and know-how across generations. *Before I am gone, here is what you need to know.* We exist somewhere between these meaningful moments and long arcs across millennia.

The hero's journey, to adventure and back again, is one fitting metaphor for our encounters with data. Each time you wade into a dataset, make some sense of it, and relay that information to the world, it is like a micro-dose of the hero's journey. You choose to confront the chaos of the unknown in hopes of delivering some order to society. The thrill of the adventure is always possible. Yet, the allure of the reward does not supersede the journey. We do not seek absolute order. The finitude of authoritarianism denies the richness of chance, diversity, and the ephemeral nature of being. Instead of arriving at some final order, we seek to straddle chaos and order to become conduits of meaning. In 1961's *The Impact of Science on Myth*, comparative mythologist Joseph Campbell described bringing scientific order to the world as a never-ending journey:

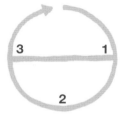

> *And is there no implied intention, then to rest satisfied with some final body or sufficient number of facts? No indeed! There is to be only a continuing search for more—as of a mind eager to grow. And that growth, as long as it lasts, will be the measure of the life of modern Western man, and of the world with all its promise that he has brought and is still bringing into being: which is to say, a world of change, new thoughts, new things, new magnitudes, and continuing transformation, not of petrification, rigidity, and some canonized found "truth."*

Explanations establish islands, even continents, of order and predictability. But these regions were first charted by adventurers whose lives are narratives of exploration and risk. They found them only by mythic journeys into the wayless open. … Knowledge is what successful explanation has led to; the thinking that sent us forth, however, is pure story.
JAMES P. CARSE, 1986

1 Separation: a hero ventures forth from the world of common day into a region of supernatural wonder. 2 Initiation: fabulous forces are there encountered and a decisive victory is won. 3 Return: the hero comes back from this mysterious adventure with the power to bestow boons on his fellow man.
JOSEPH CAMPBELL, 1949

All utopias are depressing because they leave no room for chance, for difference, for the "miscellaneous." Everything has been set in order and order reigns. Behind every utopia there is always some great taxonomic design: a place for each thing and each thing in its place.
GEORGES PEREC, 1982

Before we get too lost in the abstracts of adventure, I want to show you one of my favorite data stories. It is an incredible example of how a single image can arrange a complex topic into meaningful order. Take a moment to study the evolution of European armor shown on this page. See it through your own eyes, then we can examine how it works.

The illustrations let us know at a glance that the topic we are dealing with is the age of knights. The dots that link the helmets suggest some logical relationship between them. Further inspection

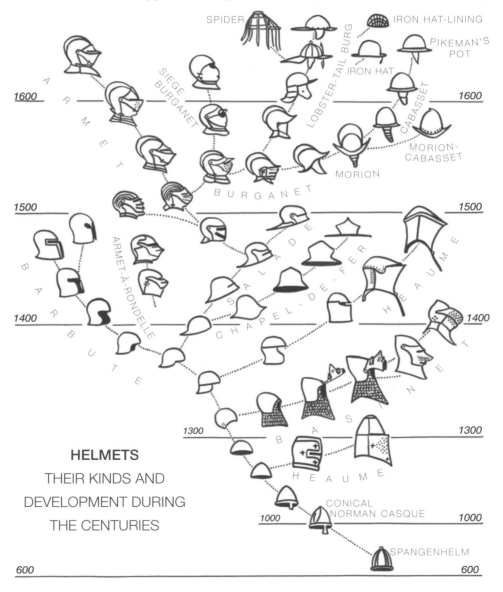

HELMETS

THEIR KINDS AND

DEVELOPMENT DURING

THE CENTURIES

reveals that connected helmets look similar to one another. The graphic's branched structure looks like a biological evolutionary tree, reminding us that technology morphs over time too.

This illustration is based on a hundred-year-old graphic by Bashford Dean, curator of The Metropolitan Museum of Art's arms and armor collection. I believe it is an elegant and effective composition because it has engaging depictions, a strong conceptual map, and enough marks (the helmets) to encourage confidence with the information. A tree with only eight helmets, each represented simply with a labeled circle, would not resonate with the same kind of power.

Bashford Dean (1867–1928) was also a professor of vertebrate zoology at Columbia University and the first curator of fishes in the Department of Vertebrate Paleontology.

The helmets open a door to the history of armor, a field I never gave much thought to before seeing this graphic. Now, I wonder if the helmets changed because of new weapons, advances in metalworking, or changing fashion. How did helmets outside of Europe influence this evolution? Did variation result from countless warriors customizing their own gear, or the designs of a few centralized armorers? How did helmets continue to evolve toward those used by today's soldiers, builders, and athletes? Plenty of keywords afford opportunities to search and learn more.

I can barely fathom the knowledge, creativity, and skill it took to produce this work. To complete data-driven hero cycles you must straddle fields that are far apart. You will need to study hard and soft sciences and the visual and communication arts. Any of these alone may not be enough to seize and deliver the treasure. History is littered with facts and figures that failed to convey understanding.

Many expressions have been used over time to label the craft that this book is about, often with a selection from the following words: analysis, communication, data, design, discovery, facts, graphics, information, numbers, pictures, presentation, quantitative, storytelling, visualization.

The interdisciplinary nature of data storytelling is quantitative and poetic, machine and human. It is a character profile that reminds me of the scientific explorers of the 1800s. Aspiring to the image of polymath Alexander von Humboldt or medical pioneer Florence Nightingale makes data storytelling seductive. A certain zeal comes with knowing that so many of humanity's tools are at your fingertips. It is your role to determine how to wield them in concert.

Each field has its own concept of graphic methods and standards of presentation and its own identifying codes, nomenclatures, or symbols.
MARY ELEANOR SPEAR, 1969

All this excitement also reveals why the craft is as formidable as it is enticing. Becoming functional in an assortment of disciplines is hard. Data processing is hard. Scientific discovery is hard. Awakening others to new realities is hard. The battle against the chaos of data is complex. And that is the magic of it all. When you venture into the craft of data storytelling, you are doing so with the knowledge that you cannot be an expert in all the skills it demands. Proceeding despite these deficiencies takes some real heart.

Courage is the ability to do something that frightens one, literally "with heart" from Latin word for heart, *cor*.

You may call the craft something else. Perhaps you prefer data visualization, data journalism, dashboard design, or infographic creation. The craft waves many banners across various communities. What matters is that you are courageously confronting the chaos of it all to improve how people see the world. That is the goal.

Our Plan of Adventure

This book is not an anthology of past projects nor is it a singular "big insight" book. It is not a history book, textbook, or handbook—although aspects of these genres play their roles. So, what kind of book are you holding?

Info We Trust is a multi-sensory voyage through the craft of data storytelling. It is organized by a philosophy of information. This understanding connects fundamentals of experience to the great saga of civilization. We will begin with numbers. Then, step-by-step, stretch all the way to creating new knowledge. One consequence of this elemental approach is that the character of the first chapters is relatively stark. They focus on the bare-bones contrast between data and information. Do not despair at the initial abundance of antiquity. We are merely setting the table for the feast that follows. Read the book straight through to appreciate the narrative of the data storyteller as a hero of the information age.

The illustrations, text, and marginalia provide multiple narratives for you to venture through.

All marginalia quotes are italicized. See the end notes for a thorough review of all referenced work.

There is an outline of how this was all composed at the back of the book for those interested in the journey that brought it into the world.

This book is empowering. It is rich with practical details that you can use to construct new ways of seeing the world. When you flip through, on your first glance or later on, this is the knowledge that jumps out. Individual chapters and many page spreads can stand on their own as helpful references. Information consumers, information operators, and veteran data storytellers will all discover new ways to bring meaning into our lives. I hope to embolden you to take action and do great things with data.

This book elevates enduring principles of information design. It grew over the last decade of my work as a data storyteller and my study as devoted disciple of the craft. The book's implicit dialog is between hundreds of years' worth of visual information pioneers and me, drawing on my own experience producing many data projects. The point of this intersection is not to chronicle history or peer at dusty charts. The aim is to elevate timeless principles for creating new ways of looking at the world. Many lessons learned while informing past generations still rule. Today, these enduring principles can guide us in an age where information is so unconstrained that it can be overwhelming.

Without spoiling any of the surprises, I would like you to know that we are going to travel to some marvelous places together. If you would like to read additional chapter-by-chapter signposting, I encourage you to return to the table of contents, which maps the sequential journey ahead. By the book's end, I hope you join me in pursuit of wonderful ways of looking at the world.

We can all be heroes who embrace the chaos and potential of data for the greater benefit. It is now time for us to step forward together. As J.R.R. Tolkien's grey wizard beckoned, standing at the threshold: *I am looking for someone to share in an adventure.*

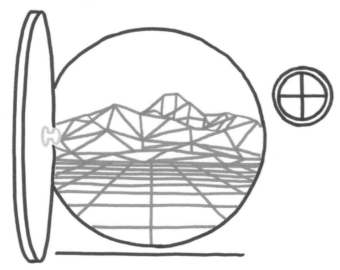

1

DATA SHADOWS

Matter and all else that is in the physical world have been reduced to a shadowy symbolism. ... The scientific answer is relevant so far as concerns the sense-impressions interlocked with the stirring of the spirit, which indeed form an important part of the mental content. For the rest the human spirit must turn to the unseen world to which it itself belongs.

ARTHUR EDDINGTON, 1929

On the evening of October 24, 1962, James Brown and the Famous Flames performed at the Apollo Theater in Harlem. It was a brief show by the standards of today's arena extravaganzas. They performed a dozen songs. None of them were new.

The concert recording was initially shelved. But, pressed by Brown's manager, King Records yielded and produced the album. *Live at the Apollo* was released the following year. It did incredible business. The album stayed on the Billboard *Top Pop Albums* chart for over a year, helping launch James Brown to R&B superstardom. Listen to that album today; his voice, the band's syncopated kicks, and the screams of the crowd still thrust you into the energy of that Harlem night. The context that swirls around *Live at the Apollo* elevates it to legend. It is a time capsule of pure American rhythm and blues, bottled 15 months before Beatlemania landed and swept the United States. Today, we now know how music, and James Brown, soared throughout the 1960s. That knowledge makes this early influential show at the Apollo even more special.

The value of a fact shrinks enormously without context.
HOWARD WAINER, 1997

How do we think about the albums we love? A lonely microphone in a smoky recording studio? A needle's press into hot wax? A rotating can of magnetic tape? A button that clicks before the first note drops? No! The mechanical ephemera of music's recording, storage, and playback may cue nostalgia, but they are not where the magic lies. The magic is in the music. The magic is in the information that the apparatuses capture, preserve, and make accessible. It is the same with all information. When you envision data, do not get stuck in encoding and storage. Instead, try to see the music.

A Curious World

When we create a statistical chart, we intuit that there is something magical about arranging data into forms that can be seen. But this notion is incomplete. It misses that data originates in the physical world. A song recording did not materialize from the ether. The song was once sung by a real person, in a real room. Likewise, our craft does not just make the invisible, seen. It makes a past reality real again.

Better data stories result when we recognize the material origins of data. Better data stories result when we appreciate how our mind interacts with the physical environment. When we acknowledge the life that produced data—the real life we see and feel—then we can better comprehend the abstract ecosystems of mathematics, statistics, and data.

Our perspective is anchored to our body and the things it encounters. Early words named objects in the physical world. As we took more notice of how physical things change over time, our language and our consciousness grew. Actions—relationships between people, objects, and environment—were named, too. Human perspective stretched outward to describe invisible social, political, and economic systems. Human perspective stretched inward to account for how these processes make us feel. Together, our experiences of physical and invisible phenomena evolved. Personal mental maps of reality and identity emerged.

Our curiosity drives us to achieve better maps of the world because they give us a competitive advantage against nature and against one another. They expand our knowledge into new domains, those of ourselves as individuals and those of our collective society. In some instances, this drive is a motivated search for answers. In others, clarity emerges organically from the chaotic environment. Curiosity sharpens the resolution of our understanding.

Each one of us arrives to data stories with a slightly different map of reality. Nerdy expertise—the kind drilled into scientists, engineers, and designers—has serendipitously prepared some for the technical challenges of the information age. These disciplines gift valuable perspectives and skills. They are uncommon perspectives if one considers the rest of the population: Only six percent of United States workers are in science, technology, engineering, or mathematics occupations. The rare technical orientation of the nerd should not be confused with the attitude of the craft. Data storytelling does not arrive from peripheral obscurity. It is born out of the common everyday experiences that we all share. Data storytelling belongs to everyone.

...the truth is nothing other than the shadows of artificial things ... Take a man who is released and suddenly compelled to stand up, to turn his neck around, to walk and look up toward the light; and who, moreover, in doing all this is in pain and, because he is dazzled, is unable to make out those things whose shadows he saw before. What do you supposed he'd say if someone were to tell him that before he saw silly nothings, while, now because he is somewhat nearer to what is and more turned toward beings, he sees more correctly...
SOCRATES TO GLAUCON, THE REPUBLIC OF PLATO

Numbered

Unary is the base-1 numeral system. The numbers 1, 2, 3, 4 are represented as: 1, 11, 111, 1111

The word for 20, a *score*, evolved from the Old Norse *skor*, meaning "to cut"— or how one might scar tally marks into a counting stick. Counting in scores, perhaps more meaningful when shoes were less common, was already archaic by the time Lincoln alluded to 1776 by beginning his 1863 Gettysburg Address *fourscore and seven years ago*. We still tally game scores on scoreboards.

The Ishango bone is a scarred baboon femur thought to be a 20,000-year-old tally stick.

We each get 10 fingers, 10 digits. Because our minds are easily distracted, we use our digits to keep track when we count. Our fingers are a versatile tool for small quantities. They help serve as an easy visual reference for what the count is. But too soon we run out of fingers (and toes) and need to externalize the count beyond our bodies. Externalizing the count also keeps hands available for other tasks. We can scratch quick marks in the dirt to help us keep track of our counting, and just like that, the history of numerals began.

The first tally marks were scrawled in dirt with a stick or drawn on rock with a piece of charcoal. It soon became useful to preserve these marks for record-keeping and communication. Ancient knotted counting ropes and slashed animal bones survive as examples of preserved counts. In the beginning, every item of the count was represented by a mark. Six is //////. These marks persist in East Asian numeral systems as the first three counting numbers: 一, 二, 三. These slash-characters are also identical to the same first three numerals in the Brahmi numeral system, the direct graphic ancestor of the modern Hindu-Arabic numerals the world uses today: 1, 2, 3. To us, these familiar numerals are abstract symbols. Today, numerals are squiggly cultural conventions no longer connected to our physical surroundings. But a long time ago, *they were*.

Tallying numbers becomes cumbersome as one counts higher. Large numbers, often multiples of 10, were abstracted with a new idea: sign values to represent a particular group. These symbols cemented our 10-fingered bodies as the base of the number system. If the number ten is † and hundred is ‡, then 114 can be recorded as ‡†////. Sign-value notation was the basis of Ancient Egyptian and Roman numeral systems. These systems yielded to a variety of additive systems which give special names to the first 10 digits (...*four, five, six...*) and important multiples of 10 (*ten, hundred, thousand*). These special names are still how we pronounce numbers in both Chinese and English today: *two hundred (and) four.*

Counting numbers struggled to account for expenses that take away more than available (i.e., debts). Another problem was that they could not clearly represent the concept of nothing. Over a thousand years, negative numbers and zero were added to address these issues. Solutions were first formalized in India, synthesized with Greek mathematics in Persia, and then slingshot through North Africa and into Europe by Leonardo fillius Bonacci (nicknamed *Fibonacci* hundreds of years later). The dominant mental picture of numbers shifted from a count of things to the more abstract number line. The positional notation of the Hindu-Arabic numerals made adding and subtracting easier. These new counting methods powered bank accounting innovations across Europe. Decimal fractions and ever-more abstract concepts, like imaginary numbers, would soon help power the scientific revolution and deliver us into the modern world.

The emergence of numbers shows how the visual memory practice of counting became hyper-externalized and abstracted to even greater benefit. As numbers evolved, they drifted away from physical reality. Today's everyday experience of numbers is surreal.

TALLY MARKS

EARLY BRAHMI

LATER BRAHMI

HINDU-ARABIC

5, 6, 7, 8, 9
At one time, there was speculation that figures past 4 had come from either the forms of initial letters or syllables of number words of the third century BC Brahmi alphabet. But they may have come from older, untraceable numerical symbols.
JOSEPH MAZUR, 2014

A symbol is a visual shape used as a conventional representation, or proxy, of an object or idea.

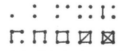

John Tukey advanced a compact base-10 tally system that built a box of dots and dashes with each additional count.

It requires you to leave your physicality behind and mentally step into an abstract world. But this has not always been so. All of mathematics began with simple vignettes, such as prehistoric shepherds looking across their flocks, counting sheep. It is all rooted in our lived experience.

Value types define how data is stored and impact the ways we turn numbers into information. Computer code often demands that certain aspects of value types be declared. Numbers and text can be quickly processed inside the computer's abstract world when they are labeled appropriately. Yet, we must appreciate even more than the computer if we are to build information. Observe the many value types expressed in this statement:

> The roar of the crowd swells as Joe Louis, the 198-¾-pound heavyweight, enters the arena for the final fight of the night, hopeful to exit the ring as the champion.

A *Boolean* will record the win-loss outcome. Zero is false. A nonzero, usually one, is true. The heavyweight *category* is stored as a *string* of text. This particular category is *ordinal* because it can be positioned in order. There is a non-arbitrary relationship between weight classes: Heavyweight is heavier than middleweight, which itself is heavier than lightweight. The fighter's name, Louis, is also stored as a *qualitative* string of text. But it is considered just *nominal*, as there is no meaningful way of ordering fighter names.

An *integer*, a *quantitative* non-fraction, counts the fights of the night. It is *discrete*, with no in-between states. A *floating point* records the fighter's weight. Floats are associated with

INTEGERS
count amounts

BOOLEANS
true or false?

FLOATS
offer precision

Many codes … exist primarily to make life easier for machines and their designers without any consideration of the burden placed upon people.
DON NORMAN, 2013

In 1847 George Boole introduced the world to the truth values of Boolean logic and their main operations of AND, OR, and NOT with *The Mathematical Analysis of Logic.*

The floating point is able to hold values that arrive from the entire depth and breadth of the number line. It is called a floating point because the value can be re-expressed using scientific notation which moves, or floats, the decimal point.

how we perceive—and measure—the real physical world: a *continuous* spectrum that can be zoomed in on. Time can be split into seconds, milliseconds, nanoseconds, and so on. Space can also be sliced into ever-smaller fractions of length or degree. Recognizing value types is one foundation for better information because it helps you see the inherent structure in the data's origin.

Enter Data

A datum is a value stored in a location. The value could be of a variety of types, but is often a float, integer, Boolean, or text string. More than one datum makes data. Data is traditionally expressed as the plural of datum. But today we also refer to it as a singular mass noun, like *sand* or *rain*. Whether we say *data are* or *data is*, each datum includes a value and a storage location.

In some cases, the data value's location is associated with an actual location in the real world. The location might be global, like a map coordinate, or local, like the position of a stent in a heart's coronary artery. In other cases, the data value's location is defined by reference keys and attribute names that have no relation to a real physical place. Data can also be characterized by how many values are stored for each location.

Just as the value types of data differ, data storage types vary as well. Two-dimensional tables of data position values into neat rows and columns. Hierarchical trees, such as your hard drive's nested folders, stack relationships. Databases manage a variety of data and programs in one unified environment; they create flexible systems sometimes explained with "object" metaphors.

The diversity of data value types and data storage types combines to help create our data, but they are often not enough. Modern data packages also contain metadata, such as summary values and data dictionaries. These metadata provide explanatory context for what the data values contain, how they relate to one another, and context for what it all means. Many datasets are complex and multilayered combinations. They may contain different

Scalar data, such as temperature, has one value at each position. Vector data, such as air velocity's direction and magnitude, has two values at each position. As such, it is often represented by an arrow. Tensor data has many values at each position. One example of tensor data is how a stress-strain tensor can differentiate how a material will behave in the three dimensions of space.

Rote learning and drill is not enough. It leaves out understanding. ... ideas and understanding are what [it] is centrally about.
LAKOFF AND NÚÑEZ, 2000

It's not the numbers that are interesting. It's what they tell us about the lives behind the numbers.
HANS ROSLING, 1995

A MacGuffin is something desired that helps advance a story's plot. The pursuit of the MacGuffin, not the MacGuffin itself, is what is important. The search for the Holy Grail motivated Arthurian legends, while the pursuit of the Maltese Falcon statue was at the heart of Dashiell Hammett's detective novel. Today, the search for a valuable cache of data, often made visible by its portable object of storage, propels action films forward. The most lovable MacGuffin might be *Star Wars'* R2-D2, the custodian of the stolen plans (i.e., data) that can *save the people and restore freedom to the galaxy.*

structures and file formats. Nonetheless, simple mental models, like the relationship tree, table array, and spatial map, persist.

How do we picture data? We might imagine imperceptible strings of zeros and ones that go on forever, written by tiny machines to solid-state drives. Data lives far away on chilly server racks, ready to serve you at a moment's notice; it is backed up elsewhere, just in case. Data can also be a precious portable thumb drive, pursued by the characters in a Hollywood action film. When we see data in the currency of its medium of storage, we block the creative work we need to do. These impenetrable images of data do not help.

The first lesson for data storytellers from James Brown's album is an easy one: The magic is in hearing the music, not the nuance of its capture and storage. The second lesson is that *Live at the Apollo* is not a perfect time capsule. It cannot be. As a sensory event, the album only transports us audibly to that room, and even then, only partially. It is not a total rote recording of that 1962 concert. It is merely a simplification, an encoding that reduced the sensory reality of that evening to a tiny fraction of its original, rich salience.

But even a virtual reality experience that put us perfectly back at The Apollo would still not be the same as actually witnessing the show. This is because you would have a different frame of reference compared to any 1962 Harlem concert-goer. Furthermore, James Brown's recorded performance will not be motivated anew by audience cheers. Reality does not happen twice. Any recording is but a shadow of the performance. It is an incomplete artifact that lives on.

The album is a sliver of what that night was, but that does not make it inferior. It is a treasure. The album is a beautiful compression of what that concert was. It helped James Brown rocket to success and still moves our feet today. No one would want to watch a continuous stream of someone's life, there is too much monotonous noise. But compress a life story into a two-hour film and you can move the emotions (and wallets) of millions.

We often wish we could remember more. Russian neuropsychologist Aleksandr Luria treated a patient whose memory was too sharp for his own good. Referred to as S., he suffered from not having the "art of forgetting"—the automatic disposal of trivial detail as we push information from short-term memory to long-term storage. In *When We Are No More*, historian Abby Smith Rumsey relates the consequences of S.'s condition of being unable to forget triviality:

> *S. suffered from a* disorder of distraction. *He could not make things dull, and had a hard time maintaining focus on anything for extended periods. He was unable to sort his impressions for value and emotional salience. To him the world was far too vivid far too much of the time. …*
>
> *He easily confused what he had remembered (because everything he encountered in his daily life triggered a chain of recollections) with what had actually transpired. Memories were so fresh in affect and spun out in his mind so rapidly that he mistook his recollections for reality. There were periods in his youth when he did not get up in the morning to go to school because even thinking about arising stimulated memories of having done so before. He thought that he had gone to school even as he lay still under the covers.*

Having only a compression—an impression, a model, a shadow—is actually the best we could hope for. Too many stimuli would bore, overwhelm, or make it impossible to understand. Distilling the performance of James Brown into an album made it possible for the performance to reach millions of people. And it makes it possible for us to keep traveling back to the 1962 Apollo.

Storytellers of all stripes must regularly compress all of the possible information their stories could contain into a manageable number of relatable details.
MICHAEL AUSTIN, 2010

To see why encoding is necessary, imagine trying to memorize an event without any simplification taking place; the result might be called a "total rote recording" or "perception without concepts" … In the real world we can't possibly take everything into account all the way down to its most microscopic details, and so we necessarily must ignore almost everything about every situation that we encounter, and that means we unconsciously make a highly selective encoding of it when we store it in memory. We have to strip everything we experience down to a caricature of itself.
HOFSTADTER AND SANDER, 2013

All data is a shadow of what has flowed before. Data is reality distilled with intention. We no longer have to picture data as an impenetrable monolith. When we think about data, we should consider the world that delivered it to us. Pause to reflect: What has been lost from the data's world? Why were some things selected to survive? How has it all been transmitted forward to us, today? Then, we can see data for what it is, whispers from a past world waiting for its music to be heard again.

INFORMATION

MURMURS

"Data! data! data!" he cried impatiently.
"I can't make bricks without clay."
SHERLOCK HOLMES, 1892
THE ADVENTURE OF THE COPPER BEECHES

Wheat centralizes power. Visible above ground and harvested all at once, you cannot evade the taxman if the entire village knows who grew what.

These plants domesticated Homo sapiens, rather than vice versa. ... The word "domesticate" comes from the Latin domus, *which means "house." Who's the one living in a house? Not the wheat. It's the Sapiens.*
YUVAL NOAH HARARI, 2015

Numero-ideographic tablets used in ancient Sumerian accounting represented discrete transactions. Each circle equals 10 in this 5,000-year-old Uruk example: 12 + 19 = 31.

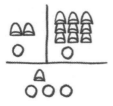

We should not take data whispers for granted. The past has not been delivering them for very long. We did not always have data, well, at least not how we do today. The impressions and compressions of life that data preserves makes the very *idea* of data beautiful. How we got data is quite a story.

A common telling of our history goes like this: Civilizations flourished across the globe with the ability to harvest and store food. Food surpluses went into centralized granaries. This accumulated wealth spurred development. Bureaucratic management, trade, and a new hierarchy emerged. Increasingly, social power wielded physical power. Caches of food, and the material luxuries they helped achieve, became targets for competing communities. Violence evolved right along with the emergence of civilization. Together, they advanced in organization and efficiency.

That caricature is one way of telling the story. Today, new discoveries are challenging long-held beliefs about life before the Fertile Crescent. Pre-agriculture humanity seems to have actually been more capable and vibrant than ever imagined. One of the reasons we credit the relationship between cultivation and civilization so much, you see, is because of a massive information-survival bias. The agricultural revolution did not just produce a lot of wheat. It also produced an enormous amount of durable information objects. The agricultural revolution birthed a wealth of data. Food, livestock, and people were counted. These numbers were first represented with small sculptures, which were then abstracted into a system of 3-D tokens. Tiny cone and ball tokens were later pressed into clay to create records. Triangular and circular indentations eventually became symbolic. The tokens were abandoned in favor of the more efficient reproduction of their indentation with a reed stylus. Writing was born.

Crops beget surpluses, which beget markets. Trade depends on people trusting one another. Individually, people are likely to forget (or manipulate) what exactly was traded. Arguments between traders do not make good markets. So, to ease friction, traders recorded agreements by documenting them at the time of the trade.

Memories were frozen by pressing them into clay. Then, these clay tablets were made public, or *published*. Abby Smith Rumsey highlights that these tablets, unlike traders, were unable to lie or forget. She calls them *objective witnesses*, *truth tokens*, and *warrants of trust*.

An army of bureaucrats grew to manage clay records. Tablets helped tax subjects, sustain communities through drought, raise armies, trade with neighbors, and glorify civilization. These records of counting were stored in vast centralized library warehouses. And data just sat in racks, curated by castes of scholars, for a long time.

The Way of the Future

In January of 1662, a London peddler named John Graunt published *Observations on the Bills of Mortality*. Hundreds of years later, we now look back and see that his book was a notable surge in a deluge that has since swallowed up the world.

In the 1600s, London suffered from incessant plagues of disease. John Graunt went to work to help King Charles II understand what was going on. First, Graunt gathered proxy birth and death data from a mess of records scattered across London's parishes. His book began with neat tables of local christenings and burials going back to the prior century. The cause of death was included when available. After organizing the newly uniform demographic data, excerpted below, Graunt included some written observations.

Clay tablets are a curiously durable method of information storage; a library fire simply hardens them.

The application of figures of arithmetic to "the condition and prospects of society," dates from those early times when families first clustered together and grew into tribes, and tribes into nations; when cities and fortified places came into existence; and men, impelled by very natural motives, took to measuring their wealth and strength. This they did by counting their tents, their herds and flocks, their camels, horses, cattle, sheep, goats, and slaves; their warriors, arms, and war chariots; their money and articles of barter. They even traveled so far on the road to development as to take censuses of their populations, and to make muster-rolls of their fighting men; and they were precise in their statements of the number of victims by their plagues and pestilences.
WILLIAM A. GUY, 1885

A TABLE of the
CHRISTENINGS and MORTALITY
For the Year 1645 and 1646

Weeks.	Days of the Month.		Christ.	Bur.	Plague
1	Dec.	25.	125	205	6
2	January	1.	143	217	2
3		8.	161	171	0
4		15.	138	241	2
5		22.	165	200	0
6		29.	160	202	1
7	Febr.	5.	146	192	0
8		12.	152	188	5
9		19.	157	171	1
10		26.	128	155	1

Graunt's *Observations on the Bills of Mortality* was a success. The book propelled its author into the prestigious Royal Society. The data tables established a foundation for future demographers. A new science of population study emerged by analyzing Graunt's data and refining his approach. Probability, the mathematics of chance, was once transfixed by the odds of gambling dice and playing cards. Now, it had a new domain to explore. Probability had empirical numbers from the real world. Probability had data.

John Graunt's tables are a notable wave in an ever-surging flood of data. Since then, data has swept many domains of life into modernity. Insurance funds emerged from studying population records. Physical sciences materialized from the numbers and diagrams in laboratory logbooks. Performance measurement rapidly improved mechanical contraptions. These machines helped an economic revolution roar out of English mines. Statecraft hatched a new political science called statistics. This is just a sample of what data helped create, all before 1800. Data, the capture and organization of facts for analysis, has ever since helped advance civilization.

Information inventions create periods of information inflation. These technology impulses include Mesopotamian writing, Greek libraries, and European movable type. Each new technology outsourced more of our memory to "ever more durable, compact, and portable" objects. Storage evolved from tablets, to scrolls, to books, to microfilm. Every time, the information surge overpowered our ability to manage information. Archaic institutions groaned under the weight of information inflation. When traditional institutions failed, people became disoriented. The public had to figure out for itself what information was trustworthy. Crises of authority ensued.

The cost of producing and caring for clay tablets (or scrolls, books, or microfilm) used to limit the rate of data production. Objects always forced us to decide what we wanted to save. Today, the latest digital information inflation has uncoupled data from physical objects. Today, we have arrived again at a world with more data than we know how to manage.

New data often arrives to us by way of tremendous exertion. At the dawn of the 1900s, Annie and Walter Maunder voyaged around the world to observe solar eclipses. One hundred years later, their efforts are mirrored by the struggle to put the enormous James Webb Space Telescope into orbit. On the ground, remote corners are photographed for street maps. Cosmic telescopes and streetview-harvesting vehicles are both visibly impressive data producers. But efforts are not always so showy. Smartphones quietly archive a trove of data about every user: what you browse, where you go, and who you know.

Incentives nudge us toward better knowledge of the world. New data is at the heart of much value creation. Today, tech entrepreneurs create new data to connect additional slices of reality to the Internet. Interesting research papers often apply rote analysis to clever data sets. Journalists fight hard for a good scoop, that is, first access to data. Unique, untouched, never-before-seen data is the foundation from which new insights and competitive advantages flow. These advantages can be secured if you generate new data yourself. I have spent years working on new datasets before attempting any serious visualization. Storytelling icing is delicious, but only if you are frosting the finest data cake.

Immersive Data

Objects and anecdotes that survive from the first data pioneers afford only a glimpse into their worlds. History lost most of the context that surrounded early data like Graunt's tables. Today, we can consider a much richer context. We have the power to expand what gets considered when we analyze modern data.

Do not expect data to tell you all the questions it has answers to. You must seek many perspectives if you are to exploit every line of inquiry. The entire world the data arrives from is a player in the story, whether we acknowledge it or not. Invite it in. Trust it as a collaborator. Let the world speak. Let it guide you to a more truthful understanding. To probe data origins is to develop a feel for the world the data comes from, sometimes before even opening the dataset. Probing reveals

The utility of new information, in a strict sense, is quantifiable. It is a foundational pillar of statistics according to Stephen Stigler who questions, *more evidence is better than less, but how much better?* The central limit theorem, first clearly defined by Pierre-Simon Laplace, implies a root-n relationship where *if you wished to double the accuracy of an investigation, it was insufficient to double the effort; you must increase the effort fourfold.*

A river cannot, we are told, rise above its source.
DARRELL HUFF, 1954

If, for example, it is a gasoline account, read books on oil geology and the productions of petroleum products. Read the trade journals in the field. Spend Saturday mornings in service stations, talking to motorists. Visit your client's refineries and research laboratories....
DAVID OGILVY, 1985

who is involved and how they think about their world. It also gives insight to what did not make it into the data set. *What hard decisions had to be made to capture this data? How was it recorded?*

Ideally, you are able to talk to the people who know the data and the data's world. A conversation might begin by trying to understand their needs and concerns. Questions that invite interviewees to visualize help me learn. *If I were to follow you, what would I see? Could you show me how you think about this?*

People who know the data's world always have something powerful to teach. It is my responsibility as interviewer to unearth the lesson. Pursue incomplete responses with curiosity. *Are there other reasons? Can you give me an example of that? Why do you think, feel, need?* Probing and open questions with no easy yes/no answer encourages interviewees to reveal more context. *Can you tell me something you know to be true that the data does not show? What do you know that you wish your boss's boss knew? That is all I have to ask— is there anything you would like to add?*

To know the human side of data is to fortify yourself against cold summaries that dehumanize it. I try to observe a real patient's experience whenever I work with health-care data. These visits are always worth the effort. I get vivid encounters with patients, clinicians, and facilities. They help correct my misconceptions and move me to better understand how the data works. Stay too long behind a computer screen and the reality behind each anonymous patient ID begins to fade. An in-person journey into data origins gives a sensory experience that you can reference across data work.

Unfortunately, these journeys are not always practical. You cannot always experience a day in the life of your Census, social media, or consumer data. But you can make some effort. Watch videos online, pick up the phone, read a few trending articles. Get to know the data's world however you can.

Trips into data origins go by many labels. "Design thinking" encourages one to become emotionally intimate with a problem's environment. Described as *human centered*, its curiosity for new insights powers energetic observations, exchanges, and iterations. The design thinker darts through the world of the problem. A journalist's trip into data origins is part of their investigative reporting. Reporting on the shifting economy might include interviews with people affected. Their testimony can give a nuanced sensitivity to what macroeconomic trends actually mean. Similarly, a consumer-product manager with widget performance data might test similar gadgets in their own daily life. To them, this is competitive research. Whatever you label it, consider threading your own life experiences through the world the data comes from. You will learn more.

Toward Information

Imagine a messy pile of books in the middle of a classroom floor. Curious, you approach the pile, pick one book out, and leaf through its pages. Setting it back down, you begin to wonder what other titles are lurking in the confused jumble. Then, you notice a nearby empty bookshelf, and decide to

clean up the mess. But how should the books be arranged? They could be simply placed on the shelf in the order you pick them off the floor. But perhaps they should be sequenced by author name or date of publication. Finally, you decide to catalog them by topic and dive in. Once done, you stand back to admire your work.

The original messy pile of books was random, unordered, and formless. Shelved, the individual books did not change at all. But their arrangement has changed quite a lot. You have put the books *in formation*. Through sorting the books, you learned a lot about what the pile contains. Now, you can read all the spines. The titles are more accessible. You can also see which topics are better represented by seeing which shelves are more full. This recognition and

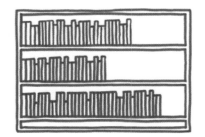

Engineers and businesspeople are trained to solve problems. Designers are trained to discover the real problems. A brilliant solution to the wrong problem can be worse than no solution at all: solve the correct problem. Good designers never start by trying to solve the problem given to them: they start by trying to understand what the real issues are.
DON NORMAN, 2013

The foundation of an edifice is of vast importance. Still, it is not the foundation but the structure built upon the foundation which gives the result for which the whole work was planned. As the cathedral is to its foundation so is an effective presentation of facts to the data.
WILLARD C. BRINTON, 1914

Facts are incomplete without context. ... "compared to what?" gives it power.
HOWARD WAINER, 1997

To see an object in space is to see it in context.
RUDOFF ARNHEIM, 1969

inspection would be impossible if we were to continue rummaging through the messy pile book by book. The shelved arrangement creates a more navigable collection for anyone to explore.

We can imagine an almost infinite number of messy piles of the same collection of books, all equally frustrating. But there are comparably few useful arrangements that afford access and show patterns. Information involves uncommon arrangements. Unlike any messy heap, the shelved form is not likely to come about by chance. Similarly, a pile of stones is not a house. The arrangement matters.

So far, we have only discussed data conceptually. We haven't looked at data directly yet because that requires something more. To see data we must have information, data in a form consumable by people. So, let's begin with some data.

\x4e\x61\x6d\x65\x2c\x32\x30\x30\x30\x2c\x32\x30\x31\
x30\x0a\x41\x6e\x63\x72\x61\x6d\x2c\x31\x35\x31\x33\
x2c\x31\x35\x37\x33\x0a\x41\x75\x73\x74\x65\x72\x6c\
x69\x74\x7a\x2c\x31\x34\x35\x33\x2c\x31\x36\x35\x34

The above snippet of data is encoded in Unicode, the global standard for handling text. Unicode was designed in the late 1980s to be backwards compatible with the previous encoding standard, ASCII, which developed from telegraph code. Why bother stripping all the way down to coded data? It lets us distinguish data from information. The Unicode is data, but it is not in a form we can consume. Form underpins our ability to interact with data. We take a big first step out of data chaos by decoding that data to text. The little squiggle symbols of letters and numerals snap data into information. Thankfully, our programs use a lookup table to decode data like this into familiar forms. These data are populations in the county I grew up in, recorded in the 2000 and 2010 U.S. Census. Spaces can make it even easier to appreciate this information.

```
Name,2000,2010
Ancram,1513,1573
Austerlitz,1453,1654
```

Name	2000	2010
Ancram	1513	1573
Austerlitz	1453	1654

Spacing helps the eye distinguish each value and keep track of which ones are located in the same column. Just like that, visual design begins to help better inform. Tabulated data is hardly the ultimate design, but it is a basic reminder of how form is elemental to any information. Better information is possible because better forms for data are possible. We can keep going.

Tables are a foundational data visual. They originated as multi-purpose tools to store and communicate numbers. Old paper tables, like John Graunt's *Bills of Mortality*, survived so future strangers could reference the data. We no longer need to rely on visual tables to store data. Today, the only goal of the published table is to inform the reader, not to store precise values for future calculation.

Graunt invited London to discover how useful a data table can be. The world's interest has not abated since. His tables made data more easy to handle by using only simple, printing-press type: letters, numbers, lines, and spacers. The same elements continue to be the building blocks of much data reading today.

The storage location of the original data is revealed by giving each value its own cell. Good table design augments our ability to read data. It also acknowledges the natural limits of human comprehension. For example, aligning value decimal points allows comparisons to be made quickly with a vertical scan.

Be careful of how many numerals express each value. As Howard Wainer advises, "Round—a lot!" Two numerals is a good target. Reduce decimal places. Switch units to thousands or millions. Do what it takes with numerals to make numbers more intelligible.

Aggressive rounding may reduce precision by a startling amount. But consider that we cannot actually appreciate more digits easily. What does the precise difference between 10,564.4 and 82,935.34 actually mean? If we compare these two numbers in our mind we retain only the gist of each, not the detail. The mind might understand that the larger number is about eight times bigger than the smaller. Skip the illusion of being able to comprehend more than you can. Express them in thousands: 11 and 83.

The word *table* references the stone tablets that information used to be inscribed upon, often in compact lists, such as in a book's *table of contents*. *Tabulate* means to put in the form of a table. The typewriter's *tabulator* helped make indentations, or *tabs*.

Basic problem: Make data more easily and effectively handleable by minds. JOHN TUKEY, 1977

A table is for communication, not data storage … for human eyes and human minds. HOWARD WAINER, 2007

Further: More precision than two numerals often cannot be statistically justified.

Superfluous precision clouds our ability to make sense of a wall of numerals. The visual weight of a seven-numeral string, like 82,935.34, reduces the impact of the numeral that matters most, the leading 8. A sheet full of similarly precise seven-numeral numbers would be impenetrable.

Thoughtful rounding and spacing improves tables. Horizontal and vertical lines can help too. Lines can communicate meaning. Do not line every cell; instead reserve them for emphasis. John Tukey advised that double lines between things should add up, like one big equals sign. Single lines should separate summary values from their input data. Heavier lines may highlight cells of special importance. These lessons applied to our slice of the population data yield an improved table, now in thousands:

Name	2000	2010	Gain
Ancram	1.5	1.6	0.1
Austerlitz	1.5	1.7	0.2
Total	3.0	3.3	0.3

Boxes, bolding, and shading can be used to direct attention to values of particular interest. Table color meaning varies across cultures. In accounting, black is positive and red is negative. Spreadsheet colors may indicate what type of value each number is: output of a formula, a hard-coded constant, an alert, or a link to another sheet.

Table entries are often arranged in alphabetical order. This default is an outdated way of presenting information, developed by scholars to catalog work for easier retrieval. Today, alphabetic order lingers in a technological age that has made search easy. Instead of the first letters of some label, try to sort categories based on their values. It can reveal groups, voids, and other simple patterns.

Spaces between rows can emphasize value clusters. Some of these practices are applied to the full U.S. Census population data for Columbia County to show how rounding, formatting, sorting (by 2010 population), grouping, and using lines to separate summary values can shape data into better information.

Town Populations				Town Populations (k)			
	2000	**2010**			**2000**	**2010**	**Gain**
Ancram	1,513	1,573		Kinderhook	8.3	8.5	0.2
Austerlitz	1,453	1,654					
Canaan	1,820	1,710		Hudson	7.5	6.7	-0.8
Chatham	4,249	4,128		Claverack	6.4	6.0	-0.4
Claverack	6,401	6,021		Ghent	5.3	5.4	0.1
Clermont	1,726	1,965					
Copake	3,278	3,615		Greenport	4.2	4.2	0.0
Gallatin	1,499	1,668		Chatham	4.2	4.1	-0.1
Germantown	2,018	1,954		Livingston	3.4	3.6	0.2
Ghent	5,276	5,402		Copake	3.3	3.6	0.3
Greenport	4,180	4,165					
Hillsdale	1,744	1,927		Stockport	2.9	2.8	-0.1
Hudson	7,524	6,713		New Lebanon	2.5	2.3	-0.1
Kinderhook	8,296	8,498		Stuyvesant	2.2	2.0	-0.2
Livingston	3,424	3,646		Clermont	1.7	2.0	0.2
New Lebanon	2,454	2,305		Germantown	2.0	2.0	-0.1
Stockport	2,933	2,815		Hillsdale	1.7	1.9	0.2
Stuyvesant	2,188	2,027		Canaan	1.8	1.7	-0.1
Taghkanic	1,118	1,310		Gallatin	1.5	1.7	0.2
				Austerlitz	1.5	1.7	0.2
				Ancram	1.5	1.6	0.1
				Taghkanic	1.1	1.3	0.2
				Columbia Co.	**63.1**	**63.1**	**0.0**

round
sort
group
gain
total
line

Can tables be pushed to convey even more? Recall that the origin of numerals lies with the tallying of observations. What if we tally each observation according to its value from the get-go? John Tukey adopted this strategy with his *stem-and-leaf* display. It tallies low-precision values in a way that invites group profiling. The same town populations from above are tallied below with a stem-and-leaf. For example, the Town of Kinderhook's 2010 population of 8,498 is rounded to 85**. To record Kinderhook on the chart, work your way up from the bottom of the thousands (k) column, the *stem*, until you come to 8, which corresponds to Kinderhook's thousands digit. Then, staying in the 8k row, place a 5 (Kinderhook's hundreds digit) in the hundreds column, a *leaf*.

1,000 is represented by K for *kilo*, as in kilogram, a derivative of the Greek word for thousand (χίλιοι) created in 1795 France.

k	**hundreds**	
8	5	Kinderhook
7		
6	70	Hudson, Claverack
5	4	Ghent
4	21	Greenport, Chatham
3	66	Livingston, Copake
2	83000	Stockport, New Lebanon, Stuyvesant, Clermont, Germantown
1	977763	Hillsdale, Canaan, Gallatin, Austerlitz, Ancram, Taghkanic
0		

Beside the leaf, place the town's name. The stem-and-leaf display is just one example of the creative possibilities of using thoughtful design to better present information.

Perhaps we still see so many tables because they match how we think about data's storage structure. Why not just print out the map of where all the data live? I think readers place their trust in tables because tables seem to give direct access to the raw data.

Indeed, tables persist as tools for looking up values in small datasets. Tables also aid simple spreadsheet arithmetic and continue to be popular visual accessories. A tiny table in the corner of a thematic map seems to prop up a general confidence by saying, *Look there. See? We used numbers to make this.* Tables appear to be a transparent way of presenting the data. No values are hidden, but unfortunately, not much else can be seen. Looking at tables of any substantial size is a little like looking at the grooves of a record with a magnifying glass. You can see the data but you will not hear the music.

CHAPTER

3

EMBODIED

ENCODING

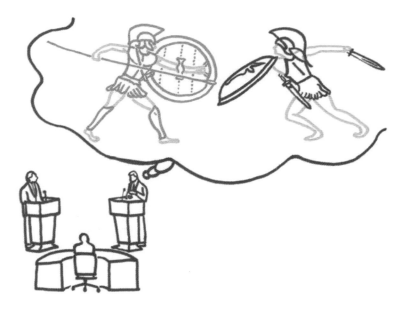

What our eyes behold may well be the text
of life but one's meditations on the text
and the disclosures of these meditations are
no less a part of the structure of reality.
WALLACE STEVENS, 1951

INFO

humanize   probe

DATA

To create better information, we must enter into a dialog with data. Creating information and exploring data are partner endeavors. Together, these activities form the *humanize-probe* cycle that powers all data storytelling. To wade into this cycle is to submerge yourself into the pool of data chaos, resurface to consider what you found, and dive in again with a better idea of what treasure might lie beneath. First, let us get our toes wet by pausing to consider how we think about, and navigate about, the world of our experience.

Stretch Cognition

When we encounter a never-before-seen object or meet a strange situation, we mostly do not panic. Instead, we stretch what we already know to help us understand what is going on. Our ability to extrapolate *what we know* to *what we don't know* is the secret of our success. This power—called analogy-making, category extension, and metaphor-mapping—helps make strange things familiar.

All of your mental categories, or concepts, are related through a dense network of relationships between your brain's neurons. In a novel situation, this network comes to your aid. It surfaces patterns from your long-term memory that might best help figure out what is going on. The first beanbag chair you ever saw was an ugly lump on the floor, unlike any furniture you had seen before. But once you saw that the category *chair* could be extended to include this new lumpy object, all kinds of chair-properties, namely that chairs are good for sitting, were suddenly mapped to the giant beanbag. The moment one realizes *chair* can be stretched to the lump, the category of chair also expands. Chairs now include lumpy beanbags. Every new encounter offers the possibility of extension.

Our brain's network helps us understand strange situations. It also filters the avalanche of stimulation that the world barrages us with, to focus us on what is important. The world presents too many objects at once for us to take in. Mental categories help make sense of the cacophony of the world by directing attention to what is useful, now. Knowing what is important allows us to ignore the rest. Many

Buridan's ass is
the parable of the
thirsty and hungry
donkey who, unable
to choose between
the equally appealing
bucket of water or pile
of hay, dies from the
parched starvation of
analysis paralysis.

things evade our notice, by design. The alternative would be to suffer like Buridan's donkey: In a constant panic of information overload, never sure of what to do, we would be unable to take any action.

Our experience of the world is naturally biased. We tune our senses to what our existing concepts consider important. A practical prejudice, which focuses our attention on what we consider useful, is necessary if we are to swim through the chaos. Along your path, interesting things attract your attention. The most compelling and novel stimulation helps cultivate and grow your personal microcosm. Some learn the hard way to not touch a glowing stovetop, but their updated model of how the world works prevents them from doing it again. The coherent reality you inhabit gets refined. By paying attention to some things, and ignoring the rest, we each thread our individual life through the world of experience. Each of our paths is a little unique slice of reality, a microcosm, of the common world we all share. It is our nature to strive for ever-more useful connections to help us better interact with the world.

Curiosity is the search for more effective categories. It often helps us also achieve a more accurate understanding too. But everyone's cultivated personal microcosm is first about guiding their own life. One quick way to gain a more effective understanding is to compare your own unique microcosm to others. No two people's lived realities are quite exactly the same. Seeing how others perceive the greater world is a route to your own improvement.

Evaluating yourself against others is productive when it helps you identify holes in your personal experience of reality. Others can teach us how to refine our microcosms so that they are more true, and more effective. From this vantage, we can imagine our way to

"You don't know much," said the Duchess; "and that's a fact."
ALICE'S ADVENTURES IN WONDERLAND, LEWIS CARROLL, 1865

All that has been learned empirically about evolution in general and mental process in particular suggests that the brain is a machine assembled not to understand itself, but to survive. ... It throws a spotlight on those portions of the world it must know in order to live to the next day, and surrenders the rest to darkness.
E.O. WILSON, 1998

From the experientialist perspective, metaphor is about imaginative rationality. ... New metaphors are capable of creating new understandings and, therefore, new realities.
LAKOFF AND JOHNSON, 1980

empathy and compassion. Together, we can close the gaps between our microcosms and inspire one another to stretch our minds in new, more useful directions. Ideally, we strive to understand the microcosms of others, and be generous and kind with how we share our own perceptions of reality. A parent not only safeguards the kitchen, but also teaches their child about its dangers, such as sharp knives, electrical outlets, and hot stoves.

So, what does this all have to do with data? A data story is a new microcosm for the reader to consider, inhabit, and compare against their current worldview. It is one way to generously share a perspective on how the world works. Whether it is a stark bar chart or a fully interactive experience, each data story invites the reader to take a new look. It is a real privilege to build and offer visual slices of the world for a reader's consideration. We hope that each data story can help others better understand what is actually going on. We hope to nudge one another toward better personal perspectives and, in the process, maybe even change who we are.

If data stories compel readers, it is because their territory is somehow interesting. People crave knowledge. We are interested by things that help us achieve more useful categories, which, in turn, help us better interact with the world. If readers sense that a data story can help them improve their mental map of how the world works, then they will open themselves up to being informed. As data storytellers, our job is to help readers in their quest to enrich their categories. We do this when we provide interesting information.

Only certain information can actually extend someone's knowledge. If it is too familiar the reader will be bored; too strange, and the reader will disengage. We ignore what we have already accounted for and what we cannot possibly understand. In 1971, Murray Davis characterized interesting things as those that credibly challenge what is taken for granted. His simple script promises your information will engage with an audience's existing mental categories: *You probably think this, but it's actually not true. Here's the proof, and here's why it matters to you.*

Stories that simply challenge the status quo certainly can attract a lot of interest. But this is only one way to make something interesting. Above all, we must appreciate that to engage an audience is to activate the frontiers of their existing mental categories.

At their best, data stories address readers where they already stand, and expand their worldview to someplace new. Making things simple is not how this is done. The mind is phenomenally complex. It deserves more respect than just dumbing down the data. Instead, we must aspire to meet readers where they already perceive the world. This way, we can inform readers in a way that lets them integrate new knowledge with their existing concepts.

Consider what concepts readers arrive with. What categories, analogies, and metaphors already steer the way they perceive? What do they anticipate? How can we account for their prior experience as beings with an embodied cognition who have lived the world?

Good data stories reflect real life. But not just because we hijack a superficial set of sensory organs used by our ancestors to look across the savanna. Good data stories work when we meet minds right where they already are, already surfing invisible worlds.

Metaphor-Mapping

Today, we are wanderers of invisible worlds. Each of us is centered by a personal identity, which cannot be seen. Its daily experience is a struggle with a swirling tangle of forces we cannot see. We have all yearned to advance our self's economic and social worth, if only we could grasp money and love.

New metaphors emerge when two ideas fire at the same time and their resemblance becomes conflated. Metaphors help expand understanding by linking the unknown to the known. As we map the unfamiliar, our conceptual sphere, our microcosm, expands. Lakoff and Johnson introduced conceptual extension with the metaphor that *ARGUMENT IS WAR: Your claims are indefensible. He attacked every weak point in my argument. His criticisms were right on target. I demolished his argument.*

For we, on our little pile of mud, can only conceive of that which we are accustomed.
VOLTAIRE, 1752

We are at our human best as creatures of the shore, with one foot on the hard ground of fact and one foot in the sea of mystery. … It is at the shore that the creative work of the mind is done—the work of the artist, poet, philosopher, and scientist.
CHET RAYMO, 1998

Embodiment expresses an abstract idea concretely, especially via relation to a person's body.

Analogy is the fuel and fire of thinking.
HOFSTADTER AND SANDER, 2013

The essence of metaphor is understanding and experiencing one kind of thing in terms of another.
LAKOFF AND JOHNSON, 1980

*The sole aim of a
metaphor is to call up
a visual image.*
GEORGE ORWELL,
1946

*One's interaction
with one's body and
one's environment
constitutes the
heart and soul of
human thought.
The concepts that
one creates, as well
as one's way of
reasoning, are seen
as emerging from
such interactions.*

...

*people do not
mentally juggle
with patterns
of unanchored,
meaningless symbols.
Rather, thought is
anchored in two
fashions (that is,
the meanings of
our concepts come
from two sources).
Firstly, thought is
anchored in the past
through analogies,
and secondly it is
anchored in the
concrete world
through the body,
which has participated
in so many
experiences.*
HOFSTADTER AND
SANDER, 2013

Metaphor is the bridge from the safety of the familiar to the excitement of the new. It powers sophisticated thought by helping us engage with, comprehend, and communicate abstract ideas. For visual storytellers, metaphor helps link ideas and what we see.

Our language is full of metaphors that rely on physical experiences. We can catalog how all kinds of bodily actions are used to describe more abstract, invisible concepts.

TOUCH: One can be *touched* by a kind *gesture*.
SMELL: One can think the plan *stinks* or *smells fishy*.
TASTE: A *tasteless* movie could put you in a *bitter* or *sour* mood.
HEARING: Wearing that *loud* outfit *sounds* crazy.
SIGHT: *Watch* the political environment to *see* how it *looks*.

By the time we begin school, we are already equipped with a library of metaphors. They arrive to us from biological evolution, culture, and our own personal experiences. Some associations are wired into us, like *snakes are bad*. Many people sense a fear of snakes even though most of us have never had a negative experience with one. Some concept associations, such as a fear of spiders or heights, were selected by evolution. They became part of our wiring because they are useful.

Other metaphors are learned during childhood as we learn our first language. Of course, many of these common cultural metaphors are also reinforced by our individual experiences. For example, Mother's warmth is associated with her affection. The conflation of warmth and affection wired our language to produce statements such as "he *warmed* up to me after being *cold* all day."

How do physical experiences influence, not just how we *talk* about the world, but also how we *picture* the world? So much of reality is consumed visually and so how we understand the world is also quite visual. Just like language, our visual cognition is supported by categories. It has been shown that cultures with more named color categories perform better when detecting color differences. A person raised in a grassland culture that has dozens of concepts of *green* (think: *lime*, *grass*, *forest*), is better at distinguishing shades of green than someone raised in a culture with fewer words to describe green. When looking at a group of similar green tiles, they pick out the one tile with a slightly different hue more quickly. More color categories and more relationships between them create a richer understanding of color. The very idea of more colors changes how the mind sees the world.

Differences between our mental categories fascinate us. But these boundary cases do not dominate the way we see the world. Mostly, people share a common set of visual concepts, a common embodied perspective, because we all have human bodies.

Today, the word *visualization* describes an external process that puts abstract data into forms we can see with our eyes. But it has not always described this activity. To *visualize* meant to form a mental image, like the imaginative visions you experience with your eyes closed. So, for a moment, close your eyes and visualize your favorite color.

What did you just experience? The mind's eye supplies mental images that we perceive without sensory input. A common example of this phenomenon is the vivid visualization that occurs as you read. We become more engaged in the storytelling of a novel if it excites us into actively picturing its world. By supplying the costumes, sets, and special effects with our own imagination, the reading

becomes more real. If an author can convince us to co-imagine the story, then we will stay engaged until the last page is turned.

What exactly is the mind's eye? Our ability to voluntarily shape these mental images varies. Some visions are spontaneous, like the imagery of dreams. Others are controlled and methodical, like the visualization we conjure up when planning a trip. Like many skills, our ability to visualize with our mind's eye can be improved through attention and practice.

The mind's eye evokes the forehead's mystical third eye. The third eye represents the attainment of higher consciousness in Eastern spirituality. It represents the wisdom of *seers* who have gained sophisticated insights into life. Wise holy people are revered because they perceive the invisible patterns of life. The abstraction they see cannot be known from simple visual input alone. The third eye opens as the consciousness awakens to a higher-order understanding of reality.

The mind's eye is a phenomenon to cultivate in ourselves and a target to engage with in others. A successful data story activates the mind's eye of the reader. It prompts them to see even more than what is on the page, just as your mental imagery runs wild while reading a novel. It is our challenge to help others see more.

Visual Encoding

Rules help us make pictures from data values. The number line's left-to-right sequence is one rule. It tells us exactly where to place each number in linear space. Familiar conventions, like the number line, can be mixed with rules we invent to see particular data better. It is up to us to choose the rules for how we generate data-driven pictures.

Like any design field, making pictures from data requires you to balance many trade-offs. This includes grappling with the weird ways people perceive the world. You see, there is not always an even linkage between the strength of a sensory stimulus and how we perceive it. A sound that is twice as loud will not be heard so. A cake that has double the sugar will not taste twice as sweet. We misinterpret the power of vibration, smell, temperature, muscle force, and many other physical phenomena. And yes, we misjudge what we see as well. The warped ways we perceive warn us to remain vigilant against lazy visual design. The message you intend to send is often not the message that is received. Encoding content into sensory packages, without concern for how their meaning will be decoded, is no way to communicate.

To choose how data gets encoded in a visual form is to choose the rules for how meaning gets packed into a picture. Encoding is all about building things. It is the most powerful agency we have to help create order from the chaos of our data. But cheeky encoding is not the goal. It does not serve the reader to present a visual contraption that requires painstaking dissection. As data storytellers, successful encoding is *not* mere witty storage.

Successful encoding yields successful decoding. Visual decoding is how readers interpret data pictures. If the audience decodes successfully, then the picture has transmitted successfully. The same perceptual skills and biases that help us understand and encode can point us to how the audience might later decode.

Regardless of individual differences in data literacy, we all share a common set of visual metaphors because we all see a similar spatial understanding of the world. Do not risk mistranslation by ignoring the spatial meanings people employ to understand graphic information. Successful encoding builds a bridge to the audience's shared graphicacy.

There is a candy shop full of ways we get to communicate meaning visually. For example, the concept of importance is naturally associated with size. *Big things are important.* Why might this be? We start off small. When you are a child, big people like your parents are important. Bigger people, the ones who were already grown up, are much more powerful. Sometimes big adults are even scary. Even longer ago, big animals, you must remember, used to eat us.

Big things, whether parent or predator or palm tree, are also important because, to our eye, big things are *closer*. Ultimately, big

The essence of a graphical display is that a set of numbers ... are represented by an appropriate visual metaphor....
HOWARD WAINER, 1997

The great criterion is the effect produced on the mind.
WILLIAM PLAYFAIR, 1801

Clever encoding does not always translate to visual decoding.
WILLIAM CLEVELAND, 1985

Seeing comes before words. The child looks and recognizes before it can speak.
JOHN BERGER, 1972

Graphicacy is knowledge or skill in the use of graphical information.

An appeal to the eye when proportion and magnitude are concerned, is the best and readiest method of conveying a distinct idea. ... The advantages proposed by this mode of representation, are to facilitate the attainment of information, and aid the memory in retaining it: which two points form the principal business in what we call learning, or the acquisition of knowledge. Of all the senses, the eye gives the liveliest and most accurate idea of whatever is susceptible of being represented to it; and when proportion between different quantities is the object, then the eye has an incalculable superiority; as from the constant, and even involuntary habit of comparing the sizes of objects it has acquired the capacity of doing so, with an accuracy that is almost unequaled.
WILLIAM PLAYFAIR, 1801

things occupy a larger portion of our visual fields. There, big things vie for more of our attention. Important big things stretch, conceptually, into our language (e.g., "I wish you would stop focusing on *small* matters and see the *giant* issue we have"). Embodied metaphors transcend language because all people have similar embodied experiences. Big things are important in Zulu, Hawaiian, Turkish, Malay, and Russian. When we make pictures of important things, we do not have to abstract all the way to language metaphors. Just draw important things bigger on the page.

Rectangles placed side-by-side can help us compare two numbers. The bigger number gets a taller rectangle. Once the two rectangles are next to one another, we automatically compare them. We all recognize the negative space between their heights. It is as if our two eyes see what is on the page, but our mind's eye notices what is missing. Strive to create effortless experiences that engage the viewer. Visualization works best when the audience, like the reader of a novel, visualizes with you.

Big things are important is just one of many visual metaphors we use to understand the world. *Similarity* is conceptualized in terms of *physical closeness*: two ideas could be close, in the same ballpark, diverging, or light-years apart. *Me-first* language assigns positivity to abstract concepts using our body's physical orientation: upright, frontward, and active.

We could go on listing correlations between the body's physical experience and how we perceive and talk about the world. But what we really need is a more direct appreciation for how this helps us read data. How do common visual metaphors guide readers to decode data stories?

COUNTING

TIME

*There were several roads near by, but it did not take her
long to find the one paved with yellow brick. Within a short
time she was walking briskly toward the Emerald City, her
silver shoes tinkling merrily on the hard, yellow roadbed.*

THE WONDERFUL WIZARD OF OZ

L. FRANK BAUM, 1900

Mathematics flow from a stack of metaphors. Near the base of this stack is the common experience of tallying objects. Counting is the first of many ways we think about, talk about, and visualize numbers. Numbers as assembly, numbers as distance, and the ways we experience time are all familiar, once you pause to notice them. We must raise the ways we perceive numbers to our attention, and onto our design palette. Then, we can use our knowledge of how everyone perceives numbers to anticipate, and better serve, our audience.

Count Me In

Children learn their numbers by counting objects. When we count, the things we actually see are represented by the idea of a single, specific number. Count four bricks, in any order, and the count remains the same, the idea of *four* persists. The set of numbers we use to count objects is the first step from concrete reality into the abstraction of mathematics. We can even apply the *object-number* metaphor to the concept of zero. Zero is the empty collection of no objects at all.

But, what if you have the same four bricks and I ask for five? You will not be able to meet my request. The solution to 4 – 5 requires a negative number and a negative brick is absurd. Similarly, what if we want to divide our set of four bricks into three equal groups? The object-number metaphor cannot support all division. It has no solution for 4÷3. Perhaps we could smash the bricks into pieces and assemble three equal groups of *pieces of bricks*. But this is not the same as groups of *bricks*. The object-number metaphor fails again.

The object-number metaphor is unable to support the fractions that division demands. We address this shortcoming with a second metaphor: Objects are assemblies. An assembled whole can be separated into smaller parts, like a toy plane made from many Lego bricks. The *assembly-number* metaphor allows numbers to be decomposed into smaller parts. This metaphor extends our conception of each object, each number. Assembly parts begin to open up the whole domain of arithmetic possibility.

To measure the length of a room, you might walk heel-to-toe, from one side of the space to the other, counting the number of feet as you go. We measure length by counting how many times the same object can be placed end to end across a span. Our own bodies were early standards of measure. In addition to our feet, we used the width of the thumb (an inch), the width of the hand (still used to measure the height of horses), and the length from fingertip to elbow (the cubit). Bodily measures were externalized and standardized as simple tools like the builder's ruler and tailor's tape. Measuring tools evolved to include many units of length and they were scored appropriately.

Whatever standard is used to measure length, whether it is a body part or not, we envision a long chain of unit objects. This chain represents a line segment, a concept with magnitude but no width. The *length-number* metaphor builds on object and assembly metaphors. It adds many useful properties to our understanding of numbers and our ability to calculate with them. Length has an inherent organization. If you count the contents of a box of four rocks, the order in which you count does not matter. Line segments are not so forgiving. Four always comes after three along the line. The length-number metaphor provides a visual anchor and conceptual home for each value. We can now see the order of the numbers.

In 1958 MIT fraternity brothers measured the length of the Mass. Ave. Bridge, which connects MIT to Boston, using a new unit of measure. One *smoot* was exactly equal to the height of the shortest freshman pledge, Oliver R. Smoot, whose 5'7" body was laid down repeatedly over the span of the bridge to determine that its length was 364.4 SMOOTS ± 1 EAR.

The rod, equal to sixteen feet, was the basic unit of land measure in the early 1500s. Since the king's foot was not practically available for every measurement across the land, an alternative solution was proposed by Jacob Köbel: Sixteen men should be lined up, heel to toe, and the length of that line would be used to measure the rod, which could further be divided into sixteen equal lengths to determine the foot. It was an early modern example of the mean (average).

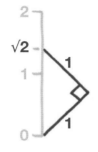

Zero also takes on new meaning with length. A wall-mounted measuring stick used to track a growing child's height gives zero the *smallest possible height*, not a *lack of height*. Zero is no longer constrained to just emptiness; it can also be the ultimate smallness. Length can also be divided, just as the assembly-number metaphor split whole objects into fractional parts. But assemblies only allow for wholes to be divided into *equal* parts. The length metaphor is able to do more because lines are continuous. Length's measuring stick shows that for every physical segment of length, there is a number. Length supports a continuity of fractional parts that assembly cannot.

Travel distance is a particular type of length that we encounter in everyday life. Sure, travel distance is usually much longer than object length. We measure the length of a garden wall in meters and the distance to the next town in kilometers. Otherwise, *measured length* and *distance traveled* seem metaphorically identical; they are not. See, it does not matter what end of the wall you begin measuring from, the length of the measurement will be just as useful. Travel, however, incorporates the value properties of length's measuring stick and then adds more meaning to the number: Distance gives numbers direction.

In Oz, Dorothy travels away from Munchkinland and toward the Emerald City. Travel implies an orientation and a destination. The *distance-number* metaphor combines the magnitudes of line segment length with the direction of motion along a path. Together, they connect mathematics to our experience of physical space. Together, magnitude and direction give us vectors.

Travel distance is one example of a broader spatial schema. The *source-path-goal* schema moves an entity from a source of motion and toward a destination goal. We describe paths traveled using words like *along*, *through*, and *across*. This spatial language is sometimes called "fictive motion." It can help us understand and describe parts of our world that do not actually move. A fence *runs* alongside the road that *goes* up the hill. Of course, neither the fence nor road move at all.

Fictive motion is one of the ways we describe meaning when we see information. Data takes on a personality that moves about the page: A trend *reaches* its peak and lines *meet* at a point. The way we talk about charts makes it sound like they are flea circuses inhabited by imaginary beings moving about the grid.

The distance-number metaphor also gives zero more meaning. When we first considered objects, zero was emptiness, absence, or destruction. Zero was the group of nothing. Then, the measuring stick helped us extend our thinking to zero as the ultimate smallness. Distance implies a departure point. Now, zero is the name of the origin of travel. Zero can finally scream out of the void. It has become a real place. Zero is the point-location at the start of the number line.

Travel along a path gives a relatable home to zero and then proceeds forward. The directional nature of travel allows us to also consider going backward on a return trip. Negative magnitude, impossible to imagine with a bunch of bricks, can now be seen. To negate is to move against the direction of the path. Existence below zero simply describes progress in the opposite direction. The entire number line can be pivoted, or reflected,

Personification is a general category that covers a very wide range of metaphors, each picking out different aspects of a person or ways of looking at a person. ... they allow us to make sense of phenomena in the world in human terms—terms that we can understand on the basis of our own motivations, goals, actions, and characteristics.
LAKOFF AND JOHNSON, 1980

Science interests me precisely because of my efforts to escape anthropomorphic knowledge; at the same time, however, I'm convinced that our imagination can only be anthropomorphic.
ITALO CALVINO, 1985

We use the same language to talk about the number line as we do geographic space: "4.9 is near 5. The result is around 40. Count backward from 20. Count to 100, starting at 20. Name all the numbers from 2 to 10."
LAKOFF AND NÚÑEZ, 2000

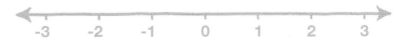

around zero to balance the environment. Negative numbers extend our basic experience of physical reality so that we can do even more with mathematics.

Time after Time

Sixty's many factors (2*30, 3*20, 4*15, 5*12, 6*10) offered a pre-fraction world several ways to slice a whole, which is why there are 60 minutes in an hour and 360 degrees in a circle.

We use the number line to understand all sorts of phenomena. Perhaps most helpful is the way its linearity has become conflated with time: the past, the future, and the space in-between that we inhabit right now. Space and time have always been mixed-up linguistically, light-years ahead of Einstein's space-time continuum. How exactly do we see time?

Time is space.	Space is time.
In the *near* future,	Turn *after* the light, but
perhaps *at* two o'clock.	*before* the statue.

The depiction of time: The process begins with metaphor. Once the metaphor is established, the images quickly follow.
KRISTEN LIPPINCOTT, 1999

We are so spellbound by our voyage through time that it is easy to forget that we have not always been along for the ride. Our linear comprehension of time is rooted in the limits of our embodied experience of the world. The evolutionary story goes something like the following: Eyes evolved to hunt for specific objects in the environment. But the most sensitive photoreceptors detect only a small portion of the entire field of vision. Narrow slices of the environment arrive to our mind in the order that we direct our focus. Moment to moment, we move our eyes and send new slices to the mind. The holistic, three-dimensional image of the world you think you see is actually a psychological trick of the brain. It is the product of combining a sequence of narrow, two-dimensional flashes.

Perception of time is not linear. In our mind, time speeds up the farther into the future we go. One year from today definitely feels closer than two years away. On the other hand, 10 years from today feels about the same as 11 years away. Both periods are one year apart, but we perceive them differently.
DONA WONG, 2010

Your ancestors' eyes darted about the landscape to find food and detect predators. Today, the analogous hunt is for the perfect piece of fruit at the grocer. Stand still in front of a display of apples. Your visual search across the bin of apples is experienced as a temporal journey, even though neither you nor the fruit ever move. The sequential cascade of images arrives across the sequential passage of time. As our eyes dart around we begin to anticipate what might come next. We begin to have foresight about the future.

Our ancestors did not just stand still, of course. Like us, they moved around. And as we move around, especially with forward-facing predator eyes, we experience time through our motion. Time, like space, is a dimension that we move through. Time is travel over a landscape. Time becomes associated with distance. A change in time is a change in distance. The passage of time is linear motion over a landscape. The number line is naturally extended to conceptualize time as distance. We are *at a point* in time, hurtling *into* the future *from* the past. Our personal mental image puts us, in this current moment, at the zero-origin, with past events *behind* our forward motion and future events *ahead* of it. Like someone looking out the back window of a car, we see the past receding in the distance, blind to what's to come.

Our motion through space became conflated with motion through time. Across evolution, our identity and concept of self strengthened. We all became time travelers who remember the past, expect the future, and move through time together, at the constant speed of reality, one second per second. And then, a curious flip can occur. As the self strengthens, we no longer move through time. Time moves through us. Time becomes objectified, even personified, and it does not sit still. Time becomes a moving object that hurtles toward us. The time *will come*, then the time *arrives*, and then it is *gone*. Because time moves, it has a front, which takes a face, just like us. We *face the future* just as the *future faces us*.

Western readers naturally begin scanning pages at the top left and move diagonally to the bottom right according to the pull of "reading gravity" first described by newspaper graphics pioneer Edmund Arnold. Eye-tracking tests confirm the top left corner is where to put the most important information.

Time travel is only science fiction when it happens suddenly.
MICHAEL BIERUT, 2005

The statement *We're looking ahead to the following weeks* seems to be metaphorically inconsistent. Something that follows should be behind, not ahead. However, this phrase works because it combines two temporal frames of reference: From our perspective, we are looking forward and ahead. From the future's perspective, the "following weeks" are the far future that is following the near future, with the entire future train barreling toward us.

THE PAST

NEXT WEEK

FOLLOWING WEEK

The year zero does not exist in the *Anno Domini* system of the current Gregorian calendar. The year 1 BC is immediately followed by AD 1. The Scythian monk Dionysius Exiguus (c. 470–544) is credited with inventing the Anno Domini era. He is also the first known medieval Latin writer to use a precursor for the concept of the number zero, which would not reach Europe broadly for hundreds of years.

As we reflect on our life, we might play with the number line's origin point. Our own life anchors a personal timeline as we count our age from birth. Our timeline extends through the current point of progress and into an uncertain future. Thinking about our own number line helps us build relationships with a continuum of versions of our self across time. It helps us recognize that the current moment is not all there is. We have an origin and a destination.

To reflect on your experiences is to converse with your past self. To make plans for the future is to make an agreement with your future self. You make little bargains with your future. *Do not eat all the food today; save some for tomorrow.* Practical and symbolic sacrifices helped us plan and improve. Paradoxically, youth represents both the past and the future. In the past you were young, but the potential of today's youth inherits the future. We can have clearer conversations across time as we learn to manage our multiple temporalities.

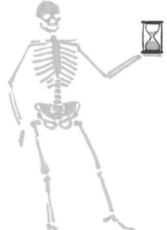

The human awakening to time is so important that it became immortalized as one of the creation myths of Genesis. Adam and Eve eat from the tree of knowledge and learn of their own impending doom. A personal relationship with time is a relationship with one's own mortality. To know time is to know that the state you exist in today will not persist forever.

Detach the timeline's origin from your personal existence. Now, you can entertain more creative possibilities for how to see time, and how time can help us see. Removing the self uncouples the number line from our personal life and sets it free to look for other sensible origins. The origin could be any date within the continuum of our world. Perhaps we select a historic event like the birth of a religious hero or the Big Bang's birth of the universe itself. Every timeline suggests a beginning and end, whether personal, historic, or cosmic.

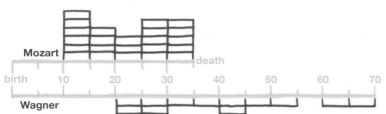

OPERAS

by age of composer, at composition

Mozart

death

birth   10   20   30   40   50   60   70

Wagner

Chronostatic time
is relative time,
determined by looking
at relationships to
other events.

Chronometric time
is absolute time,
usually described by
year, a global constant
progression of time.

We can also step outside of a single time continuity to play with many timelines at once. If we gauge distance as the time elapsed since birth, then the timeline can be repurposed to represent age instead of dates. Asynchronous lives can be reimagined as contemporary and compared using this new context.

The timeline is a marvelous extension of the number line. Timelines adapt arithmetic properties to show differences, helping us see spans of time. The number line's continuous property allows us to imagine immeasurably small slices of time. Its directionality can help us reorient what the past and future mean to any particular perspective. The timeline can even help us weave different continuities together. It is so useful and so powerful that we forget that the timeline is but one visual way of seeing time.

The time-is-distance metaphor was essential for the Newton-Leibniz conception of calculus, which begins by considering the change of distance over a change in time: $[f (x+ \delta) - f (x)] / [\delta]$ Taking the ratio of distance to time makes perfect sense if you already consider time to be a type of distance.

Any Time You Want

Beyond movement, other sequential activities reinforce the linearity of time. Counting objects and constructing shelters step by step further anchor us in linear time. Wherever sequential alphabets gained power, cultures became more transfixed by linear time. Change the order of the letters, and you get a new meaning: *canoe* is never mistaken for its anagram *ocean*. *Map* is not the same as its levidrome *Pam*. Linear time in our mind moves forward because we move forward. Linear time on the page moves from left to right because we read from left to right.

Just because the Latin alphabet is read left-to-right does not mean that reading has always been so. Before Gutenberg gave us cheap books, people did not read much. But if they did,

In all these cases, every point of view is correct. It all depends upon what you consider to be moving. What does all this mean for design? What is natural depends upon point of view, the choice of metaphor, and therefore, the culture.
DON NORMAN, 2013

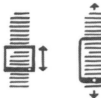

Screens orient navigation with a moving-window or moving-page metaphor.

there was a good chance that it would have been on a vertical scroll. Verticalness is fundamental to our perspective as creatures defined by an upright posture. Today, time progresses as we scroll down web pages. You advance toward the future as you read toward the bottom of an article. We can sense this weakly in English when we talk about a family heirloom being handed *down* to the next generation.

By contrast, in static infographics where the reader does not move content, such as in a printed newspaper, the most recent time is often at the top. This suggests the murkiness of the past: Sit in a boat today and look down into the water of time, where less light is able to shine on older events. So, vertical time's direction might depend on whether the reader interacts with the content. In either case, vertical time orientation should be reinforced.

Chinese Mandarin words are different from the words of Western languages. Chinese is not made up of sequential phonetic alphabet characters and so does not demand any particular lateral reading. Its traditional vertical orientation still impacts how the Chinese language orients time. The past is up and the future is down: June is *above* July. July is *under* June.

Even more important than how its characters are arranged is how Chinese words are composed. Each character is an ideogram because each holistically represents an idea without indicating the sound used to say it. They can then be poetically combined to create ideogrammatic metaphors. For example, *tomorrow* 明天, combines the ideograms for *day* 日, *moon* 月, and *date* 天. The result is a written language that, relative to Western written languages, emphasizes synthesis more than sequence. The Mandarin language does not include past, present, or future

tenses. There is no need to conjugate verbs. The entire essence of time is less linear. This perspective has preserved more appreciation in China for another ancient way of thinking about time: in circles.

Like a train running down its tracks *clickety-clack clickety-clack* the minutia of moment-to-moment experience feels like one long sequence. But what if the train track runs in a big circle? Consider any span of life and you notice recurring phenomena. A new sunrise every day. A new moon every month. A new harvest every year. Of course, we know now that all these natural cycles are created by incomprehensibly large circles in space. We perceive cycles because Earth rotates and revolves.

As hunter-gatherers, our lives revolved around the cycles of birth, life, and death. At night we looked to the stars and tracked their progression. The agricultural revolution extended our understanding of time—time is a circle—to the lives of crops and livestock. An early agriculturist's experience was not that different from the life of their parents. Unlike the last few hundred years of history, there was little discernible change between generations. All noticeable changes came from natural cycles. The health of the community depended on our ability to manage these cycles. Every spring, the rebirth of crops and new baby animals strengthened communities. If you master the circle of time, then you can rule your world.

Today, we can splice linear and circular time together by imagining a spiral. Its coils capture the essence of moving around in a circle and moving forward along a line. Like a Babylonian ziggurat, the tower spirals around as it climbs. Unfortunately, showing a Slinky-spiral form in static 2-D does not convey the visual metaphor well. Even rotating a spiral on screen somehow is not the same as rotating it in our heads. Abstracting a spiral to zig-zag lines or a sinusoidal curve may be a good compromise if we can bear over-emphasized turning points.

Right-handedness influences the direction of text. Chiseled letters, hammered by the dominant right hand, were naturally inscribed right to left. This method left a lasting mark on ancient right-left written languages such as Hebrew. Ink's invention necessitated a switch so that the pen-holding right hand did not smudge wet ink.

In [South American] Aymaran culture, the past is ahead because it is already known and can therefore be seen. The future, in contrast, is unknown and can't be seen; therefore, it is located behind the speaker. JAMES GEARY, 2011

[Australian Aboriginal] Pormpuraawans arrange time according to cardinal directions: east to west. That is, time flows from left to right when one is facing south, from right to left when one is facing north, toward the body when one is facing east, and away from the body when one is facing west. BORODITSKY AND GABY, 2010

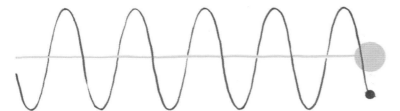

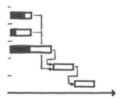

Henry Gantt developed a waterfall method in the 1910s to manage schedules. The *Gantt chart* was refined through its use in WWI to coordinate production for American armed forces. Polish researcher Karol Adamiecki had already invented a similar method in the 1890s, called the *harmonograf*.

What is the world? What is reality? In the end reality is just a flow of data. Physics, biology, economics, it's all just a flow of data.
YUVAL NOAH HARARI, 2017

A different visual metaphor for time highlights individual spans of time. It minimizes the continuity stressed by the timeline and time cycle. More and more, we appreciate the idiom that *time is money*. Today we *spend*, *invest*, and *budget* our time. We are careful how we use it because we only *have so much* and it will eventually *run out*. Time is a thing you give, lose, and expect to be thanked for.

Time as valuable currency revives the first metaphor of this chapter. Time as money, like other objects, gets counted. In today's world, our digital calendars help schedule time in minute increments. It is as if we each manage our time like Ebenezer Scrooge manages the coins in his counting house, carefully dolling out every twelfth of an hour.

Today, the work of chemist and Nobel laureate Ilya Prigogine can help us think of time in yet one more way, *an irreversible performance*. The whole universe is a stage, and all matter are its actors. The actors move about the stage with energy and the play unfolds with their unpredictable interaction. We could never give all of them, all of the matter in the universe, perfect directions for how to return to exactly where they were at the start. That would require an impossible amount of precision. As complexity expert César Hidalgo summarized, "There is no past, although there was a past. In our universe, there is no past, and no future, but only a present that is being calculated at every instant."

WORLD BUILDING

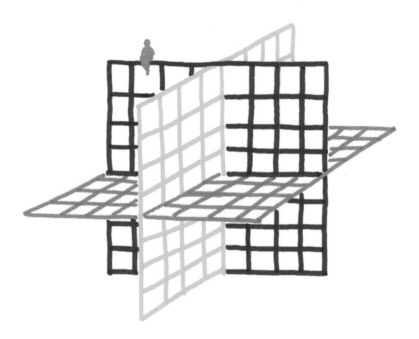

*The Grid, a digital frontier. I tried to picture clusters
of information as they moved through the computer.
What do they look like? Ships, motorcycles? Were the
circuits like freeways? I kept dreaming of a world
I thought I'd never see. And then, one day... I got in.*

KEVIN FLYNN, TRON: LEGACY

To see data, we must build a visual world for it to inhabit. The metaphors we use to count objects, measure distance, and experience time are the foundations for building these worlds. To choose the rules of these worlds is to choose how data gets spatially encoded. Further design decisions flow once we position data.

Spatial Diagrams

Think of the number line as a virtual world. Compared to the one we inhabit, it is rather simple. Yet, the number line is a self-contained world. It has order, rules, and constraints. Like a tabletop aquarium, any number line is a product of, and exists within, *our* world. Both the number line and fish tank are also distinct domains we get to play in. When we invoke visual metaphors to visualize data, it is like we are imagining an aquarium for the data to swim in. How big should it be? What does its terrain look like? Will the data look interesting in this world?

> *One might say that the world is hardly more ancient than the art of making the world.*
> PAUL VALÉRY, 1871–1945

Numbered worlds were most whimsically related by schoolmaster Edwin Abbott in 1884. In his Lineland, points move back and forth, unable to imagine the higher-dimensional world of geometric shapes. Shapes exist on a plane called Flatland. There, number lines cross to form a two-dimensional grid. Flatland is inhabited by triangles, circles and the square protagonist (named A. Square). These flat characters struggle to comprehend the three-dimensional Spaceland of spheres and cubes.

In *Unflattening*, comics educator Nick Sousanis uses Abbott's *Flatland* to show how dimensional extension can elevate us above the confines of limited perspectives:

> *Imagine a vast sheet of paper on which straight Lines, Triangles, Squares, Pentagons, Hexagons, and other figures, instead of remaining fixed in their places, move freely about, on or in the surface, but without the power of rising above or sinking below it, very much like shadows....*
> EDWIN ABBOTT, 1884

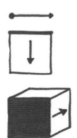

In one dimension –
moving a point produces a line.
In two, moving a line creates a square.
Moving in three dimensions,
a square forms a cube.
And moving a cube in four dimensions?

World building is essential to any storytelling adventure. When I recall my favorite childhood stories I am transported to Alice's Wonderland, Dorothy's Oz, or Wendy's Neverland. These stories have relatively simple plots. *Find your way home. Get the prize. Defeat the villain.* The light narrative burden clears plenty of room for complex, colorful, and compelling world building.

Like Abbott's spheres and cubes, we too inhabit a Spaceland. Our original look at the world is with our own eyes. They give a thoroughly unique perspective. From our self-centered vantage point, we perceive direction and distance relative to our body. Things are to the right or left of me, below or above me, close to or distant from me.

Even though we are vertically oriented creatures, our motion is often abstracted to a flat, 2-D plane. We live in a world represented by the marriage of two number lines: forward-back and left-right. Most of our spaces are

flat because it takes a lot of energy to raise our bodies against the force of gravity. The vertical dimension is only seriously considered during specific activities. We think about going up and down when we scale a hill, ride an elevator, or climb to cruising altitude. Despite our higher dimensionality, we frequently think about our own physical reality as a kind of Flatland.

Imagine walking across the neighborhood to dinner. Part of your mental vision might include some kind of avatar moving about an overhead map. Mobile web maps reinforce this view. They dynamically reposition the entire virtual Earth so that you stay at the center of the screen. You are the star of the show. This out-of-body perspective fuses our personal vantage point with a more objective frame of reference.

What do we make of our contemporary interactive maps' post-Copernican, egocentric orientation, which places you —not the earth, not the sun, not Jerusalem or Mecca —at the center? What happens when we hold in our hands manipulable maps that render space as something seamlessly traversable, rational, and exploitable?
SHANNON MATTERN, 2015

The crowning achievement of memory is the model of the world we carry in our heads, a kind of diorama that closely resembles reality and allows us to respond to events in real time … we are all born cartographers who draw mental maps….
ABBY SMITH RUMSEY, 2016

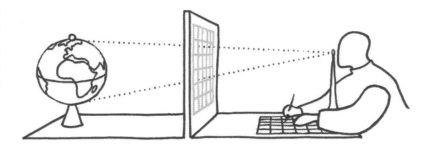

The front-back-left-right perspective is meaningful only to the unique viewer. In contrast, a north-south-east-west grid is useful to anyone who traverses its plane. Latitude and longitude's objectivity transports our personal experience from relativity to the 2-D virtual world. In either case, how we think about our multidimensional world is not so multidimensional after all.

The geographic map is populated with a variety of simple marks. Points, lines, and shapes represent roads, buildings, land, vehicles, and you. Each flat map is a *projection* of the globe designed for a particular use case. Each map projection is a tool designed for a specific purpose. All map projections are distorted because they warp the surface of Earth's oblate spheroid to lie flat on a map's 2-D plane. Projections straddle trade-offs between area, shape, direction, bearing, distance, and scale.

There are appropriate and inappropriate map projection choices. It all depends on what part of Earth you want to show, and for what purpose. However projected, physical geography is reduced to Flatland's two-dimensions. Map grids are created by crossing two axes, two distance-number lines. They elegantly mirror our embodied conception of the world around us.

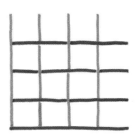

The perpendicular distance-number lines of longitude and latitude mimic the physical world and connect physical geography to the Cartesian plane. The geographic map is a gateway to exploring an endless variety of 2-D virtual worlds. Replace the longitude-latitude axes with other

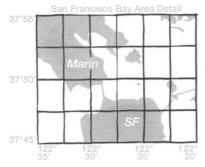

San Francisco Bay Area Detail

37°55'
37°50'
37°45'

Marin

SF

122° 35' | 122° 30' | 122° 25' | 122° 20'

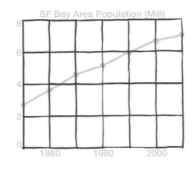

SF Bay Area Population (Mill)

8
6
4
2
0

1960 | 1980 | 2000

A mapping is a correspondence. It associates each element of a given set with one element of a second set

dimensions, such as time and performance, and the same grid can be used to explore more abstract territories. A familiar grid variant places time on the horizontal axis. This abstract grid shows us what would be difficult to appreciate otherwise. It lets us see how a value, like population, changes over the years in a way impossible without a picture. All grids are virtual worlds we interpret and navigate.

When you define the horizontal (x) and vertical (y) axes of a 2-D plane, you are world-building. Virtual environments are invoked so data can be positioned. Just as map roads and buildings demand a virtual geography, all data must have a spatial home if they are to be seen. It is like set-design for play actors. The show cannot go on without a stage. Some of these environments, like the stock market price (y) over time (x), are quite familiar. Other worlds require careful introduction. Most of these virtual worlds will build somehow on our familiarity with the number line and its conceptual extension, the timeline.

Like 2-D web maps, data worlds are not reality. They are useful virtual models of reality. It is easy to lose yourself in these virtual worlds, but we have not yet been completely consumed by them. We still look toward the horizon and picture what is on the other side of the next hill.

Descartes cemented the convention of using the beginning of the alphabet (abc) for known constants and the end (xyz) for unknown variables. It has been speculated that x is the most prominent variable in Descartes's *La Géométrie* (1637) because it is the least commonly used letter. Terry Moore argued that x is the result of Spanish scholars using the Greek X (Chi) as a phonetic stand-in for the *sh* sound of the Arabic word ﺀﻲﺷﻻ (al-shalan), which means "the unknown thing."

Ancient Romans adopted Greek orthogonal city grids. The *Cardo Maximus* was the main north-south street in the city; it was full of shops and considered the axis, or hinge (*cardo*), of the city. Today, we still call the north-south-east-west directional hinges the *cardinal* directions.

Off the Grid

Rectangular maps and charts are everywhere. Yet, Cartesian x-y axes are only one way to build worlds for data. Polar coordinates put the focus of the world on a central axis, or pole, and extend vectors away from that anchor. The polar world has two dimensions, just like its square cousin. But their meaning is asymmetrical compared to the rectangular grid. Cartesian axes are balanced in rectangular harmony.

Polar coordinates' nested circles and radiating rays are not so interchangeable. They strike a different kind of perpendicularity. Each polar axis has a differentiated ability to convey information.

Vectors are perfectly shown with the angle-magnitude dimensions of polar coordinates, but these axes can do even more. Polar charts reflect basic ways we perceive the world. They channel an outlook from a definite perspective and they reflect our cyclical appreciation of time. Furthermore, polar charts often have a compact form factor, which makes them easy additions to many graphic compositions.

The pie chart shows part-to-whole ratios. It works well for a few categories. Our mind's eye contrasts pie chart divisions against invisible 25, 50, and 75 percent portions of the circle. These reference points are reinforced by our familiarity with clock faces. Pie charts are criticized for their inability to display comparisons effectively. Indeed, they are not capable of comparing too many divisions. All things being equal, data is usually better displayed with a bar chart, but things are often not equal.

Pie charts continue to perform on thematic maps. There, they serve triple duty. First, they encode position as marks on a

Clocks runs clockwise because they mimic the directional path of a sundial's shadow in the northern hemisphere.

Pie chart slices are conventionally ordered by size, with the biggest starting at the top 12:00 position and proceeding clockwise until the smallest piece ends back at 11:59. An alternate ordering also places the largest slice clockwise from 12:00, but the second largest slice counter-clockwise from 12:00, giving both a chance to be compared against the invisible horizontal reference line that runs from 9:00 to 3:00.

Typical

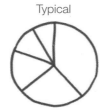

Alternate

Too Many?

greater reference plane; second, they encode magnitude with circle area size, and, third, they encode a simple ratio with the angular division of the pie. Polar coordinates make virtual a worldview that appreciates distance

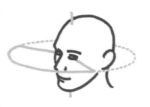

from the center. The tribal, and *polarizing*, us-versus-them attitude reflects a past reality where we did not yet have a global sense of geography. In some ways, the self-centeredness of polar coordinates is more natural. We stand upright at the center of our own personal world and turn about to look out at what is near and far. In the evolutionary extreme, polar coordinates hurtle us right back to a life jumping through the branches around the trunk of our home tree. Imagine an evolutionary ancestor's mental map of the world. The world is anchored to the safety of the tree. Distance is tracked from the tree. Direction is mapped around the tree, perhaps anchored by the position of the warming sun. The world extends cylindrically from the forest floor to the heavenly sky.

Much later, we lived in walled cities. The physical boundary protected the community from the dangers of wild animals and ravagers of the outside world. The early city, or *polis*, was safety. Its center was

sacred, and often marked with a temple altar or vertical obelisk. For its inhabitants, their city was the center of their world. Unlike the ancient tree-jumpers, early city-dwellers were already losing interest in the vertical dimension. Our love of polar coordinates is more deeply rooted than we can imagine.

As we move about the globe, different perspectives help us enhance the environments we build for data. Cartesian and polar systems are readily available codes for positioning data. Both virtual microcosms mirror physical environments. Their familiarity helps audiences navigate and interpret their way through information.

The curved surface of the globe stitches together Cartesian and polar coordinates into a conceptual harmony. A perfect polar system is seen at the poles, while zooming into where anyone actually lives shows a rectangular grid.

The polar and rectangular mental maps we already use to explore the physical world are repurposed to explore all kinds of data. Cartesian and polar coordinates are easy. They are easy to understand, and easy to implement. They ask you to simply snap data variable to axis, then sit back and relax as data pop into place. And that is wonderful, but it is also only a partial conception of how we can position data. What if these ready-made systems are not the best visual home for your data?

You Can Relate

We carry around a lot of experiential knowledge in our heads. Some of it is spatial. Our ability to traverse places that are familiar is naturally stored on a mental map. But onboard geographic knowledge is not what makes people special. Other animals, some with built-in magnetic systems, are superior wayfinders. Eels, shorebirds, bats, and even ants, all navigate staggeringly immense journeys.

What is truly special about humans is our ability to absorb, store, and transmit information that has little to do with geography. We are obsessed with invisible abstraction, long historical arcs of power, personal and professional relationships, and emotions whose essence escapes numerical capture. The abstract worlds we inhabit are what make people marvelous. Must we ground abstract information in maps that stem from the geographic world? Both Cartesian and polar systems help creators and readers, but perhaps there is a better way to show invisible worlds. What other microcosms might surpass these encoding systems?

Vertical power relationships have persisted through thousands of years of history. From Egyptian pharaohs to the medieval church to today's CEO, humans understand that power is stacked. Today, our conception of hierarchy is divorced from lived physical reality. Yet, we can still see vertical power's origin with a vision of a predator above its kill. *The powerful are on top.* This visual metaphor shapes how we imagine the power dynamics of society. Vertical power encoding logic is on display in the design of the org chart.

Information always invites us to realize it into better forms. It does not always map well to any standard linear or circular

 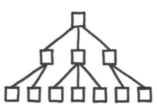 

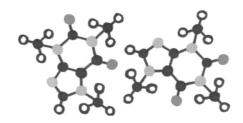

diagram. Perhaps your mind pictures it in a different way, just as the corporation is reflected in the tapered shape of the pyramid. Take a moment to pause and engage with your mind's eye. *How does my mind already picture this information? If I were to pencil a sketch of what my mind already sees, what would it look like?*

Data that does not map to familiar spatial encodings often have something to do with relationships. Relationships are documented by their nodes and whether these nodes link to one another. Then, qualities about the nodes and relationships can be added. Node-link network graphs reflect this particular data structure well. But like a table of text, these graphs often come up short showing anything of interest.

Too many network graphs are burdened with too many connections. A network hairball only reveals that the network has many connections. Respect the limits of display density. Then, network graphs may help discover groups, connecting paths, and associated nodes.

Network positions are fluid. If you remake a network graph, then its nodes may appear in a new location, as long as the

same relationships are preserved. This is different from the geographic map, where the same city will always appear at the same latitude and longitude. For example, consider the chemical bonds of the caffeine molecule ($C_8H_{10}N_4O_2$). The entire molecular network can be rotated because the relationship links are still maintained. You may never see the same network the same way twice. Caffeine is still caffeine, wherever the nodes get drawn.

This freedom of positioning can be problematic. We yearn to catalog, categorize, and fix things in space. Recall how we extend existing familiar concepts to learn new knowledge. If we recognize something new as belonging to an existing category, then we can project our existing category knowledge to the new thing. Consistent positioning gives us something familiar to compare new things against. Unreliable, always-changing network positions take away the opportunity for a spatial baseline reference. Changing positions reduces

Adjacent

Shortest Path

Ring

Topology comprises geometric properties and spatial relations unaffected by the continuous change of shape or size of figures.

A testament to our
fondness for spatial
information, the
*memory palace
technique*, also called
method of loci, helped
ancient orators deliver
long speeches from
memory by associating
conceptual chunks
with objects located
in an imaginary
architectural space.

One idea, say *Playfair
invented the bar chart*,
might be associated
with an imaginary
deck of cards placed
on an imaginary table
in the middle of the
imaginary entrance
hall. Chunks can be
retrieved as needed
by mentally "walking"
through the space and
recognizing objects.
Sometimes, these
spaces reflected real
places already familiar
to orators. Often, they
were constructed
(and expanded with
additions) to perfectly
accommodate
memories.

The used-future
world of *Star Wars*
helps create the
magic, but it is not
the main event.

our ability to visually compare the new to the familiar. The spatial freedom of network graphs also runs against how our mind actually pictures relationships. The mind may not see networks as tied to any geography, or even a numeric scheme. The mind may also not be able to picture many relationships at once. But, the mind's way of thinking about relationships often has some kind of meaningful order. You do not change the cubbyholes mentally reserved for your high school friends with those reserved for your family members. You anchor classes of relationships according to some kind of schema. Just as power relationships were likened to physical domination that put the subjugated below the powerful, conceptual rules can be unearthed to help position network graphs. Positional logic boosts context and helps keep design consistent for later reference. The chaos of the ever-morphing network graph can be tamed if we build it a more meaningful world.

Our first set of visual metaphors traces an evolution of human cognition: outward facing polar diagrams, geographic maps, timelines, number lines, and the spatial freedom of network graphs. They all began with how we understand our own physical reality and then advanced toward abstract visions of invisible worlds.

We have introduced these different positioning schema one by one. But they need not be isolated in practice. They are at the ready for you to smash together into new spatial schema. It is up to you to craft the most effective virtual world for your data to inhabit and your audience to explore.

We are now more familiar with how our physical reality is linked to different conceptual frames, especially how we think about numbers. We have a sense that these perspectives can help us build better worlds for data. Better worlds fit how we already think about things so that it is easier to learn something new. But world building is not the endgame. We build worlds so that we have a place to layer meaning. We build worlds so that we can see data.

6

INFUSE

MEANING

That was an instance of the charts meaning
something for everyone, that they excluded nobody,
that they allowed several layers of understanding.
MARIE NEURATH, 1898–1986

How do we convey meaning inside visual worlds? Well, there is a universe of possibility to consider. Position, so crucial to world building, is also one of the strongest conduits of meaning. It is joined by many other factors, such as color and size, to provide a multifaceted creative toolbox for linking visual cues to nonvisual concepts.

The canvas, printed page or digital screen, gives us only two dimensions to play with. Each dimension comes with a significant amount of baggage. Some ubiquitous visual metaphors, such as *time goes to the right* and *good goes up*, are natural to even data-illiterate audiences. They pack meaning into the Cartesian grid before we even get a chance to do anything with it. Once we know these biases, we can incorporate them into our design to ease audience's reading.

Upwards

The vertical dimension has been associated with emotionally reading a person's body language, *looking someone up and down*. The *horizontal* dimension, associated with scanning the horizon, has been associated with the focus of the hunt.

The direction of up is usually relative to gravity's downward pull. Our upright posture was critical to our ability to scan the horizon, become the greatest endurance runners on the planet, and free hands for other tasks. Higher altitudes evoke the positivity of the mythological tree home, whose axis stretches against gravity, from downtrodden animalistic roots up to angelic heavens.

Today, we live in a rectangular world. Buildings rise perpendicular to the horizon. They help tune our senses to detect even small deviations from a perfectly vertical line. Upright orientation has also impacted how we think about a myriad of abstract concepts. When we are happy we actually stand taller, things look *up*, and our spirits *soar*. When sad, we slouch, feel *depressed*, and our spirits *sink*. Consider these other vertically oriented dualities of good and bad:

HEALTH	MORE	VIRTUE	RATIONAL	PRESTIGE	CONTROL
Peak health.	Income *went up*.	*Upright* morals.	*High*-minded	*Lofty position*.	Control *over*.
Top shape.	Prices *soared*.	*High* standards.	intellectual.	*Rise to the top*.	*Height* of power.
Fell ill.	Stocks *fell*.	*Beneath* me.	*Rise above* your	*Fell* in status.	*Low man on the*
Dropped dead.	Turn heat *down*.	*Low-down*.	emotions.	*Bottom of ladder*.	*totem pole*.
SICKNESS	LESS	DEPRAVITY	EMOTIONAL	TRIVIAL	SUBJECTED

In 1980, linguist-philosophers George Lakoff and Mark Johnson introduced these and many other primary concepts in *Metaphors We Live By*. It revealed how our own spatialization helps us make sense of abstract and invisible worlds. Topside positive connotation is nearly universal across a spectrum of social categories. For data stories, the top of any visual canvas naturally communicates positive emotion.

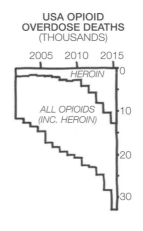

USA OPIOID OVERDOSE DEATHS (THOUSANDS)

Piling more deaths downward invokes the *down is bad* conceptual metaphor.

On the one hand, the vertical y-axis is traditionally associated with the dependent variable. This means the vertical dimension is where a lot of the excitement happens. The horizontal x-axis, on the other hand, is the independent workhorse of the story. It keeps steady time like a metronome while the response gets to go up and down on the vertical y-axis. Both directions are critical to data stories.

We can choose to design against spatial biases in pursuit of more novel storytelling. But this may increase the risk of confusing the message. Creative experiments are laudable, but only when we recognize the responsibility that comes with going against conventions. They may need compelling design and added explanation to be successful. Deploy planar axes judiciously. You only get two and they each wield enormous power.

Onward

The horizontal x-axis is associated with time, just as metaphoric linear time stretches over the horizon. The x-axis is called independent because it often holds values that are not affected by circumstance. Independent values are self-governing. The x-axis often represents the regular frequency of data collection. We record the high temperature every single day, no matter how hot or cold it is. As the timeline introduction stated, we attribute the direction of time to how we read and write. We usually proceed through time to the right. Its vertical flow can go up or down. Western future is rarely on the left.

The principles:
1. Smooth, flat, horizontal shapes give us a sense of stability and calm. I associate horizontal shapes with the surface of the earth or the horizon line... We humans are most stable when we are horizontal, because we can't fall down. Shapes that lie horizontal look secure because they won't fall on us, either.
2. Vertical shapes are more exciting and more active. Vertical shapes rebel against the earth's gravity. They imply energy and a reaching toward heights or the heavens... These structures require a great deal of energy to build—to become vertical. They will release a great deal of energy if they fall. Vertical structures are monuments to kinetic energy of the past and the future, and to potential energy of the present.
MOLLY BANG, 2000

The archetypal display of time is the x-axis time-series chart. It tracks a value as it fluctuates up and down through time. There is a practical limit to how quickly data is sampled. We do not actually measure anything continuously. Smaller divisions of time can always be measured. So we choose a data-collection frequency that is precise enough. Showing a phenomenon with a continuous line mirrors our own uninterrupted experience of time, even though we record actual data at discrete moments. We see time-series data as an uninterrupted flow that proceeds to the right, just as we imagine the adventures of a storybook hero like Alice, whose journey progresses to the right as we turn the pages. Time-series charts consider the data's temporal density, value variability, and completeness. We must match the qualities of our data to the way we already perceive time. Visualization expert William Cleveland categorized ways of showing time by how each helps better show the data:

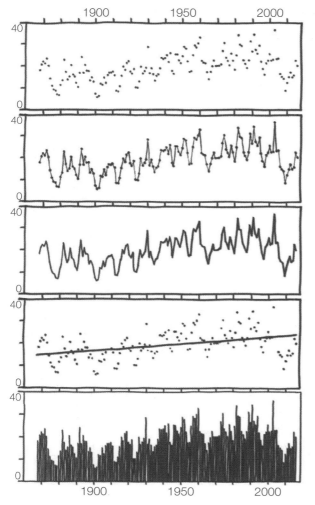

SYMBOL GRAPH
Shows long-term trend
of low-frequency data

CONNECTED SYMBOL GRAPH
See data points and their
ordering through time

CONNECTED GRAPH
Smooth series for when perceiving
individual values is not important

SYMBOL GRAPH WITH TREND
Helps assess a long-
term linear trend

VERTICAL LINE GRAPH
Highlights max and min
extremes while still showing
individual values.

This data shows a measure of the disturbance level of the Earth's magnetic field. Learn its backstory in the endnotes.

Another way to achieve continuous flow is to use a summary curve. They are generally constructed with some type of moving average. In this way, they differ from a mathematical trend, which uses a formula to fit a single straight line to the data. A smoothing summary curve may benefit data that is too noisy. However, not showing the noise of all the data points can suggest a cleaner story than is actually there. Also, be careful that the summary line does not conceal significant gaps in the data. If you connect sparse points you might suggest more data than is actually available. It is better to leave gaps empty or straddle them with a dashed line.

Even seemingly simple line charts can confuse or, in very poor designs, lead to faulty decoding. Data journalist Dona Wong advocates that axis scales should be segmented into the familiar multiples people already use when thinking about numbers. We often count in fives or tens, but elections sometimes come in four-year cycles. Time should be in days, weeks, months, or years. Line charts do not need to have a baseline at zero, but their baseline should not confuse. Extend axes to zero rather than stopping at a baseline that is *close to zero*. A zero baseline may be emphasized as heavier, a non-zero baseline should have the same weight as other grid lines.

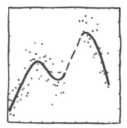

The dashed line gives us a way to express the idea that something is not concrete. Something impermanent. It may be temporary; it may not currently exist (it will in the future or it did in the past); or it may be invisible or hidden. One way or the other, it represents what it is—not solid.
CONNIE MALAMED, 2012

Ratio scales... have a meaningful zero point. Weight, height, speed, and so on, are examples of ratio variables. If one car is traveling at 100 mph and another one is at 50, you can say that the first one is going 50 miles faster than the second, and you can also say that it's going twice as fast.
ALBERTO CAIRO, 2016

100°F is not twice as hot as 50°F because temperature zero points are arbitrary. 0°F was originally keyed to the temperature of brine by the inventor of the first modern thermometer, Daniel Gabriel Fahrenheit.

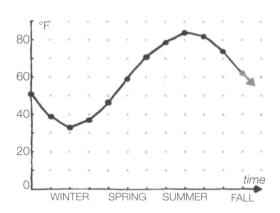

Sizing Up

We already had a glimpse of the power of size. Recall that *big things are important* because a bigger object takes up more of your visual field. Bigger things demand notice. When objects are collected into groups, the largest group commands more attention. A taller pile of things has more things in it. More products, more land, more people, more money, and even more

The *International System Of Typographic Picture Education*, or Isotype, is a method of pictorial statistics developed by Otto and Marie Neurath. It used a single symbol to represent a fixed quantity. Greater quantities are shown by the repetition of that symbol, rather than scaling the size of a single symbol.

time: We can convey all flavors of *more* with larger size.

The basic metaphorical linkage between physical size and numeric magnitude seems easy enough. However, the way you actually make shapes bigger with data in order to show more is trickier than meets the eye. We are pretty good at decoding linear position along the number line; four looks twice as far from zero as two does. However, decoding the same numbers in two dimensions, with sized areas, is fraught with pitfalls.

When we encode values in spatial dimensions, we must admit and reconcile the dimensionality of our data. A single column of number values is one-dimensional, no matter what the data is a measurement of in the real world. If our only task is to show values, then we can locate each one on the one-dimensional number line and call it quits.

Points on a line are, of course, just positions. Each point has the same size, no matter how large the value it represents. Mere position misses the opportunity to distinguish values using the visual weight of more ink, or more pixels. Harness the visual importance of size by connecting each point back to its baseline. Now, value is also represented by length. If we increase the connector's thickness, then we increase the visual impact of each value's length. The steadfast bar chart appears. *Voila.*

In order for each bar length to encode the value it represents, it must encompass the *entirety* of the value, all the way from zero. Truncate a bar with a non-zero baseline and its size ceases to have meaning. It is perfectly fine to leave the data as points if you want to focus on a narrow range of positions, but, once you introduce the physicality of length, you have to show it all. Otherwise, the length is worse than meaningless; it is misleading.

Bar charts can have horizontal or vertical orientations. The dominant horizontal metaphor is that of progress towards a goal, often a target of 100% completion. Horizontal bars, like the  number line, convey travel away from an origin baseline. They are like runners on a straight dash or miners cutting tunnels into the sheer side of a mountain. Horizontal progress bars are one of the most often experienced data visualizations. Horizontal bars also make great companions to the horizontal text of category titles. However you lay your bar, remember that its journey, how far it has come, is more meaningful if you can see where it began.

A different conceptual meaning is conveyed if the horizontal bar chart is rotated to create columns. The dominant visual metaphor for the vertical bar chart is a stack of stuff. Each column represents a total number of things, items that are often not actually stackable in the real world. A row of columns can show time progressing to the right. Like the horizontal bar chart, each vertical column must extend all the way to zero or it will lose its meaning. You would not be able to appreciate the height of a stack of stuff if you were only allowed to see its top.

As long as visual comparisons are of the *more-or-less* variety (e.g., 18 versus 13), not the multiplicative *x-times more* (e.g., 18 versus 1), we are pretty good at reading

Pierre E. Levasseur referred to vertical bar charts, in 1885, as *columns of stacked facts.*

Suppose the money received by a man in trade were all in guineas, and that every evening he made a single pile of all the guineas received during the day, each pile would represent a day ... so that by this plain operation, time, proportion, and amount, would all be physically combined.
WILLIAM PLAYFAIR, 1786

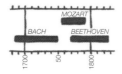

linear comparisons for what they are. A pair of bars, one longer than the other, whose lengths are encoded with values, one larger than the other, has a good shot at being decoded by the reader accurately.

Both horizontal and vertical bar charts encode numeric magnitude with length, a one-dimensional size encoding. But bars and columns must be drawn in two dimensions so that they can be seen. So, the bar widths are held constant, only their lengths change. Sizing only one dimension requires that the encoded-value be one of the two positional axes, even when we work in polar coordinates.

RADIAL HISTOGRAM   POPULATION PYRAMID   RADIAL BAR CHART   WATERFALL CHART

Using only a single dimension to convey importance is not always satisfactory because it constrains design. We can layer more data into our story with other methods. It is time to reach for more.

Area of Influence

The 1-D length of lines, bars, and columns can be exchanged for the 2-D area of shapes. This can be an appealing trade. Shapes are often better fits for design because shapes have a more even aspect ratio. Circles and squares are more compact than long lines. Shapes are also more freely scattered about the page. Unlike a bar chart, shapes do not have to be anchored to any position baseline. Compactness and freedom combine to allow more information to be

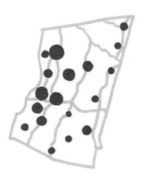

packed into a design. Shapes spread around can layer more meaning onto a canvas. For example, the geographic map of Columbia County at left locates cities while circle size tells you how many people lived in each one in 2010. Two axes, x-y or longitude-latitude, encode position while sized marks add a third dimension of meaning.

Mere 1-D length, compared to 2-D area, also misses an opportunity to reflect the dimensionality of the real world. A list of numbers is one-dimensional, but its associated units often allude to something more in the real world. The area of a plot of land, a single number, is seen in our head as a two-dimensional field. The weight of an animal, also a single number, comes from the amount of matter the animal has, something we experience in the real world as a complex 3-D shape. Money is an abstract idea. It is best compared in the single dimension of the bar chart. But in real life, money can be seen as the 1-D height of a stack of bills, 2-D area of a sheet of bills that just rolled-off a mint's printing press, or 3-D volume of a pallet of currency waiting to be robbed from a bank vault in a Hollywood heist film.

We use 2-D size to layer more meaning into a data story and reflect the physicality of the real world. To gain these benefits we must consider the total graphic design. We do not encode in isolation, but across an entire graphic composition. How do we expect the reader to decode meaning from size?

Small dots indicate points in space, even though points actually have no form at all. Points on the 2-D plane exist where two lines intersect. By themselves, points have no area. They have only positions. But if we want to see points in space, we have to mark them somehow. Just as we gave 1-D bars a constant width so we could see their length, we need to mark points. A small dot does the trick.

[Euclid] gave his famous definition of a point: "A point is that which has no parts, or which has no magnitude." ... Euclid's notion of a point only becomes clear when one reads beyond the definition and sees how points are related to lines and planes and circles and spheres. A point has no existence by itself.
FREEMAN J. DYSON, 1988

All locations around a circle's edge are equally far away from the center point. Unlike other shapes, the circle has no orientation. It has no sharp corners. There is nothing distracting about the circle. We like circles because they are *almost* formless.

To help layer more data onto each point position, it is natural to enlarge each dot to represent a value. Bigger circles attract more attention, so they must be more important. It is considered best practice to encode the data value in the circle by sizing its area, not its diameter. Our eye sees all of the 2-D circle's pixels, not just the pixels across its 1-D diameter. So we relate each of the circle's

pixels, its entire area, to the data value. This creates a power relationship between a set of data values and the radius (r) of their associated circles because the area of a circle equals πr^2.

Unfortunately, even with the recommended encoding of area, it turns out that we are not particularly skilled at decoding quantitative values from circle areas. Circles engulf many pixels in increasingly larger rings that get added on to represent higher and higher values. It is easy to underestimate a circle's area that is storing a relatively large value. For example, each ring depicted here has the same area as the inner circle. See how quickly they thin. Imperfect decoding of circle area makes us aware of area encoding limitations. Do not encumber your reader with the task of discerning precise values from circle areas. Instead, use circles when they can enhance a design by enabling rough comparisons. To convey precise values, augment circle area encoding by directly labeling them with the encoded value.

If two-dimensional area is problematic, decoding values from three-dimensional volumes is impossible. Spheres and cubes are no good on 2-D screens and sheets of paper. Too much of any volume just cannot be seen at any single time. Each vantage hides more than it shows. For example, how could we even begin to know how much more volume is packed into the larger of these two spheres?

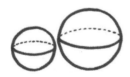

The argument against encoding data in volumes goes on. Surprisingly, we do not actually see 3-D. Every instance of sight is 2-D and, quickly over time, we build 3-D models of the world in our mind. Most of what lets us build our mental model of the world is missing from the 2-D page. The page lacks natural depth cues such as lighting, shadows, and nearby familiar objects, which we use for size comparison. Stereoscopic two-eye perspective and the different views we get by moving through the environment are also real-world aids missing from our experience of the 2-D page. In the real world we can concentrate our eyes on objects near and far and learn about their distance as they come in and out of focus. It is impossible to replicate these non-pictorial experiential cues on the canvas.

Finally, recall that a column of data values is one-dimensional, no matter what real world physical thing it represents. We may stretch this 1-D data into a 2-D area, but extending a single value into 3-D is a dimension too far. Did you guess that the larger sphere has triple the volume of the smaller? No chart is more easily mocked than a 3-D chart. Not only does it make data decoding ugly, but critics will always be able to snicker that 1-D data could have been more easily and more accurately presented in a 1-D bar chart. Do not wade into 3-D representation of numbers unless you are prepared to mount a strong defense.

The circle is an amiable introduction to why encoding data with size is troublesome, and why 3-D shapes are best to avoid. With each dimension added to form, the visual impact of the data becomes compressed. Below is one more comparison between dimensions. The gist of both the 1-D bar chart and 2-D area plot is created by grouping the same set of marks into different forms. See how rearranging the same parts into different wholes changes the nature of the comparisons made.

Assembling smaller shapes into bigger patterns can enable a variety of multi-layered data storytelling. By showing all the parts that make the whole, you reveal something more about its makeup. By creating an array of marks, you also have a set of miniature canvases on which you can encode even more data detail.

Imagine you were being chased through a hedge maze by a psychotic axe-wielding maniac. Wouldn't it be nice to have a 2-D overhead view to complement your rich multidimensional experience?

Most of us must undertake a mental exercise to relate a given figure of density to a meaningful experiential context.
ALBERT BIDERMAN, 1963

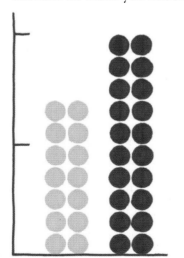

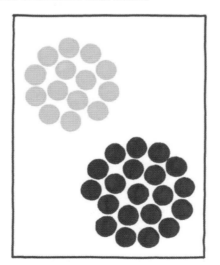

The 1-D linear comparison of the stacked bar chart puts the difference between the total values at center stage. On the one hand, the 2-D packed circle comparison can only help us see that one group is bigger than the other, but leaves us guessing by how much. On the other hand, packed circles are ready to be positioned wherever we want, while bars should remain anchored to the same baseline. Trade-offs in size encoding abound. The ability to make precise comparisons must be evaluated against everything else the design needs.

TRUE

COLORS

Man lives with what he sees, but he only sees what he wants to see. Try different types of people in the midst of any landscape. A philosopher will only vaguely see phenomena; a geologist, crystallized, confused, ruined and pulverized epochs; a soldier, opportunities and obstacles …
They all experience a certain arrangement of colors; but each one immediately transforms them into symbols....
PAUL VALÉRY, 1871–1945

The Grey

Eyespots are tiny light sensors. They help single-cell organisms like green algae get into position for optimal photosynthesis. Primitive biology is able to detect the intensity of light, and we can still accomplish a lot by swimming between black and white. Today, the human eye has millions of photoreceptor cells called rods. Like their eyespot forerunners, rods sense lightness. Concentrated on the periphery of the back of our eye, they have little to do with our modern color vision.

Alone at night in the woods, listen for clues about what nocturnal predator might be staring at you. The fear of being prey is manifest by darkness. The original experiential duality is symbolized by the Chinese yin and yang, literally *dark* and *light*. Our oldest visual archetype is rooted in life's daily journey. Through the mysterious night, into the revelation of the sun, and then back into night. Metaphoric light is the antidote to darkness because it lets you see what is going on. With light, real predators are detected, and imagined predators vanish. The sun's warming rays are the source of energy for life on Earth. No wonder so many ancient religions worshipped the sun. No wonder so much symbolic light shines throughout religious texts.

The archetypal colors, black and white, can distinguish two groups. But we can also segment them into shades of grey to do even more. This is like increasing how many flashlights shine against a white wall in a dark room, increasing the ratio of white to black in a paint mixture, or increasing the number of pinholes in a screen. Black has a lightness of 0 percent and white has a lightness of 100 percent. The continuous spectrum between black and white can be keyed to a single dimension of data by stretching a set of greys across a number line. As with area, easily encoded numbers are not always

Light detection generally begins with the absorption of a photon, which causes the electron of a molecule to attain a higher, and unstable, energy level. Return from this higher energy level begins a cascading chain of electron transfers.

Eyespots to eyeballs: A layer of retina cells

recessed into a cavity with a pinhole opening to allow directional sensitivity. A transparent lid covered this hole to filter light and keep out parasitic invaders.

The cornea split in two. The inner layer became a lens that could be manipulated by tiny muscles to better focus light.

The contrast ratio between foreground and background can be calculated to avoid reducing readability. The ratio compares the relative luminance value for each color, with darkest black = 0 and lightest white = 1

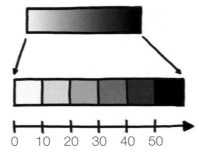

easily decoded. The way we make sense of different lightness is mostly relative. When we compare two shades, we can discern that one is darker than the other, but only if they are located near one another. Too much distance removes too much context, and distorts the comparison.

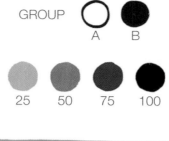

Qualitative palettes identify named categorical groups.

Sequential spectrums highlight values at one extreme with a "more ink for more numbers" metaphor.

Diverging palettes highlight values at both extremes, a pair of sequential spectrums.

The background color behind the encoded lightness spectrum matters a lot. The background determines contrast and gives context. Data values of higher interest, usually higher magnitudes, should be more salient. They receive higher contrast. Alternatively, both high and low extremes may deserve attention. Then, greys can appear to diverge by choosing a background with an average lightness. Now, middle values will have the lowest contrast and shrink from notice. Today, digital screens have removed the printing constraints that made full color expensive. Greyscale is a stylistic choice. Still, the minimalism of black and white helps focus design. It avoids the busyness and distraction that the freedom of the full color palette can introduce.

Greyscale allows us to isolate a single dimension of color, lightness, to see how to relate data and color. Quantitative values can be mapped to color spectrums. Background and nearby context is essential to appearance. We must be intentional in how we design sequential and diverging palettes. But who wants to live in austere, desaturated minimalism all the time? And working with color's other dimensions can help us increase the total number of discernible categories. These greyscale lessons can accompany us as we step out of the proverbial black-and-white Kansas farmhouse and into the wonderful world of color.

The sequence from dark to light is *lightness*. *Brightness* specifically refers to the absolute brightness of a light source. In color theory, measured position along the black-to-white spectrum may be referred to as *intensity* (light power) or *luminance* (intensity relative to the eye's spectral response). *Tone* mapping helps keep lightness consistent across different formats. In the HSV color model, *value* characterizes a range for each hue from black to most-saturated. The simplest value scale is greyscale. *Tint* lightens and desaturates by mixing with white. *Shade* darkens and greys by mixing with black.

Species of Wheels

Primates, including humans, are pretty good at seeing color. The popular theory why is that our color vision evolved to help us pick out colorful ripe fruit from surrounding foliage. Predators, like cats, do not need color vision to catch their prey. Grazers, like cows, do not need color vision to keep eating grass.

Birds, who need vision to fly, exceed our vision capabilities in many ways. Across avians we find three eyelids, binocular vision, nocturnal vision, oil droplets for haze, large relative eye size, asymmetric focus between eyes, a second fovea for sideways viewing, and UV-sensitivity.

The world is full of colors that convey categorical, or qualitative, meaning. Some, like the stop-go palette of a traffic light, are more universal than others, like the uniform colors of two competing football teams. A handful of very different colors can convey category groups. They must be very different because the goal of a qualitative palette is to make categories visually distinct from each other. The color wheel sweeps through color hues. Or, perhaps it is better to say *a* color wheel. You see, connecting the

COMPLEMENTS

world of color to only a single model is like connecting the globe to only a single map projection. Many color models exist for different purposes, for different technology, and from across the history of always-progressing color science.

Distinct hues are farthest separated from each other around a color wheel. Complement pairs are the most distinct, they straddle the wheel. Distinct palettes interest us because we perceive color according to difference. From a survival perspective, colors are most relevant relative to their background. Throughout the day, and throughout the year, lighting conditions change the perceived color of objects. We have adapted to be sensitive to difference, not absolute value. Imagine you are hunting for ripe apples against a field of tree leaves. To contrast the red color of desire against other environmental cues, we change our pupil size and photoreceptor sensitivity. This lets us hunt for apples at noon and dusk. We change to make effective comparisons across a variety of lighting conditions.

Except for a pure laser beam, the colors we see are actually ranges of the visible spectrum. Many perceived colors, like magenta, do not exist at any specific wavelength or in any natural rainbow. These *extra-spectral* colors are like the musical chords of the color spectrum, wholes perceived from physiological and psychological mixtures of light.

SUBTRACTIVE PIGMENTS

ADDITIVE LIGHT

After difference, learnability is the next quality of a good color palette. Colors and categories must be mentally linked, remembered, and referred to in conversation without confusion. Palettes should be comprised of hues that suggest familiar names. Intuitive color palettes that reflect some semantic meaning, such as making bodies of water blue, also helps. In addition to mimicking how we experience the natural world, semantic color builds on other palettes readers have seen before.

Typically, a categorical palette must be limited to a handful of colors. Hues are impossible to distinguish if they are packed too closely around the wheel. Too many colors will make it difficult to remember which colors map to which categories. Shades of the same hue might imply that one category is a lesser version of another. It is difficult to assemble a palette of many more than six hues that does not run into problems.

But we do not always have to be typical. Grouped color schemes can increase the number of color categories beyond a handful. They do this by arranging categories into a conceptual hierarchy. Each chunk of the hierarchy gets one of the main colors. Then, inside each chunk, varieties of that named color can distinguish more. For example, consider this map of my Hudson River Valley hometown. Blues are water. Greens are nature. Warm colors are buildings. Greys are paved surfaces. Browns are crops. It really is a colorful little village.

Berlin and Kay reported that a set of 11 basic color names appear in all mature languages, usually beginning with words for dark-light, then the four opponent colors (red-green, blue-yellow), and finally purple, orange, pink, brown, and grey. Their findings still resonate with many color enthusiasts, despite being scaled back since original publication in 1969.

Hue is an attribute of color dependent on wavelength, not color intensity or lightness. The word is originally linked to skin complexion (animal *hide* shares the same root).

A highlight color is a type of category used to distinguish a single class from all others. It is often a more visually striking version of another color, or an alerting color such as red or yellow.

WATER
FALLS

PARK
WOODS

HOMES
SHOPS
PUBLIC

ROAD
PARKING

CORNFIELD
ORCHARD

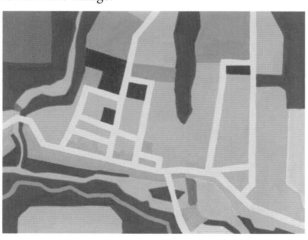

Take a brightly colored object such as a bright red ball. It is a saturated red hue all over, independent of the changes in color caused by the play of light and shadow upon it. That is, hue and saturation are inherently defined by the object color, not its lighting. Across the shaded surface of the ball, the lightness and chroma will vary. Make the lighting twice as bright, and the ball will appear more colorful and brighter. Dim the lighting and it will become less so. But, the lightness and chroma will remain the same because they are relative to the light.
MAUREEN STONE, 2003

Tetrachromats have four independent channels for conveying color information, a condition present in some animals and studied as a phenomena in a small percentage of humans who are able to detect a greater variety of colors than common trichromats.

Printing, like this book, can only display certain colors (colored at right). A screen has its own limited gamut (the RGB triangle). Neither can show all of the colors human eyes can see in nature, represented by the area under the arch, from about 450–650nm.

Color demands respect for how an entire stack of technological, biological, and cultural systems conspire against successful decoding. Our technology is not perfectly aligned with our biology. Biology varies across all readers. Each person's mental processing of color is different. It is easy to miss how wacky the handshakes are between our data, color mapping, the way colors are displayed, and the way they are perceived.

magnified 64x

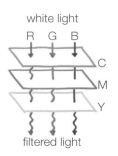

white light

filtered light

The real color spectrum is expressed with different color models for different purposes. The most familiar models help us program machines to display color. RGB instructs screens how bright to make an array of red, blue, and green light sources, like the iPhone diamond matrix here. The CMYK color model dictates where to print cyan, magenta, yellow, and black (*key*) ink on the page. No print or display technology is capable of producing all of the colors our eyes can detect. Both RGB and CMYK are languages convenient to machines, not to the human eye. How we actually perceive color makes things complicated because everyone sees differently. We are each equipped with a unique set of biological hardware. Incredibly, our brain generates our rich color experience from relatively simple sensory input: long, medium, and short (LMS) cones, named for the profile of vis-

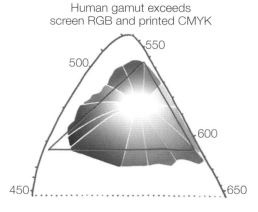

Human gamut exceeds screen RGB and printed CMYK

ible light wavelengths each is specialized to detect. The density of our eyes' rods and cones varies amongst all *trich*romats, people with normal three-cone color vision. Some, mostly men, only have two types of cones. These *di*chromats suffer some impairment in the perception of the red-green spectrum.

With only three types of cone, we get far more than just three colors. Our brain's visual system interprets the difference between the three LMS cone signals. We can imagine these signals locating colors across a multidimensional space, similar to how multiple satellites can triangulate a specific position. The combinatorial way we see, from cones to color, has import-ant implications for design. Sensory input from all three cones fuse to make us best at seeing gradations along the dark-light *achromatic* range (shown as the horizontal axis in the below diagram). Even with full color, lightness is still most important.

Example distribution of human cones

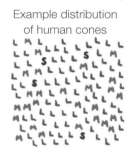

Perceived lightness, called luminance, should be consistent across color palettes. The HCL (hue-chroma-luminance) color model pursues even perceptual distance across its color volume. It arrives by way of more than a century of color science innovation, which included incorporating more computing power and running more experiments where people perform color differentiating tasks, such as determining the "just noticeable difference" between shades and adjusting colored light to make differently painted swatches match.

The eyes we design with are not the eyes of the reader. Design-ing for human vision reminds me of old graphic design handbooks. They warned: Expect your work to be mangled by photocopiers. As you work with color, simulate how design appears to different color deficiencies and on different devices. No colors, even reds and greens, have to be abandoned. They often just need to be tweaked.

From LMS cones to 3 channels: yellow-blue, red-green, light-dark

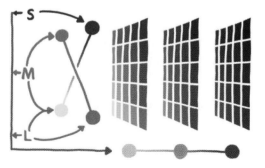

A color scale should vary consistently across the entire range of values, so that each step is equivalent, regardless of its position on the scale. In other words, the difference between 1 and 2 should be perceived the same as the difference between 11 and 12, or 101 and 102, preserving patterns and relationships in the data.
ROB SIMMON, 2013

LMS (long, medium, and short) cones are popularly associated with the colors of red, green, and blue, but this threatens to mask how much their ranges overlaps.

The population ratio of LMS cones varies from person-to-person, but we generally have more L than M, and few S. This relative scarcity of short cones impacts our ability to appreciate intensely blue colors.

The "opponent process" theory of color is responsible for connecting the overlapping spectrums of our LMS cones to how we perceive color. The resulting three color pairs are called opponent, or antagonist, channels: yellow versus blue, red versus green, and light versus dark.

HUE BACKBONE

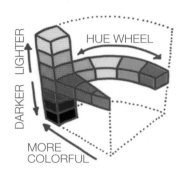

LIGHTER
DARKER

HUE WHEEL

MORE
COLORFUL

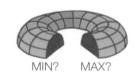

MIN?   MAX?

0   50   100

Paint by Numbers

Quantitative color palettes map a change in numerical value to a change in color value. Many palettes vary only one dimension of color. An increase in number, as we saw, can correspond to an increase in darkness. Color models are often represented by a perfect cube, cylinder, or other tidy volume. Digital tools often have us navigate 3-D color space by using the hue dimension as a conceptual backbone and presenting us with the remaining 2-D slice of color fixed to that part of the backbone. Each of these perfect volumes reflect the computer-centric regularity of machines and their controlling mathematics. Some creative palettes map data across a spline that cuts through a color volume, varying color in all three dimensions as values change. Through experiments of how people actually see, we have learned that the actual shape of our perceptual field is quite irregular. Human color space is lumpy.

The color wheel's full circle, with no beginning and no end, is a strange friend for data. Indeed, quantitative rainbow palettes introduce a conceptual paradox. Data minimum and maximum values should be visually distant because they are numerically distant. Rainbow max and min, however, are colorfully right next to each other. Using the full rainbow is like exiting a tunnel and finding yourself back at its entrance.

Color transition points can help indicate meaningful thresholds within a data range. Diverging scales direct attention toward extremes by using a neutral color for the hinge value. The color legend at left emphasizes height above and depth below sea level. Quantitative colors do not always need to be evenly distributed. The example below allocates a warm palette strategically. The only data of interest, the top 10 percent, is highlighted, while the bottom 50 percent is colorfully weakened. This intentional palette stretching blends the benefits of qualitative and quantitative approaches.

Sometimes, a fluid color spectrum is created by interpolating hundreds of color variations along a color ramp. Our ability to actually differentiate between noncontiguous colors is poor. It hovers somewhere around three or four shades of saturation or luminance. Paradoxically, dividing a rich spectrum of hundreds of colors into a few discrete bins can help people discern more colors. Go ahead and use a color ramp for aesthetic reasons, but know that it is at the expense of decoding information. Instead, bucket (or *step*) quantitative palettes into discrete (or *quantized*) bins.

More colors is not the same as more discernible colors.

Total Color Challenge

Color can be defined numerically at so many different stages: wavelength of light emission, absorption and reflection, design mapping, red-green-blue pixel encoding, our eye's reception, and our mind's perception, which takes into account complex factors such as how nearby colors interact and the relative size of each area of color. Numerical systems help us produce color, but none of them perfectly match how we think about color.

Perceptual effects [can] strengthen or destroy a design.
MAUREEN STONE, 2003

How colors are perceived, not how they are generated, is what matters most. Successful color decoding happens when we account for the reader's eyes, mind, and experience. We want color to support a successful encoding-to-decoding chain, but we also want color to help make our design look good. These two goals can create tension. A group of six distinct colors will differentiate data well, but may look garish. Color palettes often shoulder even more responsibility, such as advancing a corporate identity. Everyone associates certain colors with their experience of the world. This is why it is so much easier to make intuitive color palettes for maps, as we saw in the blues and greens of my hometown.

Pleasing colors blend and do not provide good visual discrimination.
WILLIAM CLEVELAND, 1985

As we age, our eyes change. Our eyeball lens hardens, making fine print harder to see without reading glasses. Early onset of conditions like cataracts or glaucoma can also make it harder to see. Consider how color contrasts across your visual. A thin grey font on a white background might look slick, but it might also slow down readers.

To label (color as noun), to measure (color as quantity), to represent or imitate reality (color as representation), and to enliven or decorate (color as beauty).
EDWARD TUFTE, 1990

At minimum, an effective color palette does not turn the viewer away. Ideally, it helps attract and hold attention while also informing effectively. You must balance many demands across color pursuits. The technical best practices—not too many categorical colors, bucketed palettes, steady luminance, meaningful associations, and sensitivity to impairments—are all good guardrails against making color mistakes. Some programmed default color palettes clear these best-practice hurdles, but risk leaving too much value on the table. All defaults are uninteresting because they are overused. Defaults are often poorly linked to the semantics of the data because defaults are not designed for the information your data might convey.

Your human consideration is needed to color data. Begin by referencing inspirational sources, including existing visualization and other graphic design. Then prototyping, demonstrating, and technical guardrails can help the palette be refined into something that is technically, semantically, and emotionally superb. Superior colors encourage readers to engage and help data soar.

Color is one of the most powerful channels we have. It can convey categories, quantities, and emotions. Color is also one of our most unwieldy tools. It requires more navigation of the encoding-to-decoding process than position or size. Remember, the same single data dimension can be mapped to multiple channels to reinforce the message. Do not choose between circle size or circle color to represent a quantity if both can be used in harmony.

Together, position, size, and color give us the tools necessary to *humanize* data and see information. Next, we are going to take these tools and use them to *probe* data for better and better forms.

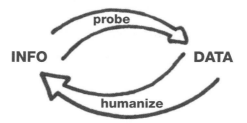

Whenever possible, make intuitive palettes. … It's not always possible, of course (what color is electrical charge, or income?) but a fair number of datasets lend themselves to particular colors.
ROB SIMMON, 2013

Recognize that it's hard and that it's going to take time and effort. Point that out to your stakeholders, schedule some time for it, don't just brush it off. One major reason why people are so bad at color in data visualization is because they don't budget any time for it.
ELIJAH MEEKS, 2018

CHAPTER

8

EXPLORE

TO CREATE

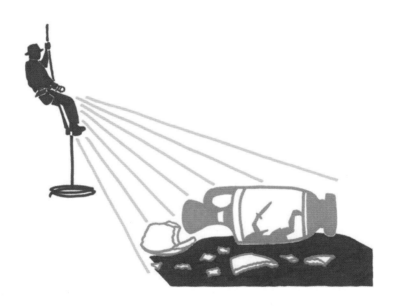

And this I believe: that the free, exploring mind of the individual human is the most valuable thing in the world.

JOHN STEINBECK, 1952

A bearded man sits down at a long table in the middle of a rowdy hall, orders wine, and unrolls the packet under his arm. People take notice of the drawing supplies now covering the table. They peer over his shoulder and ask questions as he studies the revelers around him. Their likeness is captured with quick strokes. We are in Rome. It is 1511 and the man is Michelangelo. He is studying the faces of real people in pursuit of improving his apostles for a new commission from Pope Julius II, the Sistine Chapel's ceiling.

Data Sketches

The artist makes quick, rough, unfinished drawings for many reasons. Sketches hone technical skills. They also help one imagine, invent, and discover. Postage stamp-sized doodles, cranked out by the dozen, give flight to the exploration of ideas as mind and pencil meld. Sketched lines can be altered, darkened, or abandoned in favor of starting anew.

Live figure drawing classes often begin with the model executing many poses in succession, sometimes for only a few seconds each. These "gesture drawings" serve many purposes. They warm-up the artists as they connect the model to the page for the first time in that session. They distill the figure drawing to its essence as there is only time for simple curves and shapes. The dynamic energy of the pose is frozen on a static page.

An idea transformed to the page escapes the impermanence of your own thinking. Outsourcing idea storage frees up your limited working memory for new thoughts. The sketch also makes an idea more real. You can point to it and say *there it is*. Something new has taken on its own identity. Once externalized, a sketch may serve as spark for more ideas. For artists, sketching can also help focus subject, position, and composition—before attempting canvas or marble. Like them, you have to figure out how to generate better ideas faster so you are not dragged down by the burden of full production.

The germ of an idea may often come in a reverie as a purely cognitive act, the major work of creative design is done through a kind of dialogue with some rapid production medium.
COLIN WARE, 2008

Data sketches are little pictures that help reveal what the data has to tell you. They are not the only way to investigate data, but they are a unique way of investigating data. Data sketches do not have to be pretty or conclusive. We are not yet polishing for presentation. That can wait. The purpose of sketching is to encourage you to ask more questions of the data so that you can create more sketches that are even more revealing. That is why this creative dialog must extend through many iterations. No single picture shows all. Position, size, and color give us all the tools we need to begin sketching. Start with whatever chart type is easiest to generate. It is often a chart that aligns closely with the data's native structure. Peek at the profile of a single data column on a histogram. Scatter two-dimensional dots on a plane. Raise categorical bars on a graph. Connect nodes by their links. See where points land on the map. The first step is to produce a picture of some data—any data dimension(s), any picture. At the outset, what matters most importantly is that you create something you can see so you can proceed to the next step: React to the first sketch.

John Tukey introduced the world to exploratory data analysis (EDA) in 1977 by likening it to quantitative detective work. When we explore data, we search for clues that reveal. How you explore for clues is up to you. The London Bobby and Texas Ranger each have localized skills. Methods are likewise not identical across data explorers. The health-care coder and financial analyst have different approaches to different data for different reasons. Still, there are strategies we can all consider, whatever our line of inquiry. Data exploration demands a basic ability to produce simple charts from data, and this requires some technological fluency. It does not, however, require you abandon drawing by hand. A hybrid approach can lead to creative avenues of inquisition. Alternate between data-driven computer charts and hand sketched ideas you would like to populate with on-screen data.

Data exploration can be intensely private or embarked upon as a team. In either case, we are not yet trying to communicate anything beyond the investigation. We are also not yet trying to establish any confidence. The detective hunts for clues—footprints, bloodstains, and cigarette ash—while trying to crack the case. We hunt by playing with different forms, data dimensions, and even data sources. Later, we will turn to what the evidence may prove.

Your first step might be to ask the data some establishing questions. *Tell me a little bit about yourself. Where did you come from?* Look at the data to see what kind of shape it has arrived in. What is the terrain like? Not all questions stem directly from the dataset. It provides one stock of raw materials to work with, your knowledge of the world provides the other. Exploration, Tukey summarized, "is a creative act." The sparks of creative exploration fire when you strike your data. Good data sketches deliver answers, great data sketches inspire more questions. Our goal is to find something worth further investigation and further sketching. What can we hope our data will reveal?

Let's Compare

We are comparison-making machines. The world assaults us with more information than we could ever pay attention to. A short walk to your kitchen for a glass of water brings few details of the journey to your attention. You are already habituated to everything you see. But, spot an unexpected silhouette with your peripheral vision and your focus will automatically rocket into high alert. The difference between your environment and your expectations is what counts.

Deviations capture our attention. Every viewer arrives to a data story with expectations about the world of the data. Sometimes, this prior knowledge provides enough context for the viewer to make sense of a lonely number. But to rely on only this flavor of comparison risks too much. This is why the singular *datum* is an anachronism. On its own, just one data point has no meaning. Good data stories supply both sides necessary for a comparison. If you are shown two stacks of stuff, you will automatically focus on the void of negative space that separates them. *How much more is needed to make both equal?* These

comparisons can make data stories interesting. So, what makes a superior comparison? Consider two of NASA's early human spaceflight programs: Apollo and Gemini.

The Apollo program crew had one more astronaut than Project Gemini. Apollo's Saturn V rocket had about seventeen times more thrust than the Gemini-Titan II.

The language used to describe these differences illustrate two types of comparisons. For the crew we say one *more*, or add. For the rocket thrust we say seventeen *times more*, or multiply.

Add and subtract comparisons like the crew comparison —a few more, a few less—are easier for us to wrap our heads around. This makes them more useful comparisons. Presented visually, these *additive* comparisons are appreciated with little effort. You are in fact born with the ability to instantly do addition and subtraction with a small numbers of objects, years before you know anything about numbers, numerals, or arithmetic.

Relative to additive comparisons, multiply and divide differences are more difficult. It is hard for us to make sense of them, even visually. Comparisons that are expressed as ratios—a few *times* more, a few *times* less—all land too quickly into the mental bin of "well, this is just a lot bigger than that other thing." What does it mean to have seventeen times more thrust at lift-off? It is just a big number. Without very specialized knowledge, 17x means the same to us as 15x or 19x.

The two types of comparisons, additive and multiplicative, hit us differently because multiplication is cognitively more abstract than addition. Addition is natural. Add or take objects away from a group and the size of the group increases or shrinks accordingly. You can see it. Multiplication is a conceptual extension of addition and that makes it harder to see. We interpret the operation of *three times four* with either "pooling" or "repeated addition." If solving the problem with pooling, we see three small sets of four objects each, and mass them into one large group of 12. Alternatively, in repeated addition we imagine adding four objects into a box, three times. In either case, we no longer manipulate objects directly. Instead, we

Project Gemini

Apollo Program

Subitize means to instantly determine how many objects are in a very small collection, up to four. In studies, newborns have been seen to "count" and perform simple addition and subtraction with small groups of objects.

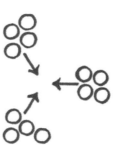

are adding a number of sets, which are themselves each represented by a number. Multiplication's *number of numbers* kicks us, conceptually, into a higher abstraction. Multiplication is one more level away from physical reality. That makes ratio comparisons difficult to comprehend. Seeing the NASA 17x thrust comparison (33 versus 1.9 mega-newtons) emphasizes how the difference between the crews is more natural.

If it is not too much bother, could you please remember the number forty-one for me? You see, after the challenge of multiplicative ratios, we must consider one more common comparison struggle. Our experience of time is a strange phenomenon. Carrying numbers in our memory relegates all comparison to the imagination. Now, contrast that original number to twenty-four. You see? Carrying numbers forward in the mind slows thinking, introduces error, and makes comparisons more difficult. There is no reason to memorize; forget that number.

One of the reasons we have pushed beyond text-riddled data tables and toward visual presentation is to reduce reliance on working memory. Do not shuttle numbers between moments if a comparison can be made in an instant. Jacques Bertin extolled the power of the "image" of the mind: a temporal unit of meaningful visual perception. We must learn how to create comparisons within single mental images. Even William Playfair wrote, back in 1801, about the "pains and labour" that memory requires. John Tukey said it best, "learn how to make one picture do." William Cleveland distinguished two types of visual comparisons: juxtaposed and superposed. Juxtaposition places items next to one another. Like numbers in a table, juxtaposed graphics require you to shuttle information between moments. Juxtaposition's spatial gap creates a perceptual gap in time. Superposition closes the gap by layering graphics on top of one other. Together, the layers share the same reference scales, the same context. Inside their common world, from two given elements a third materializes, the negative space of the comparison between them.

Patterns beyond Compare

The word *behavior* suggests how people conduct themselves over time. More generally, behavior is concerned with the way a subject acts. What does it mean for data to behave? It implies a connected performance, often sequenced over time. But we could also consider how low a cantilevered beam bends under a heavy load as a type of behavior. Whether we appraise behavior across the length of a beam, or across a length of time, the anchor is the same: a dimension that provides connective tissue. The third meter of the beam is connected to the second meter, just as the third day is connected to the second day. Behavior has a natural structure. Tomorrow's activities may not have anything to do with what happened today, but we initially sequence days in the order they are experienced. Because of its association with time, we usually position the connective variable on the rightward, horizontal axis. It is the foundation of the image. The *performant* variable can then be raised vertically against this horizontal foundation, creating the familiar Cartesian plane. This Flatland presents an opportunity for a special kind of visual exploration: the search for familiar patterns.

We are able to distinguish objects because we sense patterns. The mind ingests many pixels of color from the real world. It groups similar nearby pixels into contours and regions, and then tries to match these with the shapes of known objects stored in our memory. This all happens automatically, of course, and our mental storehouse of patterns is refined across our lives. *Patternicity* allows us to pick a friend out of a crowd from the memorized gait of their walk and skim through pages of text in search of a target word. When we explore data for patterns, our goal is to recognize behavior that can clue us in to what is going on.

The mark is a wonderfully useful commodity. At its egalitarian best, each data point receives its own mark, most often a tiny circle placed at a precise point. Many marks combine to show a large quantity of data in a very small area. Together, marks display distributions that may reveal outliers, clusters, and asymmetries.

Trend: Something practically everybody is interested in showing or knowing or spotting or deploring or forecasting.
DARRELL HUFF, 1954

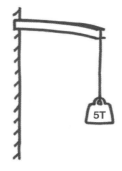

Patternicity is the tendency to perceive meaningful patterns, whether they are actually there or not. We are particularly fond of recognizing faces.

Coup d' œil is a glance that takes in a comprehensive view, literally "stroke of eye" in French.

Binding is combining different features that will come to be identified as parts of the same contour or region.

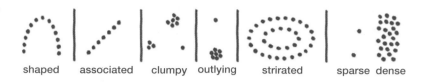

shaped   associated   clumpy outlying   strirated   sparse dense

By plotting marks on the rectangular canvas we can highlight some familiar patterns.

Your mind can already recognize many data patterns, like the happy upward trend. Learning additional patterns will help you better explore data, just as your ability to recognize objects from real life expands as you build out your library of memories. Some patterns are specific to your field. A physician must study many time-series of the electrical activity of the heart in order to rapidly interpret electrocardiogram records. Other patterns reappear across data worlds.

See how simple design decisions impact the nature of how a pattern appears to us, below. Presenting the same data with visually different slopes shows us that a spotted pattern may not be inherently interesting. It also reveals that an interesting pattern may be lurking in the data, but not apparent on a given canvas. Once any pattern is recognized, you must help determine if it is relevant by

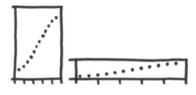

The aspect ratio, canvas height-to-width, can make the rise of the same data appear severe, or not.

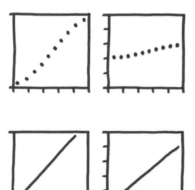

Similar effects can be produced with an increase or decrease of the empty space that surrounds the data.

Whether the slope is above or below the canvas diagonal is seen (especially when it is 45°), but it is difficult to be more precise.

providing context. Does it agree with or disrupt your prior beliefs? If a strong relationship is expected, then the absence of a pattern may be the most intriguing picture. Or, if a strong relationship is already known, then the outliers that do not conform may hold the real story. Deviation from the expected continues to fascinate.

Throughout this book, the mean (average) is barely mentioned. It is a potentially dangerous summary that flies against the spirit of looking at all the patterns the data has to offer. The mean twists the impact of outliers, variation, aggregation, and sample size. It is guilty of aiding and abetting many numerical paradoxes and traps we must be on the lookout for. Summaries, abstractions, and simplifications threaten to bury the unexpected. See how the mean misrepresents the actual data in each of the examples below.

Summaries, graphic and otherwise, are not the enemy. Geographic regionalization and best-fit curves are essential to helping us probe data. But, because summaries conceal by design, we risk error if we rely entirely on them. Take a look at the most granular level of data available. Otherwise, you might miss a clue that sparks further creative exploration.

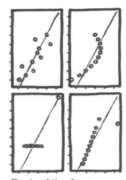

Each of the four datasets yields the same standard output from a typical regression program, namely: number of observations, mean of x's, mean of y's, regression of coefficient (b_1) of y on x, equation of regression line, sum of squares, regression sum of squares, residual sum of squares of y, estimated standard error of b_1, and multiple R^2.
F.J. ANSCOMBE, 1973

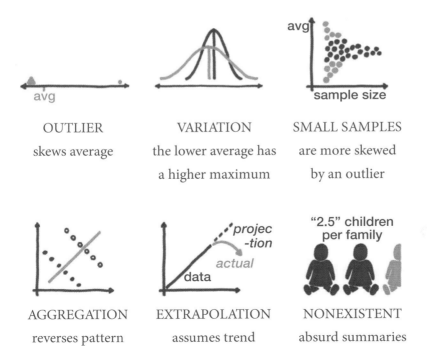

OUTLIER
skews average

VARIATION
the lower average has
a higher maximum

SMALL SAMPLES
are more skewed
by an outlier

AGGREGATION
reverses pattern

EXTRAPOLATION
assumes trend

NONEXISTENT
absurd summaries

Average daily bridge traffic would miss the rush hour jams.

The median is the middle term in a series ordered by magnitude. The outlier impacts the mean, but not the median, in the following two series:
2, 4, 6, 8, 16, 17, 32
2, 4, 6, 8, 16, 17, 92

Drawing with data is an invaluable tool to discover what is unique about the numbers at hand. It helps to reveal new possible analyses to perform: Instead of being overwhelmed by the size of a dataset and by millions of numbers, we focus only on their nature, their organization, and doing so often opens new opportunities originating from this vantage point.
GIORGIA LUPI, 2017

The greatest value of a picture is when it forces us to notice what we never expected.
JOHN TUKEY, 1977

The eye cannot look on similar forms without involuntarily as it were comparing their magnitudes. So that what in the usual mode was attended with some difficulty, becomes not only easy, but as it were unavoidable.
WILLIAM PLAYFAIR, 1801

Instead of the mean, consider the median. It is called a resistive summary measure because it is not impacted by outliers as quickly as the mean can be. Also, you can point to the median in the dataset and say *there it is*. The median ushers us toward a much more honest and direct visual description of the data.

It's been a few pages since we last left Michelangelo. Recall why the artist sketches, and why we explore data: to familiarize yourself with the subject, to experiment, and to find interesting things you never expected. We sketch to discover and develop a vision for what we are going to say. Exploring data visually takes us to new understandings economically. Simple data sketches, comparisons and patterns, are the first steps into a universe of exploration.

Remember how we originally differentiated information from data. Information puts data into forms that are readable to humans. Data often does not display interesting patterns out of the box. We cannot always pick out visual clues based on the first plot of marks. Perhaps too many dots overlap in the corner of a plot, the population of a city dwarfs its associated landmass, or the network is a tangled hairball. Data sketching pursues new, weird, and better forms that let us take a more meaningful look.

It is true that we are painfully limited creatures. We are unable to fully appreciate ratio comparisons. We only detect familiar patterns. Clues that are there may be too subtle for us to see. Their signal is too weak to our naked eyes. But, also remember that we are superior tool makers. Difficult cases are to be expected, and can be greeted with a smile. It is our opportunity to help the data show us more. Through a variety of methods, we can bring hidden comparisons and patterns into the light.

9

CREATE TO

EXPLORE

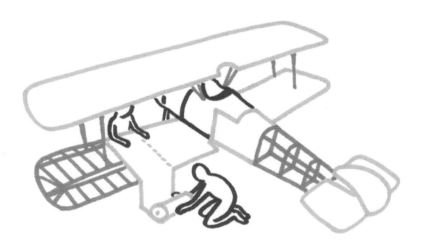

When the human realm seems doomed to heaviness,
I feel the need to fly like Perseus into some other space. I am
not talking about escaping into dreams or into the irrational.
I mean that I feel the need to change my approach, to look
at the world from a different angle, with different logic,
different methods of knowing and proving.

ITALO CALVINO, 1993

Sometimes, the first data sketches we make sing, "Hey explorer, look over here!" But we should not always expect to see meaningful patterns at first glance. Data often holds more than first visions reveal. Data needs our help to probe its murky depths. Operations —analogous to counting, subtraction, and multiplication—can help produce more visual meat for our eyes to bite into.

Profile

The search for patterns can be augmented. Layered guides, like mini-maps to the data, help bring features of interest to our attention. We may be tempted to hijack any of the following devices as standalone summaries of the data, but it is far too early for that. Profiles of data, just like profiles of people, conceal essential details. We are still wearing our explorer hats and digging for treasure. No data point should be hidden. For now, each profile is an accessory guide that will help us supercharge our inspection.

Profiles show how data is distributed. They help make sense of where marks are located. We already had a first encounter with the histogram profile via Tukey's stem-and-leaf plot. Skillful design of density-summarizing histograms comes down to playful bin sizing. There is no best bin width, just different aspects of the data that can be revealed. The histogram gives a rough sense of the shape of the data by showing relative frequency. Is the data symmetrical? Is a center of mass detectable? Is the data lopsided? Are there any unexpected humps? Perhaps these are not yet precise quantitative

Histogram was coined by Karl Pearson in 1891 from *historical diagram* because it is a simplified, or diagrammatic, view of what has happened

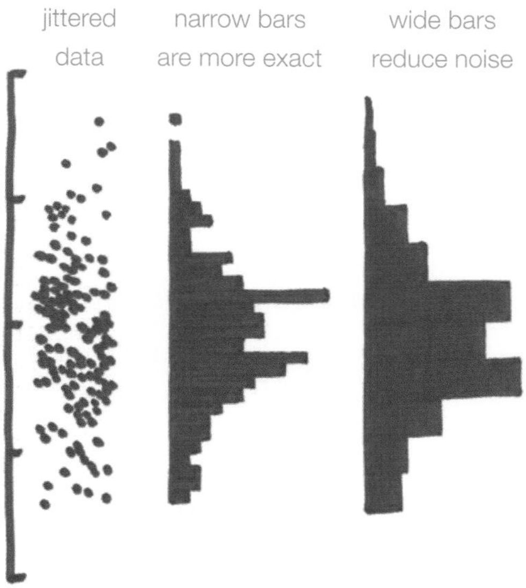

Histograms reduce information in the data... choose interval based on tolerable loss of accuracy.
WILLIAM CLEVELAND, 1985

jittered data

narrow bars are more exact

wide bars reduce noise

characteristics. But, taking a visual inventory of a histogram, like you would the profile of a trail ridge before a hike, can give a good sense of what kind of journey is ahead.

The mountainous bins of the histogram can be traded for a more numeric view of the data's center, symmetry, and spread. The box plot stakes its heart at the data's median, boxes the middle 50 percent, extends its whiskers to a chosen wider range, and shows whatever outliers remain outside. The box plot delivers focus, but its abstraction loses the shape of the histogram. Is it possible to get the best of both worlds? A violin plot mirrors the curves of the histogram and smooths its bins into an organic shape Stradivari might approve. A heatmap shades cells to indicate aggregate density.

Visual profiles provide a sense of the distribution of our data: where it is, where it is not, and where we might need to focus attention. Profiles augment our ability to see the data, but only in one dimension at a time. To probe in 2-D requires something more.

Modal means a local maximum, or peak. *Unimodal* means just one peak. The normal distribution is a special unimodal distribution. Distributions may also be *bimodal* or *multimodal*.

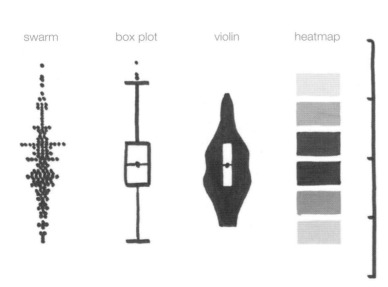

swarm   box plot   violin   heatmap

$^{0}\ \diagdown\ _{25}\ \diagup\ ^{50}\ \diagdown\ _{75}\ \diagup\ ^{100}$
The hinge diagram takes only the key numbers from the box plot: the minimum, median, maximum, and hinge data points just inside the 25th and 75th percentiles that define the middle box. Together these five points create an efficient summary of the distribution. For some applications, and with practice, perhaps the tiny

MIN $\diagdown$ $\diagup$ MED $\diagdown$ $\diagup$ MAX
HINGE HINGE

is all you need.

Translate

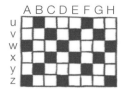

Reorder the grid
categories to reveal:

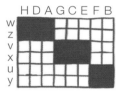

Recall that alphabetic order was developed by scholars to catalog work for easier retrieval. Today, we miss out on what an information-based order may reveal if we resign to being governed by first letters, or any other default. Groups, voids, and other patterns may appear once we begin moving categories about in search of better forms. Jacques Bertin showed how reordering "simplifies the images without diminishing the number of observed correspondences." We are free to reorder alphabetic category labels any way we please. But, what can be done with numeric data that has a built-in ordered and connective structure?

We previously considered five different ways to show time using different 2-D plots of the same data. Here is a portion of that same data, with a single, straight summary line that fits the

Linear regression minimizes the total vertical distance between the data points and best-fit line, often by minimizing the sum of squared distance, emphasizing the impact of data points far away from the fit.

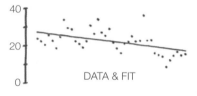

entire scatter of marks. It is a fine way to summarize the overall trend, but the fit does not have much to offer regarding what happens along the way.

If we truly want to uncover the comparisons that data offers, then it might help to focus our vision explicitly on those differences. Consider a basketball scoreboard. Whether it reads 109–107, or 72–70, the accumulated points total is not interesting in the last moments of the game. It is the two-point spread that makes the final possession by the trailing team exciting. The

DATA
− MEDIAN
RESIDUAL

residual is the difference between a data point and a summary

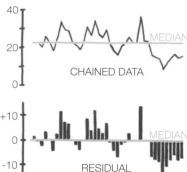

value. It helps elevate variation to our eye. Here, the same data is chained and its median is highlighted. Then, the median is subtracted from each data value to find the residual at each point. The new scale focuses our attention on variation.

An alternative to the straight line fit is the *smooth*. The smooth threads a single curve through data according to a calculated running average. The smooth can be augmented too. The distance between each data point and the smooth is a particular type of residual Tukey called the *rough*. Whatever the summary line, consider separating it out in order to take a more focused look at the variation about it. Subtracting summaries from data to see the residual is just the beginning of how simple arithmetic can help us explore. Many data behaviors vary with regular time intervals.

DATA & SMOOTH

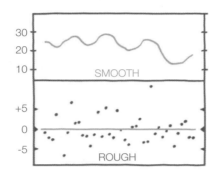

SMOOTH

ROUGH

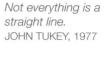

Not everything is a straight line.
JOHN TUKEY, 1977

Some change naturally, like temperature across the year. Other behavior, like weekday rush hours, vary depending on culture. Distinguishing regular cycles and long-term trends can help us understand if a small-scale fluctuation is expected or worth more investigation. Noisy data can be decomposed to its seasonality to show influencing cycles and spotlight unaccounted-for variation: Data equals trend plus season plus residual. It is all done using the same additive spirit of showing the residual.

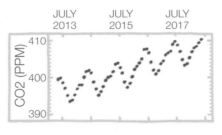

CO_2 readings, in parts per million, across the last five years at Mauna Loa, Hawaii.

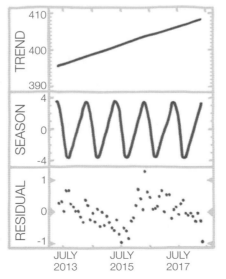

The overall trend is separated by finding a linear fit to the data.

Notice how the following vertical scales change. Seasonality, the pattern that is the same every year after accounting for the trend, is determined by averaging monthly readings.

The residual is what is left from the data after subtracting the trend and seasonality.

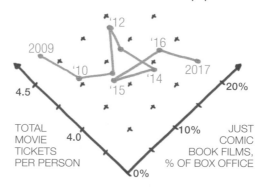

As USA went to the movies less, comic book films became more popular.

'12
2009
'16
'10
2017
'14
4.5
'15
20%

TOTAL
MOVIE   4.0
TICKETS
PER PERSON

JUST
COMIC
10%
BOOK FILMS,
% OF BOX OFFICE

0%

What if instead of translating the data, we move the entire plane? The connected scatter plot is one of my favorite charts. It reserves both axes for performant variables by connecting marks through time. Unfortunately, this places one of the two performant variables on the horizontal axis, where it is easily mistaken for time. We could skip the hassle of correcting this confusion and remove the x-axis entirely. An unconventional design rotates the entire graphic so time goes right.

Reordering and accentuating differences with translation helps us notice more with our eyes. A single image can tell a lot, but it cannot tell all. Just as a telescope cannot help you diagnose a fractured bone, each view of the data can only reveal a slice of reality. Data exploration is an iterative and playful dialog between your curiosity and your data. Playtime is about to get fun.

A changed approach is precisely the goal for the journey ahead: to discover new ways of seeing, to open spaces for possibilities, and to find "fresh methods" for animating and awakening.
NICK SOUSANIS, 2015

Transform

The entire problem is one of augmenting this natural intelligence....
JACQUES BERTIN, 1967

Translations, which use addition and subtraction to focus our eye, can only take us so far. Many of the comparisons our data have to offer are of the *multiplicative* nature. Ratios, like the rocket thrust comparison, describe *A is this many times bigger than B*. Reshuffling categories, removing medians, or rotating planes do not help make more sense of these abstract comparisons.

In Greek mythology, Procrustes was a rogue who mutilated travelers. He stretched them, or cut off their legs, until they perfectly fit the dimensions of his iron bed. Procrustean sadism is a fitting metaphor for transformations that torture insights out of data. You see, the number lines that help us illustrate our data can likewise be stretched and compressed in pursuit of more clues.

Most of modern statistics is built around data that are normally distributed— if not normal, at least symmetric. But data don't always arrive on our doorstep like that.
HOWARD WAINER, 2017

Scales define data worlds. They are very often number lines along horizontal and vertical axes. Recall how these perpendicular rulers mimic our own daily experience. We walk about the surface of the earth inside our own personal compass roses. We cannot change the laws of our world, but we can control the rules that govern the land of our data. It is time to stretch beyond the default scales data arrive with, and start playing with the shape of data worlds.

In Russian formalism study of narratology, the *fabula* is the chronological raw material of a story and *syuzhet* is the way the story is organized.

Think of data as the content and the number lines we use to plot data as the form. The content-form pair is analogous to water and the vessel that holds it. The same content looks different in different containers. The next technique shows you how to manipulate form to create a better view of the data.

If the way the numbers were gathered… does not make them easy to grasp [then] we should change them.
JOHN TUKEY, 1977

Suppose you position a few data points across the number line and notice that an outlier causes some of the marks to bunch up, or overplot. Sketched here are the five most common elements in the human body, by weight in kilograms. A person contains about 43 kilograms of oxygen (O). This outlier causes two of the less abundant elements, nitrogen (N) and calcium (Ca), to overlap.

Abundance of Element (kg)

0   10   20   30   40   50

Ca H   C   O

0 4 9   16   25   36   49

See calcium (Ca) and nitrogen (N) overlap at the lower end.

A second scale highlights the perfect squares of the original abundance to help make the visual connection to the square root transformation, below.

The gap between the top outlier, O, and the bottom cluster is so large it could be expressed as a ratio. This difference will persist as long as we retain the native scale. This axis is our number line; it obeys our command. We can change the scale if we apply the same mathematical operation across all of the data. Since we have a top-tail outlier, we need a transformation that shrinks large numbers more than it shrinks small ones. Let us reposition the marks by their square root ($\sqrt{x}$). Now, oxygen is still separated, but not at the visual expense of its peers.

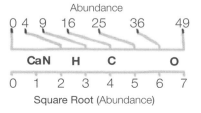
Abundance

0 4 9   16   25   36   49

CaN   H   C   O

0   1   2   3   4   5   6   7
Square Root (Abundance)

Element marks are repositioned according to their square roots, removing the overlap between Ca and N.

The square root is a good transformation, for this small dataset. But maybe a different warping effect would be better? Why, we could raise our data to a power (x^2, x^3, …) or take its inverse ($1/x$), or try some combination (like $1/\sqrt{x}$). You see, once we entertain the possibility of transforming our scales, the effort threatens to spiral into a multiverse of possibilities. How can we rein in this power before we lose control?

Overlapping marks, empty voids, and ratio comparisons can all hinder our ability to see the data before us. However ugly the data arrives, the *ladder of transformation* can help find better forms for visual exploration. If your data (y) has outliers on its lower end, a bottom-tail, then try walking the data up the ladder: $y \to y^2 \to y^3$. This sequence of powers impacts larger numbers more and helps pick apart clusters at the top end of your distribution. If the data has a top-tail, outliers like the 43 kg of oxygen, try walking the data down the ladder. The Procrustean ladder lets us warp the number line world in pursuit of seeing what the data is hiding.

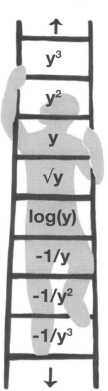

Left-skewed "negative" bottom-tails can be moved up the ladder

Right-skewed "positive" top-tails can be moved down.

If one of our biggest problems as humans is grappling with ratio comparisons, then what we need is a system of "ratio-numbers." This system would express ratios as differences, the kind of comparison we like. That way, we would be able to consume ratios in a more visually discernible way. Lucky for us, this "ratio-number" already exists. In fact, it has been helping us for over 400 years.

The ratio-number, or *logarithm*, has a tricky technical definition. How it works can prevent us from appreciating why it works: Logs were invented to transform ratios to differences. Too often, we throw a logarithm at a scale because we know it will compress a wide range of numbers to a narrower field. This may motivate you to try a log transformation, but it is only a partial victory if you miss the magic of what happens. For that, let's plot a short series of doubling numbers: 8, 16, 32, 64. Each step rises by 100 percent, a constant

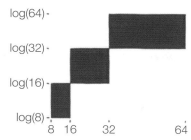

increase in ratio from one pair of numbers to the next. Above, the visual distance between these numbers is emphasized with filled boxes. Along the horizontal, the distance between each number doubles, because the number doubles. Along the vertical, we plot the logarithm of each number. The vertical visual difference is the same, because the ratio is the same. The world of the logarithm is built for comparing ratios. This is just what is needed to address troublesome comparisons that are so hard for our mind to make any sense of.

The example transformation below expands the original set of elements of the human body to several dozen. Now, elements that have only a trace abundance, like lithium and arsenic, are included too. Each element is represented by a dot, which is enough detail to show a ladder full of transformations. The most abundant element, oxygen, is again in the rightmost position. It is kept fixed there at every rung of the ladder. The 37th least abundant element (molybdenum) is kept fixed at the leftmost position. See how oxygen causes most of the elements to overlap on the blue w-rung (I chose *w* to represent *weight*). Transformations reshape how the distribution appears. Different views reveal different aspects of the distribution. It appears the log(w) transform de-clusters best.

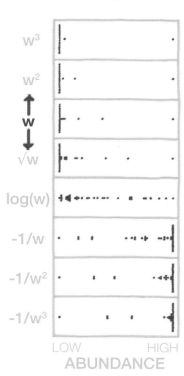

Logarithm is from the Greek words *logos* (ratio) and *arithmos* (number, also the root for arithmetic: the art of counting). John Napier published a set of logarithms in 1614 and they evolved to Leonhard Euler's 1748 standard definition.

The log's quotient property states directly that the ratio of division becomes the difference of subtraction:
$\log(x/y) = \log(x) - \log(y)$

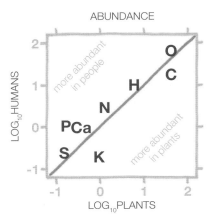

ABUNDANCE

The whole canvas often gets consumed to show a narrow diagonal band of data. Empty corners are wasted real estate once we account for the trend. Data translation, transformation, and logarithms can combine to serve our comparison-seeking eyes.

The same shape persists no matter what logarithm base (10, e, or 2) is used.

Augment human capabilities rather than replace people.
TAMARA MUNZER, 2014

Here we compare the abundance (percent by weight) of the seven most common chemical elements in people *and* plants. The diagonal represents an equal relationship between people and plants. We can trace our eye down the diagonal to see that we share with plants the same sequence of most abundant elements: oxygen (O), carbon (C), hydrogen (H), and so on. Notice how the even 1:1 diagonal relationship leaves a lot of the canvas rectangle empty.

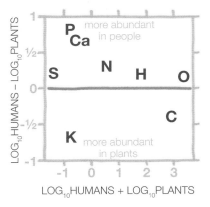

These differences can be visually exaggerated if we rotate and expand the data so that it fills all the available space. This is done with Tukey's sum-difference graph. By re-plotting the elements on an adjusted frame of reference, we can accentuate visual comparisons across the data. This gives our eyes more meat to dig into, affording a better shot at seeing what is going on. The log is one special rung on the ladder of transformation. We plot data because we want to explore it with our eyes, and the ladder makes that possible. The picture changes but the data remain the same.

We have seen how to alter the position of points, but we could go further. Do you remember how large values can get visually buried when encoded in the area of shapes? We could also change how data drives other properties, such as shape area, line weight,

In 1905 Max Lorenz compared the cumulative share of income earned to the cumulative share of people, from poorest to richest. The *Lorenz Curve* highlights the deviation from the 45° line of equality.

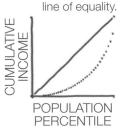

and color value, using the same ladder of transformation. This is particularly useful when mapping populations as sized circles. A transformation can keep city populations large while also letting you see small towns. As you probe, transform to reveal more.

We have warmed up to data exploration with only a handful of data points at a time, across only one or two dimensions. These examples spared the room necessary to introduce, but your exploration may not be so straightforward. Many variables create complexity that is difficult to untangle. We naturally experience a multidimensional world, comprised of our many senses and a maze of memories. Yet, we are limited to only two spatial dimensions, the horizontal and vertical, to explore our data. The third dimension, depth, does not exist on paper, and is practically missing in the virtual plane of digital screens. The fourth dimension, time, is an unreliable vessel for analysis because our experience of time is so subjective. We are stuck exploring many dimensions in Flatland. What can we do?

Climate is as reasonably a complex arena as any to take a first step into combining, expanding, and getting creative with our data sketching. It can help us add one more favorite technique on top of what we have covered so far. The scatter plot matrix is a marvelous way of scanning many pairwise patterns and comparisons across the constraints of the 2-D page, all at once, in pursuit of identifying where to dig deeper.

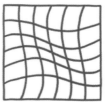

And chaos theory teaches us that straight linearity, which we have come to take for granted in everything from physics to fiction, simply does not exist. Linearity is an artificial way of viewing the world. Real life isn't a series of interconnected events occurring one after another like beads strung on a necklace. Life is actually a series of encounters in which one event may change those that follow in a wholly unpredictable, even devastating way.
IAN MALCOLM, JURASSIC PARK

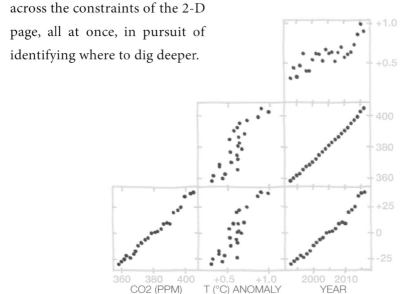

When we explore data, we can imagine ourselves translating and reordering like bulldozers pushing piles of rock around a quarry. Or, we are warping axis scales like time travelers morphing the fabric of space-time. You can explore beyond the techniques we have reviewed to encounter even more computational and creative approaches. As you voyage through the worlds of your data, you will go beyond these shores, learn more, and invent new ways of finding interesting patterns and comparisons.

Whatever the metaphor, interrogating data can be hard. Wrangling data can be a messy, iterative, draining ordeal. The energy required can tax the spirit. Remember, you are trying to bring some new insight into the world by mining chaos. It is difficult because it is a worthwhile endeavor.

Across the last two chapters, we considered how to investigate with unbridled enthusiasm. In the words of Italian writer Italo Calvino, we have flown to take a look at the world from different perspectives. I hope your data sketches are rich with wondrous comparisons and patterns. Your visions have charged you to go forward with a trove of insights. But before you fully return, you might ask, *was any of it real?* Maybe you were just seeing things.

Our brain is wired to see patterns even when they are not there. Critical suspicion helps protect us against becoming victim to our own statistical hallucinations. Just because a pattern appears does not mean we should believe in it.

Your trust in the data is the bedrock of any belief you can have in your data sketches. Understand the road the data traveled to get to your workbench. Where did it come from? How did it get here? Who touched it? Then, temper visual conclusions with a vigilant skepticism of what you think you see. But after all that, how exactly are we to evaluate the veracity of all these comparisons and patterns?

10

UNCERTAIN HONESTY

Doubt is not a pleasant condition,
but certainty is an absurd one.
VOLTAIRE, 1770

Certain. Probable. Confident. Reliable. Meaningful. Significant. These are some of the words we use to talk about how trustworthy a picture's messages are. Each one of these qualifiers is an abstract and non-visual concept. Sometimes, these words are coupled with numeric precision. They are often left naked. You do not see these qualifiers directly in the real world. For us, they are non-visual checks against our visual perception.

Philosopher of science Karl Popper expressed that "observation can give us 'knowledge concerning facts' but does not justify or establish truth." Qualifiers, like significance and confidence, characterize how truthful observations are. They are defined by abstract narratives that fill pages with verbal arithmetic. Cultural norms litter their history. Recall the model of time that Ilya Prigogine inspired; time is a stage where every instant calculates reality. The calculator takes inputs from that last moment in order to spit out the next. In a past world, certain measurements were frozen as recorded data and delivered forward to us. In the current moment, we can use data to understand the past time it came from, and use it to make guesses about what future might arrive next.

We stand today like the ancient Roman deity Janus, the god of gates, transitions, time, beginnings, and endings. Janus is depicted as having two faces, one to look into the past and one to look into the future. We do not have the luxury of perfect knowledge of other times. But we can use data to build better relationships with the past and with the future.

The desire for truth so prominent in the quest of science, a reaching out of the spirit from its isolation to something beyond, a response to beauty in nature and art, an Inner Light of conviction and guidance—are these as much a part of our being as our sensitivity to sense impressions?
ARTHUR EDDINGTON, 1929

I say not that it is, but that it seems to be....
HUBERT N. ALYEA, 1903–1996

Janus is sometimes shown with young and old faces to represent straddling time. Or Janus is represented with male and female faces to represent straddling dualities. The gateway between the old and new year, January, honors the god.

Why is it so difficult for the mind's eye to see truthfulness? Let us pursue this question by looking at several statistical concepts used to improve our relationship with the truth. Together, we can develop a careful appreciation for how to qualify visual discoveries. Then, together, we can strive to picture what is so hard to see.

Probable Possibilities

Prediction is our first step into the world of truthfulness. Conversations about the likelihood of future events often rely on fuzzy, imprecise language. *The candidate will likely win on Tuesday.* Expressions such as *highly unlikely*, *probably*, and *almost certainly* nudge our understanding. It is an understanding with a crude specificity. Unqualified expressions often only give us a binary, more-or-less insight into what is going on. Mostly, they just tell us whether the speaker thinks one way or the other.

Subjective language expresses a psychological feeling of belief or doubt. It does not have much scientific value. Subjective language is fuzzy, and fuzzy things are hard to refute. A word like *improbable* could describe a chance of 15 percent or 35 percent. A one-in-six chance could be *doubtful*, *unlikely*, or have *little chance* of occurring.

Imprecise expressions reveal how we think about probability. They tell us that the context for a prediction matters a whole lot. 20 is high if you were expecting 5. But 20 is low if you were expecting 50. We often talk about probability relative to some kind of unspoken expectation. Speakers use fuzzy language because they do not have any precise numerical insight. Listeners, in turn, may not even know how to understand a specific number if they heard it. Together, they form a cabal of double-imprecision. But if a specific value is not known, then fuzzy language might be more honest than some alternatives. An analyst who conveys an uncertain result with too many decimal points invites more trust than what is warranted.

A prediction with a precise value is obtained by considering how many cases of interest there are, compared to how many equally likely cases there could be. This probability, a numerical

A true story: I, too, have turned to lying—a much more honest lying than all the others.
LUCIAN, c. 125–180

CIA analyst Sherman Kent observed that Cold War policymakers interpreting the statement "serious possibility" would assign different chance values to the probability, from 20 to 80 percent.

Part of our knowledge we obtain direct; and part by argument. The Theory of Probability is concerned with that part which we obtain by argument, and it treats of the different degrees in which the results so obtained are conclusive or inconclusive. … in the actual exercise of reason we do not wait on certainty… All propositions are true or false, but the knowledge we have of them depends on our circumstances.
JOHN MAYNARD KEYNES, 1921

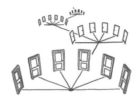

prediction, refers to a group of possible events, not a single instance. The probability of rolling a two on a six-sided die is 1/6. This statement describes the expected reality of an entire sequence of rolls. Eventually, the total quantity of rolled twos, divided by the total number of all rolls, will stabilize at about 1/6. The next roll of the die is merely one member of a series of possible events.

Prediction is a prospective measure. The set of six possible die rolls is a group of fictions, only one of them will actually appear next. Prediction stands us at the threshold of the multiverse, unsure which door will pull us forward. When we evaluate a prediction, we are asked to appreciate a group of scenarios, even though we only walk one path. But prediction's possible scenarios, the multiverse of possibility, are not always so obvious as the die's six options.

The die's probability is a result of the physical symmetry of the cube. Sometimes, the set of potential outcomes is fabricated by a possibility factory. Whether we are forecasting election results or hurricane paths, statistical models work in a similar way. They simulate many possible futures, each simulation the result of slightly different initial parameters. The outcomes of these different futures can then be tallied. For example, across 1,000 simulated hurricane paths, 341 show the storm hitting the coast and 659 do not, yielding a 34 percent chance of landfall occurring.

Like a toy train, models are incomplete simplifications of reality. They rely on assumptions. Models also harbor the biases of their human tenders. They do not fully capture the richness of the world. But, neither do our minds! Like our own understandings, models are approximations, hopefully good-enough for the task. And models can get better over time as they are fed more data. But here

is the visual challenge: models are popularly thought of as black boxes. The dominant way of describing them is an object which you cannot peer into. At their invisible worst, a statistical model is proprietary. But even the mechanisms of a published model are obtuse unless you work in its field. Models often require some kind of faith that, behind the curtain, a fair multiverse of possibilities is being created. The model asks you to trust

that its input data, assumptions, and rules are all designed well enough.

Eventually, one of the possible futures of the multiverse actually manifests. But we, the audience, may still not know much more about the validity of the model. Imagine a binary choice between success and failure. Model A predicts a 60 percent chance of success. Model B predicts a 90 percent chance of success. If the event is a *success*, was model A or B more correct? We cannot know with only a single event. The event would have to be run again and again to determine if the success rate were closer to 60 or 90 percent.

The way we interpret numerical probability is also fuzzy. It is too natural for us to translate a number to a feeling. If you read that "a team's chance of winning the game is 83 percent," you might translate this to a subjective statement such as *my team is probably going to win*. You might even believe your team is certain to win. A more fair digestion of 83 percent might be: *If the same game happened six times, my team would lose once.*

Consider a candidate with a 44 percent chance of winning an election. The first way you might see this number is some kind of progress bar, almost halfway to 100. We obsess over the halfway mark. The chance of winning is confused with the 50 percent share of the vote needed to win the election. The vision of the progress bar arrests our appreciation of what this probability really means. Instead, imagine blindly throwing a dart at a board that is 44 percent covered in blue for the candidate. Now, fine differences in probability, and proximity to 50 percent, do not seem to matter as much. So, when are these specific numbers any use? No surprise, we engage once we are able to compare.

Just as the ability to devise simple but evocative models is the signature of the great scientist so overelaboration and overparameterization is often the mark of mediocrity. Since all models are wrong the scientist must be alert to what is importantly wrong. It is inappropriate to be concerned about mice when there are tigers abroad.
GEORGE E.P. BOX, 1976

If a meteorologist says there is a 70% chance of rain and it doesn't rain, is she wrong? Not necessarily. Implicitly, her forecast also says there is a 30% chance it will not rain.... [people] always judge the same way: they look at which side of "maybe"—50%—the probability was on. If the forecast said there was a 70% chance of rain it rains, people think the forecast was right; if it doesn't rain, they think it was wrong.
TETLOCK AND GARDNER, 2015

We can only reasonably predict so far into the future. The *Lyapunov Time* helps define the prediction horizon, how far into the future we can hope to make predictions for a system: millions of years for a planet's orbit; a few days for the weather.

Now, consider two candidates chances of winning: 44 versus 43 percent. Suddenly the contrast gives context, a comparison for us to bite into. Numbers become much more interesting if we can focus on their difference. Similarly, a change in prediction for a single candidate— 40 percent last week, 44 percent this week— provides an easy narrative: *The candidate is trending up.* A single number lacks precise meaning without context. Two predictions create an environment where precision suddenly seems to matter a great deal. But we should not forget that without the comparison, specific numbers are lost on us.

Elections send us forward with a question about the mental pitfalls of reading statistical claims. How do we factor in trust? Is there any use in reporting a one-point difference between candidates if the margin of error is three points? Comparison without context about certainty creates a false sense of confidence.

Percentiles, the multiverse of probability, black-box models, and our subjective reading of it all combine for quite a quagmire. The language of truthfulness gets mixed up with the language of belief. What exactly constitutes confidence? At what point is something significant? Is the margin of error significant? How exactly do we measure trust?

Without Truth

Why do we even put up with these abstract expressions of trust? Well, precision is expensive. Absolute certainty is often impossible. You cannot measure the entire universe, so you look at a slice, a subset—a shadow of the world that has already passed—and learn to make do with what the sample tells you. Sampling theory is not only important to data storytelling, it is also wrapped up with the entire epic saga we call science.

Science progresses on the principle of falsifiability. Karl Popper's landmark *The Logic of Scientific Discovery* explains, "Science never pursues the illusory aim of making its answers final." A scientific claim is a statement that could be proven wrong.

In contrast, existential claims are unscientific because they cannot be falsified. "There is" statements, such as *there are blue giraffes*, are unscientific because they are not falsifiable. We cannot search the entire universe to check if they exist, have never existed, and will never exist. Science cannot help us evaluate these kinds of statements.

Science is a method of rejecting carefully qualified opinions with new evidence. As exceptions are discovered, general claims get knocked down to more specific cases, or abandoned entirely. There are no truths in science because a truth cannot be overthrown. Science trades in corroboration, truthfulness, and trust —not absolute truth.

There is also no absolute precision. Even simple physical measurements, the wellspring of so much of our data, are not absolutely precise. When we measure the length of an object with a ruler, the number we report falls somewhere along the narrow width of a single tick or between two tick marks. In either case, the single number recorded actu-

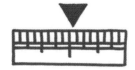

ally represents a range. We could narrow the range by measuring with more precise equipment, but we do not bother because our measurement is good-enough as is. Measurements are not absolutely true, but they are true enough for what we need.

A scientific view is interested in claims that can be proven false. A scientific view embraces numeric measurements as ranges. A scientific view knows our goal cannot be absolute certainty. That is why we must consider expressions like error, confidence, and significance. When we acknowledge the limits of truthfulness, we are able to offer stories as worthier of trust. When you grapple with uncertainty, you put yourself directly in the middle of the struggle between the world as it really is— reality—and the world as we perceive it. We strive to bring them into a little more harmony.

With Certainty

I recently went to an evening lecture about Enlightenment thinking with a friend. Before the talk started, she asked me what I thought the ratio of men to women attendees was. The effort of counting everyone in the theater would be silly—we did not need an exact ratio to satisfy our curiosity. So instead, we each counted the men and women in a couple of sections and together determined that the room was about two-thirds men. The estimate from this quick sample led us to then discuss why there might be an imbalance.

Statistical confidence relates a random sample to the actual larger universe it came from. Measuring the entirety of anything is expensive, often impossible. To get a sense of a candidate's chances you do not call every voter with polling questions. A scientist's experiments cannot continue forever. Even if you could record a complete snapshot of the entire universe, where would you store it? In fact, if we learn how to have confidence in the relationship between the sample and the true world, then we do not have to measure the entire universe. In 1937, statistics pioneer Jerzy Neyman explained this sample as an "estimate, which presumably does not differ very much from the true value of the numerical character."

Confidence is expressed as a duo: level and interval. The confidence level is a percentage, often 95 percent, picked prior to analysis according to some cultural norm. The confidence interval is a range of values, calculated using the predetermined level and the sample data. The interval is supposed to help us understand the range within which the actual parameter is estimated to occur. *Supposed to.*

A 95 percent confidence level is *not* the probability that the actual parameter lies within the confidence interval. Instead, it is a probability statement about future imaginary confidence intervals. Like I warned, statistical confidence contains imaginary futures and layers of abstraction. Just like the chances of two candidates winning an election, confidence quickly becomes a comparison game. We only really make any sense of confidence once we are able to contrast one interval against a cultural norm or other competing range.

No theory that involves just the probabilities of outcomes without considering their consequences could possibly be adequate in describing the importance of uncertainty to a decision maker. It is necessary to be concerned not only with the probabilistic nature of the uncertainties that surround us, but also with the economic impact that these uncertainties will have on us.
RONALD A. HOWARD, 1966

Clinical significance describes the practical importance of a treatment's effect on daily life.

A 95% confidence interval conveys that there is a 95% probability that the calculated confidence interval from some future experiment encompasses the true value of the population parameter. It is a ratio of the number of imaginary confidence levels that contain the true value to all imaginary confidence levels.

The credible interval is the Bayesian analog to frequentist confidence interval. It determines the probability of a parameter falling within a predefined range of values.

We often mention the confidence level in a footnote and depict the confidence interval directly on the graphic. Suddenly, we are back home as we compare tall and short bars—but do not miss how conceptually convoluted what you are comparing is. The confidence interval may do a good impression of Tukey's box plot, but what it indicates is far more abstract.

Significance characterizes truthfulness based on how likely a finding is merely a product of random chance. It works by a kind of reverse logic called *reductio ad absurdum*: If it were not true, things would be absurd. Significance is often used to evaluate the relationship, or correlation, between two data variables in pursuit of making predictions about the future. But, an observed correlation does not necessarily make for an interesting correlation.

Imagine that childbirths increase in the spring, the same time of year that migrating storks return. This does not indicate that the birds brought the babies. Spurious correlations occur when events appear to be causally related due to coincidence or the presence of an unseen factor, called a lurking variable. Children's intelligence is not caused by the size of their feet. But, reading ability and shoe size both increase as a child grows up. It may appear that *A* causes *B*, or *B* causes *A*, when *Z* causes both. Connectivity does not have to dip into the illogical for us to question causation. Chicken-and-egg interdependence makes one unsure of which variable is responsible for the other. Writer Darrell Huff described, "The more money you make, the more stock you buy, and the more stock you buy, the more income you get; it is not accurate to say simply that one has produced the other."

All this shows how important it is to keep your wits sharp and not forget common sense as you voyage through statistical truths. So, what about some of the other measures associated with numerical trust? The margin of error is just half of the confidence interval. Like its parent interval, smaller margins of error indicate more confidence. Say you were sailing the Caribbean and knew a treasure was buried on one of 10 possible islands. One spy tells

The confidence interval around the mean is often represented in the same way a box plot displays the interquartile range around the median.

Significance level is the complement of the confidence level:

Conf. Level
+ Sig. Level
1

Reliability is a coefficient that indicates consistency or agreement. How reliability is calculated depends on the situation.

you he can help narrow it to five of these islands. Another spy tells you she can help you narrow the hunt to just two of the possible 10 islands. She is more confident and having fewer options on the chart is good if you are racing to find the treasure.

On the number line, shorter ranges indicate more confidence. But a visual representation that is physically small and meaningfully large goes against the *bigger is more important* convention. We should want our eye to be grabbed by things we are more confident in, but here the opposite occurs. We must rise to the challenge of spotlighting confidence using visual channels beyond size. Try playing with density, as if the true position is lost in a blurry haze and we can merely paint a picture of the cloud.

Remember how troublesome the mean (average) is. It is often packaged with certainty-inducing qualifiers or distribution summary metrics, such as the variance or standard deviation. Remember that summaries, especially nongraphical summaries, reduce. If you are going to accept any of these intimidating statistical qualifiers without a picture, you better be able to supply the right context that lets you make a real human comparison. Otherwise, do not give blind faith to what looks like an impressive fact.

Certainty, our last term, is a generic word that has no consistent meaning across fields. Yet, our craft is often called upon to communicate uncertainty. We now know what a complicated, challenging, and worthwhile task this is. In 2009 Howard Wainer taught that effective display of data accuracy must:

Remind that the data contains some uncertainty

Characterize the size of the uncertainty with respect to the inferences made

Help us avoid incorrect conclusions through the lack of a full appreciation of the imprecision of our knowledge

Statistical trust reveals how tricky truthfulness can be. It is difficult to meaningfully illustrate some of the basic concepts that statistics uses to convey trust. Be careful you are not dazzled by their abstraction as you qualify how findings relate to past and future worlds. We cannot ignore statistical trust. Uncertainty is a critical part of the message that must be conveyed.

Return of the Hero

At a certain point in any voyage of discovery, the ship's hull can fit no more. It must sail home to tell stories of adventures and deliver precious cargo. We explored how to make meaningful pictures with data using position, size, and color. Then we got a better sense of how to conjure more interesting comparisons and patterns, with an eye for understanding what truthfulness is all about. We have now circumnavigated the probe-humanize cycle.

So, how do you know when it is time to step out of the cycle, and turn your attention toward shore? In the best of circumstances, you discover something so exciting that you cannot bear keeping it to yourself. Full of energy, you rush to tell the world. Often though, you will have merely attained a personal comfort in your familiarity with the data. You develop a good sense that it does not have any more secrets to share right now. Sometimes you just run out of time and have to push on, unable to carry all of the treasure home.

We shall not cease from exploration And the end of all our exploring Will be to arrive where we started And know the place for the first time.
T.S. ELLIOT, 1942

John Tukey used to end discussions with: *I am convinced that this is as good as we can do so far.* Inquiries into data, like so many creative endeavors, are never completed, just abandoned (or sometimes, taken away). By the end of it all, you will know your data better, perhaps better than anyone ever has. You will know what it can and cannot tell you about the world. Perhaps it has revealed something astonishing. Our attention will now turn from exploring data and toward informing the world.

Now, a little surprise. So far, we have clutched our data and method-
ically advanced toward the moment when we inject it into the world.
Before we do, let us first step ahead and marvel at the rich landscape
of information already there, serving your authentic experience as
a creature of the world. Your embodied cognition powers successful
data storytelling, but it also delights in dancing, music, and laughter.
It is time we flip our perspective.

All of the world, in some way, is serving you signals all the time. Most of them are not data-driven insights; very little of the world arrives on a statistical platter. Yet, you crave it all. Broader human experience has lots to teach data storytellers. We will now sample a handful of the many ways we receive all kinds of information. Doing so will help us examine higher concepts that relate to our own craft, such as engagement, emotion, and explanation. It will also reorient our perspective from inward data facing to outward

people facing. Data storytelling is often an insulated practice. It is just you and the data and maybe a small team. But it is ultimately a people-facing art. Each of the following five chapters is a focused sample of a specific, non-data domain that can illuminate our craft. Some connections will be made directly back to data storytelling, but I can promise you that it would be impossible to catalog them all. There is a world of rich experience for you to draw from.

ENCOUNTER

A cool marble doorway separates me from a velvety black space. I step in. Walking forward, I look up and notice I cannot see the ceiling, there is just inky black. As my eyes adjust to the darkness, a dozen halos of light sharpen. Approaching the nearest one, I see it is an exquisitely lit glass box with a small clay vase inside. It is decorated with iconic geometry in madder red, burnt orange, and black. Not much bigger than my hand, the vase is at the perfect height for me to view.

The atmospheres of some museum galleries invoke temples of worship and their spiritual predecessor, the cave. Museums, in fact, *are* temples. Ancient Alexandria's Temple of the Muses, called the *Musaeum* or *Mouseion*, was a vast institute that attracted many scholars. Today, behind-the-scenes activities

liken the museum to a library or archive. On display, museum exhibitions compete with other entertainment outings, such as going to the movies. This public-facing function is the side that interests us most.

Museum curators and exhibit-designers create spaces that manage visitor attention. Where maps imitate and reflect the real world of experience, museums actually do it. They are real-world experiences. Examining how museums inform visitors can inspire better data storytelling. The principle distinctions between our craft and museum design is just the nature of the canvas, and the dimensionality of the data. Artifacts and objects, like the small vase in the dark gallery, are the museum's raw data. New acquisitions are studied, cataloged, preserved, and, mostly, tucked away in storage.

There they wait in climate-controlled boxes and racks for a probing researcher or creative curator who might need them.

Each museum object is an information vessel. A physical description, such as the vase's size, color, and material, is the foundation for many types of data. Archeology is layered on to these physical features. The vase I admire was found in southern Italy, but from its material composition we are sure it was created in Greece, probably Attica, 25 centuries ago. These object-specific qualities can then be connected to the greater flow of history. We know this vase's form. It is a *lekythos*, used to perfume brides with oil. We know this name because others like it were labeled: *This is my lekythos*. What does this example tell us about other vases? What does it tell us about the people who owned it?

The object, you see, is the key to a trove of information. When the object is put on display, its data goes on display too. There, it collides with the knowledge of the visitor, and new ideas emerge. When I gaze at the vase, I see its heroic imagery, geometric patterns, and elegant contours. I imagine sun-soaked rituals above Mediterranean shores and reflect on the milestones of my own life. A single museum object channels a spectrum of information, from its own physicality to what it means to the visitor. Likewise, the museum audience will consist of a wide spectrum of interests and capacities for interacting with that information.

A single vase may strike you with awe, but traipse through a storeroom of thousands and you will go numb. Experience psychologist Stephen Bitgood characterizes the success of exhibits to good management of visitor attention. Any higher goals, such as learning, is a byproduct of attention. To manage attention well, we must understand audience and setting factors. "Museum fatigue" is a low-energy exhaustion where your body and mind beg for a break from cultural enrichment. Also called information overload, it can arrive in a number of ways. Satiation occurs from repeated exposure to too much of the same thing. Distraction occurs when you are overrun with stimuli begging for your gaze. Dazzled by the options, the excitement of exploration quickly recedes as each additional decision saps energy from your visit. *What room should I visit next? What art should I focus on? How do I get to where I want to go? Why is this meaningful? What if I don't see everything?* The more times we pause to figure out what is going on, the more we are pulled out of the flow of interfacing with the objects. So then, how does a designer help fight museum fatigue?

Museum curators come to the rescue by easing navigation, not only as we negotiate the physical rooms of the building, but also as we explore psychologically and intellectually. Curators do this with careful planning of architectural layout, selection and arrangement of objects, signage and labeling, handheld brochures, and even lighting and wall color. These elements are put to work to maximize visitor interest, curiosity, and satisfaction, while minimizing visitor time and effort.

A high-value experience begins in the museum lobby. It performs the same function as the entrance antechamber of a temple or hallway concession area of a movie palace. Lobbies offer a place to help transition visitors from the frenzy of the outside world, and orient them to be receptive to the experience ahead. A lobby calms and encourages you to take a moment and determine. *What is there to see and do? Which direction should I explore?* This orientation is enhanced by personal greeters, handouts, and signage.

Some museums are able to orient visitors simply with their architecture. A high-ceilinged expanse that is beautifully ornamented puts you in a state of wonder and slows you down. From lobby center, with the museum entrance to your back, you might get a glimpse of what each gallery option holds: a monolithic seated Egyptian pharaoh statue if you go right, a Greek column to the left, and a gold-framed European painting if you go straight.

One may think of an information forager as an information predator whose aim it is to select information prey so as to maximize the rate of gain of information relevant to his or her task. ... Our notion is that the proximal perception of information scent is used to assess the profitability and prevalence of information sources. These scent-based assessments inform the decisions about which items to pursue so as to maximize the information diet of the forager.
PIROLLI AND CARD, 1991

What information consumes is rather obvious: it consumes the attention of its recipients. Hence a wealth of information creates a poverty of attention, and a need to allocate that attention efficiently among the overabundance of information sources that might consume it.
HERBERT SIMON, 1971

NYC's Metropolitan Museum of Art calls its lobby The Great Hall while London's British Museum calls their lobby The Great Court.

Large objects can act like billboards, they inform and beckon you to come closer. You do not even need a map to begin. These points of prospect give you the space and time needed to consider options. Good entry points are inviting and easy to access. They give an emotional first impression and tell you a little about what lies ahead.

Effective entry points act as *progressive lures.* They first attract people to enter and then gradually disclose more about what lies ahead as you get deeper into the experience. Information overload is prevented by displaying only what is necessary. But progressive lures can also deceive, such as when you turn a corner to discover that the line you are waiting in is much longer than anticipated.

Wayfinding is how a visitor navigates, or finds their way. Long sight lines, right-angle turns, and human-scale distances all make it easier for visitors to construct their own mental maps of the museum's galleries and paths. Frequent "you-are-here" locator maps and well-labeled landmarks help visitors check in with, update, and expand their personal maps. Together, these design cues help the visitor navigate, circulate, and keep track of how much there is left to see.

There is more to making a museum mental map than traversing an architectural floor plan. That is just a spatial layout. We are much more concerned with the meaning we wish to experience during our visit. Each institute will be a little different, of course, but many fine arts museums show how space can be used to weave meaning into our mental maps. From the museum lobby, you step onto an enormous timeline that snakes through collections that are juxtaposed according to a higher plan. You can then take an uninterrupted stroll through a complete survey of Western art in the order that it was created. Start by admiring ancient Greek sculpture and then proceed to the next gallery to see all their Roman copies. Accelerate through medieval and Renaissance painting, through French Impressionism, and into abstract contemporary art. Gallery flow creates a time-travel experience that reinforces the artistic traditions connecting the works and subtly strengthens mental maps.

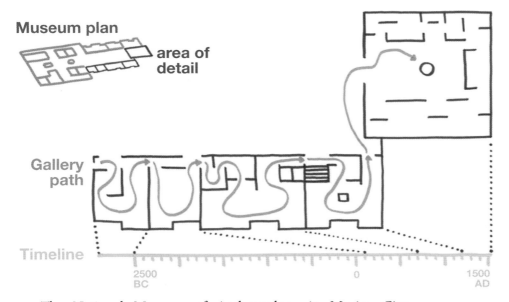

Museum plan

area of detail

Gallery path

Timeline

2500 BC

0

1500 AD

The National Museum of Anthropology in Mexico City presents an exquisite collection in a way that uses space to pile on layers of meaning. The first gallery sets the stage by showing what we know about prehistoric life in the region. Then, you proceed counter-clockwise and chronologically, beginning in 2500 BC through exhibits on great preclassic, Teotihuacana, and Toltec civilizations. With each new gallery, you advance forward in space and time. Finally, you arrive at the heart of the museum and its most amazing room, the Mexica gallery, which spans AD 1200–1521. At the center of this gallery is the museum's most iconic object, the Sun Stone, which is 12 feet in diameter. After not spending enough time in the Mexica gallery (there is never enough), you can continue exploring Mexican history, eventually finishing back in the present day, where you started your journey.

Successful museums have thoughtful route design that reduces the friction of the visitor-object interface. You mostly do not notice these cues, by design. They are there to reduce your mental burden, after all. We can more directly sense other efforts by museum curators by recognizing the tools they equip us with, such as handheld maps, good signage, audio and guided tours, and smartphone apps. The best place to see how they help us achieve an exceptional experience is in an individual gallery.

A favorite detail of mine about the National Museum of Anthropology in Mexico City is that funerary objects of each culture are housed in underground galleries. You must descend to meet the art of the dead.

Space is the medium in which ideas are visually phrased.
ROBERT STORR, 2006

Where museums use timeline layouts, zoos use maps. Each can be conceived as a little Pangea, grouping species within continent-themed zones that are smushed together.

Inside a particular gallery, our search strategy begins with a simultaneous gestalt view of the entire space that drives our attention to a large or prominently placed object—such as a painting in the center of a wall or statue in the middle of a room. Then, we often shift to a sequential visual processing of other objects in the room. These are often grouped thematically to highlight a certain form of fabrication, geographic origin, or chronological story. Objects are arranged in an aesthetically pleasing way that is in harmony with the room's design.

The most important and frequent visual queries should be supported with the most visually distinct objects.
COLIN WARE, 2008

We engage with objects that are able to hold our attention. To do this, an object must first be detected. Detection is a function of salience, which in turn depends on size, contrast, color, distinctiveness, and from how far an object is visible. Once detected, the object is judged based on our perceived value of it vis-a-vis our time. Will the benefit outweigh the cost?

Detection + Value = Attention

Good gallery signage and labels provide context. In an art museum, I appreciate one or two paragraphs of introductory welcoming text that orients me to what is going on in the room. Some items are so salient that we will read their individual labels. Beyond aesthetic beauty we yearn for context and labels can give it. They open access to the metadata that the object attracts us to. *What is this called? How old is it? Who made it?*

More distance can be introduced between the painting and its label, such an entire gallery room's worth of labels in a single location, usually by an entrance. But this physical distance introduces a cognitive load to anyone who wants to know more.

But labels can also distract and interfere. You go to an art museum to see art, not to read labels. One approach advocates that visitors should first experience art with their own eyes before being influenced by the curator's written narrative. Ingrid Schaffner, Carnegie Museum of Art curator, describes an ideal interaction where you take in the art, read the label, and then return again to the art. She explains that "the standard placement of labels follows this simple rule: because we read from left to right, the label should appear to the right of the object, at eye level, where it appears like a footnote to the work of art." Appreciate the art, the raw data, for what it is first.

I appreciate museums that go to the effort of giving each individual object a few sentences so that the nonexpert (me) can be clued in to *why* it matters. Ingrid Schaffner advises that these labels begin with information specific to the work and continue to knowledge that helps link the work to the broader exhibition. Finally, the label can conclude with a call to action, as advised in Coleman's *Manual for Small Museums*: "If the concluding sentences of a label are written with a view to persuading the visitor to do something about what he has learned [like look at another picture in the show…], the label attains to the greatest usefulness."

Imagine approaching the label of a piece you are curious about but do not quite understand, and then reading only the artist's name and a non-descriptive title, such as *Untitled #73*. Not only are you dissatisfied, but you probably feel alienated and stupid, too. Composer and critic Virgil Thomson cautioned against the possibility of these types of experiences, advising to "never overestimate the information your readers have, but never underestimate their intelligence."

Museums have delighted me since childhood. Studying how they work has caused me to enjoy them even more and to reflect on lessons for the craft of conveying information: Layer information. Give direct access to raw authenticity. Help orient a viewer to many dimensions. Text can augment understanding, but not at the expense of letting people discover and see things on their own. Several paths to meaning can be contained in a single space. Give access to all of them. Create opportunities for return visits. Use subtle design to reduce navigation friction. Help audiences find their own context and meaning.

When I lived in Boston I returned to its Museum of Fine Arts many times under different circumstances. It was the quiet backdrop for a Sunday afternoon read, the promenade for a romantic stroll, preparation for a trip to a foreign city, destination to see a touring exhibition, and place to learn from an expert's gallery talk.

Beyond *how* museums work, *why* museums exist connects them even more closely to data storytelling. The spirit of ancient Alexandria's *Musaeum* was resurrected in *Wunderkammern*, Renaissance cabinets of wonders. These private collections of curiosities were assembled by the affluent, centuries before state institutions like the Louvre Museum and British Museum were founded. Cabinets of curiosities contained objects of science like fossils, minerals, animal specimens, instruments of discovery, architectural models, and diagrams of how things work. This collection of examples and conceptual diagrams is the physical predecessor of the infographic collage, a sensory attempt at taking many angles on a topic.

But the cabinets also included biological oddities, religious icons, and mythological images. In short, items that tried to provoke curiosity and help make sense of what was not understood well. Today, science and art are firmly divided, but back then they were united in serving the same sense of wonder. Swiss curator Hans Ulrich Obrist sheds light on these prototypical museums as tools to "organize and explain the world's copious and strange complexity … and luxuriate in what cannot be understood." In search of better understanding, we naturally delight in playfully confronting the unknown.

Gesamtkunstwerk is the desire to produce a total picture or to realize an entire universe, originally from Richard Wagner's ideal work of art where all parts serve an integrated whole.

Many museums (and theme parks, another playful encounter) steer you to exit through the gift shop. More than a money-grab, the gift shop gives you a chance to immediately relive it all again, by way of images and other objects related to your adventure. You decompress from your experience and begin to transition back to the rest of the world, with a renewed sense of awe.

Our tour of encounter design might feel incomplete and that is O.K. Remember that sometimes the best experiences leave you wanting more. There is more informing for us to explore.

CHAPTER

12

LISTEN

A story comes alive in the imagination of its listener. A life becomes real once it is narrated. Without a story, you would dart from moment-to-moment, embracing pleasure and fleeing hardship as each stimulus went in and out of focus. Without examination and interpretation, life reduces to mere biology.

Your experience of reality is a never-ending story. Stories give you a place in the world and a place in time. Stories are how you remember the past and expect the future. Every moment, a story organizes your life by accounting for all that you see and all that you cannot see but truly believe.

Information has not done its job until it impacts the story running in a person's mind. Only then has information informed. If we understand story, then we can help data come alive in a person's mind too. So let us take

a critical look at the (sometimes irrational) art of storytelling.

The more you know, the better you can navigate the obstacles of life. But there is a natural limit to the knowledge one can learn from their own experience. We each get only one lifetime, and that makes time precious. Stories give access to the accumulated knowledge our ancestors spent their whole lives acquiring. We get to benefit at a bargain price. That is the story of the last 5,000 years of civilization.

Stories help us see what could be. Fiction is like a laboratory for life. It helps us develop alternatives and store solutions for what might happen. Stories teach us how to interact with one another. They reinforce esteemed models of behavior and chastise misdeeds with scorn.

Millions of people believe they are all part of the same tribe because they all believe in the same stories.

Stories are storehouses, conduits, and expanders of knowledge. They help connect staggeringly large social groups. Stories are useful. O.K., fair enough. This does not yet address the aspect of stories that offends the empiricist. Somewhere, we know that the nature of storytelling does not prioritize the truth. It prefers the sensational, the exaggerated, and the exciting. Why are stories like this?

Consider an evolutionary perspective. Today, truth helps us understand reality. But the truth did not always help us survive reality. Here is a story:

> It is the end of the dry season and the sun is heavy. I take hold of my cane and call for my dog. Parched, we set out together across the savanna in search of water. There is no shade along the hard-baked path, just a sea of yellow grass. Walking along, all I can think about is the cool taste of water on my lips. I hardly notice the bird circling overhead, or the pair of antelope bounding away, into the hazy heat. Finally, we emerge out of the dry grass and into a clearing. There it is. I can see the watering hole. Suddenly, the dog stops. In an instant she is more alert than usual. Maybe she heard a rustle in the grass. Maybe she smells something in the air. Maybe the watering hole is just a little more quiet than usual. Looking around, things feel… different.

What do they do? Approach the water or turn back? What would you do? Odds are, there is nothing awry at the watering hole today. It is unlikely that, say, a lion is waiting for the thirsty pair to step forward before it pounces. But, even a 99.9 percent chance of survival is bad odds. A one in a thousand chance of becoming lion chow can get you spit out of the gene pool.

The truth—whether there actually is a lurking predator—takes a backseat to the goal of not being eaten. Total consequences win, even if the odds are small. It is better to walk away from nothing a thousand times so you can be right that one time your hunch turns out to be real. From an evolutionary perspective, the truth is a luxury good.

Our biology did not keep up with how rapidly we conquered nature. The world we are wired for lags behind the world we exist in. We are no longer prey to man-eating lions, but instinctual threat detection remains. The stories we tell each other and ourselves speak to certain biases that used to help us prevail.

In stories, *speculation beats truth-seeking*. The truth takes time and risks exposure. It is safer to assume and move on. In stories, *exaggeration beats subtlety*. If you are wrong and flee, you live. If you are wrong and stay, you die. In stories, *excitement beats monotony*. Adrenaline-juicing encounters demand our attention, then they live on as the slices of life we remember most vividly. In stories, *self-deception beats rational analysis*. Passionate belief in a thing is sometimes the critical piece required to make that thing real. In stories, *expectation beats living in the moment*. Life is hard. It helps you endure to know that traumatic experiences, eventually, end.

These elements make us doubt storytelling. Stories are irrational, perhaps even animalistic. Yet, stories help us to do things that only humans do. We make meaningful connections across thousands of years. We organize massive social groups. We feel most alive when we are part of something much bigger than our individual selves.

Our complicated nature prefers certain experiences. And they can tell us a little about the entertainment we enjoy. Comedies make us happy. They produce more smiles and laughs than other film genres. Yet, passionate dramas, violent adventures, and even horror films sell tickets. We yearn to be terrified, safely. We delight in scandal and surprise. We crave fake anxiety. As storytellers, we must pay attention to the natural impulse for anxiety simulation. Do not sensationalize. Do not deceive. But also, do not be afraid to entertain. If you want someone to hear you, then you must have an ear for what they listen to.

Modern man is in fact a curious mixture of characteristics acquired over the long ages of his mental development. This mixed-up being is the man and his symbols that we have to deal with, and we must scrutinize his mental products very carefully indeed.
CARL JUNG, 1875–1961

Useful fictions: We perceive truth and utility to be much closer than they really are. ... Given a choice between a useful fiction and a useless fact, natural selection will choose the useful fiction every time.
MICHAEL AUSTIN, 2010

The character of a society is largely shaped and unified by its great creative works, that a society is molded upon its epics, and that it imagines in terms of its created things—its cathedrals, its works of art, its musical treasures, its literary and philosophic works. One might say that a public may be so unified because the highly personal experience is held in common by the may individual members of the public.
BEN SHAHN, 1957

Good stories build energy across their telling like a train going faster down the track toward its destination. Along the way, good stories cause the audience to endure an enjoyable amount of anxiety. Good stories also give you a reason to climb aboard for the ride. If a story moves *and* engages the intellect *and* the heart, then it is well on its way.

Your mind experiences time in sequence, so it receives story in sequence too. Every story arrives across a linear flow, one beat after another. A storyteller can command this flow precisely to hold a listener's attention and bias their experience.

Narrative flow puts content in the right order. It makes salient what matters for each moment. It banishes anything irrelevant from view. A tight flow can meet a listener where they are, and step them to a place otherwise incomprehensible. From the familiar to the unknown. A similar controlled sequence allows a teacher to progress students toward new knowledge. We reach new domains and higher levels of abstraction by extending what we already know. Storytellers and teachers both have a vision for where they want to take their audiences and focus their attention until that goal is achieved.

If the flow is smooth, the world of the story engulfs the listener's identity, and they can enter into a flow state. It is as if their mind has stepped up to the very horizon of the story's imaginary world to absorb the narrative rush through them.

How is this done? You cannot show everything, an actual experiential flow. That would bore anyway. Instead, give the listener the necessary connective tissue to keep up as the story leaps forward. In film, spatial and logical context move us forward shot to shot. If we know a hero is going on trial, we are not surprised when a scene opens on a courtroom; it is a logical connection. A wide establishing shot of the entire courtroom lets us know where we are spatially before seeing a close-up of the hero taking the stand. Both logical context and spatial orientation help us go with the flow.

Connective tissue is the foundation of the escapism that takes filmgoers and novel-readers on a ride. The ride gets exciting if you can get the audience to guess where the story is heading. That is called engagement. It is great if they are guessing, but no fun if the whole story is predictable. That is called a dud.

At the other end of the spectrum, a narrative with weak connections is difficult to follow. If the flow is confusing, the audience gets snapped out of their flow state. They wonder what is going on. Their identities distance themselves from the story and turn critical. To engage, the narrative must land somewhere between boring and confusing.

Conventional stories order events the same way we experience them, over time. *First this thing happened, and then that, and then this other thing.* The familiar structure steps a protagonist through a setup-conflict-resolution arc. One adventure leads to the next in a chained sequence of cause and effect.

Story sequence can illuminate many more kinds of phenomena beyond temporal continuity. Sequence can also show effect, *then* cause. In education, effect-cause is called an explanation. In storytelling, it is called a flashback. Sequences can contrast unlike things. Sequence can elaborate, exemplify, and generalize. Sequence can surprise by violating our expectations. Take a look at the variety of plot structures below, each paired with a classic film from cinema history.

A linear ordering of phrases which conveys a gnarly network of ideas … a writer must constantly reconcile the two sides of word order: a code for information, and a sequence of mental events.
STEVEN PINKER, 2014

[The narrated story is always] more than mere enumeration in a simple serial or successive order of incidents or events. Narration organizes them into an intelligible whole. … The plot is a synthesis.
PAUL RICOEUR, 1986

When we look at a painting, there is also a linear experience because our eye sees the painting over time; the storyteller just has less control.

3-ACT
each scene
demands the next

SINGLE STREAM
every moment is
most important

TWO TIMELINES
linked emotionally,
not causally

BACKWARDS
concealed
beginning

CIRCULAR
ends where
it starts

REPETITION
same story,
over and over

HYPERLINK
multi-causal
network

FLASHBACK
how did we
get here?

Even more structures exist if we look across communication arts that seek to persuade. Formal arguments lay out a claim, provide supporting evidence, refute objections, and swell all of that into a big conclusion. I prefer the more straightforward model taught by Nancy Duarte. She shows how the best speeches toggle between what is and what could be. They begin with a long exposition that characterizes how unsatisfied we are now, establishes a vision for where we could go, and then, faster and faster, switches between the two until everyone is ready to embrace the new world.

Why three acts? Because the audience needs an intermission from sitting for so long, just like how television shows need breaks so they can show some commercials. There is no specific number of anything needed for good storytelling.

Endings satisfy. Our nature is to be curious and we are willing to stick around to find out how situations will resolve to get closure. Along the way, tension, suspense, and anticipation mount as we make short-term predictions about what will happen. Anxiety builds as we wait for the outcome. It is painful to walk away from an open question.

Why do we crave closure? As mentioned before, closure helps us endure struggle. Knowing that the pain will stop makes it bearable. The unknown is the worst torture. The villain you cannot see is the most terrifying. Our need to stick around for the ending seems to go against what was said earlier about prioritizing utility over the truth. Here is the difference: Closure seems to be all about forward-looking expectation and especially concerns the social world. Truth is all about backward-looking explanation and especially concerns the physical world. Knowledge about the future is more immediately critical to survival than knowledge about the past. We care a great deal about the future and will speed into it, regardless of how well we understand the past. We look forward to the fulfillment of the end.

How do we motivate an audience to desire a story's closure? If we are blunt, we raise questions directly, as I just did. More elegant stories convince the listener to ask questions on their own. The story about the watering hole never explicitly states *there might be a lurking threat* because it does not have to. You do that work.

The engaging story is a woven mesh of audience-imagined questions and answers. As a story unfolds, and questions (Q) are answered (A), new questions are asked. Multiple levels of curiosity propel us through the story. Some take the entire work to satisfy.

PRIVILEGE

Creates suspense
by burdening
audience with more
info than hero.

CALLBACK

Question,
once thought
abandoned,
is answered.

ELABORATE

Question
detail and
meaning build
over time.

SURPRISE

Answer thwarts
expectations. Adds
anxiety if narrator
is untrustworthy.

If a film is fast-paced and builds some anxiety-inducing curiosity, you will stay until the end. You might not watch it ever again, but you will not walk out. But those two elements—linear momentum and closure—are not enough for you to finish a whole television series. You also need to care about the characters. The story has to have meaning.

Our concern for an imaginary person's safety is a strange phenomenon. But is it? We can already see the thirsty pair on the savanna in our mind, even though the story did not tell you anything about what they look like. Fictional characters live exclusively in the heads of listeners. But they sit right next to historic figures, contemporary celebrities, and memories of old friends. Are your internal images of George Washington, Tom Hanks, and Harry Potter all that different from each other? For the devoted fan, Harry might be most real.

We never get complete knowledge about anyone. So we take the given story character and blend it with what we know about the world. Together, the story and our own experience synthesize a gestalt being. Our imagination projects a complete person, bringing the character to life in our minds. If the story activates you to create more, then the story becomes more alive in your head. This is how books can produce more escapism than film. A good book, even with less sensory stimulation, can be more real.

Characters, real or not, are real in our imagination. We are filled with empathy for the people we project with our imagination. We recognize when another being is in pain and imagine what that hurt is like. Their experience, fiction or not, affects us. In some ways, it is easier to map your own identity to a fictional character than to a real person. Storytellers design characters specifically to receive your concern. Why does the thirsty character have a dog? I included a dog because I want you to care more about my protagonist.

Empathy goes beyond feeling sorry for characters. We are also invested in them because vicarious living is fun and useful. Anything learned by experiencing their journey can help us in our own future trials. Movies can inspire us to be more romantic, more

Endings, frankly, are a bitch. A proper ending for film is one in which an expectation is fulfilled for the audience. But once they get a sense of it coming, often they're ahead of you. You don't have to rush. But you must never waste even a single shot—because I think the ending requires the most delicate and thoughtful writing of any part of a movie.
WILLIAM GOLDMAN, 1983

[A] familiar pattern merely shows us what we already expect and does little to raise expectations or contribute to narrative motion.
STEVEN KATZ, 1991

The art of creating suspense is also the art of involving the audience, so that the viewer is actually a participant...
FRANÇOIS TRUFFAULT, 1983

Comics panels fracture both time and space, offering a jagged, staccato rhythm of unconnected moments. But closure allows us to connect these moments, and mentally construct a continuous, unified reality.
SCOTT McCLOUD, 1993

daring, and even more creative. We are social creatures, interested in better navigating our tribe. We gossip to learn about people. We follow stories to learn successful behavior strategies. Once again, story is a way to expand our knowledge.

Feeling for a character is a reliable way of building meaning into a story, but it is not the only way. Let us look at another dimension of meaning with a pair of statements by E.M. Forster. First:

The king died and then the queen died.

Here we have two events, the king's death and the queen's death. We also have a continuity relationship between the two events. One after the other. Two facts, one relationship. Now, see what Forster does by adding one little detail:

The king died and then the queen died of grief.

Wow. Those two little words, *of grief*, change everything. We have one more fact, the queen's grief. It has a causal relationship to the queen's death. But that same grief also creates an additional correspondence. Now, we also know more about the queen's relationship with the king. His death destroyed her. One additional detail creates two new relationships. This is very different than if it had said the queen *died of old age*. That would not tell us much about how the king and queen got along.

The real magic is that the connection between the queen and her beloved king is not explicit. You intuit it. Great stories are rich with opportunities for the listener to make connections on their own. These self-made connections help the story leap off the page and into the reader's imaginative reality. The more the story comes alive in the reader's head, the more meaningful the story becomes.

It is the storyteller's challenge to convince the listeners what to be curious about. The storyteller cannot tell listeners if the story is meaningful or not. That is up to them.

We have referred to the audience as readers and listeners. But really, we should only be using the singular form: reader or listener. Having an audience of thousands does not mean you are going to address the entire mass as a crowd in a stadium. People experience stories alone, in their heads. But what if you did address a stadium of 30,000 people? The magic of story would still occur in 30,000 individual imaginative minds. Address each listener on a human, one-to-one level.

Novice storytellers think mechanically. Their currency of thought might be camera station, shot size, and camera angle. Master storytellers determine these details based on the relationship they want to create with the viewer. Instead of camera station, what point of view should we have? Instead of shot size, do we want to feel distant or close to the subject? Instead of camera angle, how should we perceive the subject? In good stories, narrative decisions drive technical execution, not the other way around. You see, the discourse is not the main event. What happens in the listener's head in response to the narrative is most important.

Story activates and creates ideas unknown to the storyteller. E.M. Forster knew his queen's grief would make us feel differently about her relationship with the king. But he could never know that his little line would call forward my own grandparents' loving bond. My grandmother's lonely hardship after my grandfather's death is now somehow better illuminated to me. This feeling is a special product of my imagination. It is a private meaning, uniquely mine.

A master storyteller engages the listener's imagination to bring stories to life. Their listeners intuit internal connections between story elements. A legendary storyteller goes beyond. Their listeners discover personal knowledge that is meaningful outside the story. These are the stories that cause us to feel more alive.

Stories that make us feel alive are often symbolic. Symbols imply more than is obvious; they cannot be fully explained. They can be interpreted in many ways. Symbols can mean

A text is not an entity closed in upon itself; it is the projection of a new universe, different from the one in which we live. Appropriating a work through reading it is to unfold the implicit horizon of the world which embraces the action, the personages, the events of the story told. The result is that the reader belongs to both the experiential horizon of the work imaginatively, and the horizon of his action concretely. ... the reading itself is a way of living in the fictitious universe of the work; in this sense we can already say that stories are told but also lived in the imaginary mode.
PAUL RICOEUR, 1986

On myths and mythology: What would we be without the help of what does not exist? Not very much, and our very unoccupied minds would pine away if myths, fables, misunderstandings, abstractions, beliefs and monsters, hypotheses and the so-called problems of metaphysics did not people the darkness and the depths of our nature with abstract creations and images.
PAUL VALÉRY, 1871–1945

different things to different generations. Paradoxically, the universal symbolic is achieved with precise description. Strong story symbols are rich with specific detail and are often very personal to the creator. In contrast, the generic is impersonal. It has no emotion. The generic affords no opportunity for the individual to connect, empathize, and imagine.

Powerful symbols are sometimes called archetypes, a concept I think best to let Carl Jung explain:

> [Archetypes] are pieces of life itself—images that are integrally connected to the living individual by the bridge of the emotions. That is why it is impossible to give an arbitrary (or universal) interpretation of any archetype. It must be explained in the manner indicated by the whole life-situation of the particular individual to whom it relates...

> They gain life and meaning only when you try to take into account their numinosity—i.e., their relationship to the living individual. Only then do you begin to understand that their names mean very little, whereas the way they are related to you is all-important.

Stories are engines of knowledge creation, especially self-knowledge. They help us discover more. Sequence, closure, and meaning help bring story flow alive. And if stories are alive, then the successful stories are the ones that survive. A successful story is the one that keeps getting told. These are the stories that do not just help us thrive, but make us feel alive, too.

FREEZE

Frederick Siebel's poster plunged the 1942 American public into the sea to face a young man gasping for life. The drowning sailor makes eye contact, reaches out (or is he fingering the gossiper?), and spits out water to use what might be his last breath to warn: *Do not gossip, you might be leaking military intelligence to enemy spies.*

This singular image weaves setting, hero, conflict, and outcome. We know where we are (the aftermath of a sunk ship), who we care about (the archetypal sailor, who represents all servicemen), and gain an insight to how this happened (SOMEONE TALKED!). It only takes a few brushstrokes to convey high-stakes emotions, stoke your adrenal system, and speed your heart rate. We leave the piece with new resolve against careless gossip.

Still images do not move, but they can send our minds on causal journeys. Narrative photographs, paintings, and magazine illustrations engage us intellectually and stir our emotions. The frozen stories this chapter is about threaten to drown us in an entire survey of the visual arts. We will resist this deluge and focus on just a few media that help us better connect data to audiences. Not all data stories are frozen, of course. Many interactives, animated films, and presentations sequence data-driven content over time. Yet, each of these build on still comparisons and can benefit from considering the singular image.

Narrative art is art that tells—or narrates—a story through imagery. The power of a story is in how and what it makes us feel. Images ignite imagination, evoke emotions and capture universal cultural truths and aspiration
LUCAS MUSEUM OF NARRATIVE ART

Illustrator Norman Rockwell became famous for visual stories that caught characters at just the right moment. In *The Shiner* (1953), a young student sits outside her principal's office with a black eye, smiling. In Rockwell's *Freedom From Fear* (1943),

parents tuck sleeping children into bed, with violent newspaper headlines in view.

Many Rockwell illustrations appeared on the cover of *The Saturday Evening Post*, a weekly magazine that contained another kind of effective visual story, the print advertisement. Advertising has always been on the cutting edge of attracting attention, conveying messages, and motivating action. Across the last hundred years, ads have kept pace with communication technology across newspapers, radio, television, and the Internet.

Advertisements blend aesthetics with utility. Pleasing and beautiful design encourages reader engagement, acceptance, forgiveness, and satisfaction. However, a merely stimulating ad is not a successful ad. Radical designs delight creators and win awards, but confuse audiences. Instead, the advertisement that influences is the real success. So it is with data storytelling. If our design is too bold, we may confuse. If we get lost in aesthetics, our efforts to covey information may be reduced to mere decoration.

The classic print magazine advertisement is the most relevant analog to our craft. Its format consists of a headline, image, and body text. Advertising tycoon David Ogilvy had advice on each ingredient. Whether it is an advertisement, newspaper article, or data story, large portions of audiences will only consume the headline. Headlines work well if they promise a benefit, and even better if they communicate news. Headlines should offer *helpful information*, be written in familiar and descriptive language, and appeal as specifically to the target audience as possible. In advertising, bad headlines do not mention what the product is or what it will do for you. Horrible ads have no headline at all.

The best visuals arouse curiosity. The reader who wonders *what's going on here?* is the reader who will stay to find out. We like looking at ads that depict individuals we can identify with, not crowds. Babies, animals, and sex still appeal. Photographs often perform better than illustrations. As data storytellers, we must consider how to grab the reader who only gives us a glance. This can be accomplished in many ways: include a summary comparison, annotate an exemplary data point, or call out a specific insight. Orienting readers to how the chart works is good, but showing something useful the chart can do is better.

A celebrity's image slapped onto an advertisement might grab the reader's attention, but they will depart the engagement thinking about the celebrity instead of the story you want to convey. Quick, superficial decoration is not the same as design elements that lure you into meaningful engagement. Getting the reader's attention is not the same as informing them. Our challenge is to connect the busy reader to the essence of what the whole piece is about. For an advertisement, the essence has something to do with a story that the reader identifies with or aspires to. For a data story, the essence is usually about improving how the reader perceives some aspect of the world.

If a scene with clearly expressed gist is combined with an object that is incompatible with that gist, the results will be a cognitive effort to resolve the conflict in some way. The advertiser may thereby capture a few more cognitive cycles.
COLIN WARE, 2008

A superficial feature is an aspect of a situation that can be modified without touching the core of that situation.
HOFSTADTER AND SANDER, 2013

An imitation may be described as an identity manqué. It is artificial. It is not fortuitous as a true metaphor is.
WALLACE STEVENS, 1951

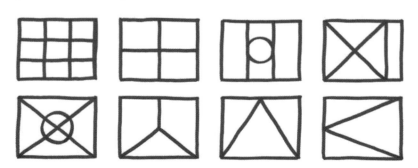

Grids provide a structure for organizing elements into a properly related and harmonious composition.

Glossy magazine pages arrive from a broad tradition of graphic design that evolved from colonial broadsheets, yellow journalism newspapers, and Belle Époque posters. Since then, posters have been used to promote films, propagandize wars, organize protests, and decorate public spaces. Poster design guidelines help concentrate our attention on composition lessons:

FOCUS. A clear focal point directs viewers where to look first and keeps them from wandering off the page. Does the eye naturally land on the introductory element?

DIAGONAL. Diagonal lines break the rectangular grid and help the eye cut across the frame, creating a sequential experience. How does the eye move about the panel?

DEPTH. Overlapping objects create a 2.5-dimensional visual hierarchy without the perception problems that mimicking 3-D volumes introduces. Objects in front are elevated to our attention.

STORY. The content of a single frame can communicate setting (context, where are we?), character (what do we care about?), conflict (what contrast and pattern can we see?), and satisfaction (what new knowledge have we learned?).

Depth is combined with color, line weight, scale, and placement to organize visual elements into a successful composition. For data storytellers, these visual elements include common graphic items, like headlines and captions, and items specific to charts and maps, like an interesting comparison or perceptual cluster of marks. In either case, the human brain can only hold a few elements at once in short-term memory. So, how can we preserve complex visual stories that are comprised of thousands of elements?

A chunk is a unit of information that can be stored in short-term memory. We first saw the concept of chunking with the grouped color categories on my hometown map. In 1956, psychologist George Miller introduced us to the idea that we can only hold about seven chunks in our head at once. This total has since been further pared down; researchers now think we can hold only three or four chunks at once. One trick to complex storytelling is to package a set of ideas into a chunk. Then we can navigate the chunks and break them into their sub-elements as necessary. Cognitive psychologist Steven Pinker explains:

> We can only hold in mind just a few of the letters from an arbitrary sequence like MDPHDRSVPCEOIHOP. But if they belong to well-learned chunks such as abbreviations or words, like the ones that pop-out when we group the letters as MD PHD RSVP CEO IHOP, five chunks, we can remember all sixteen. Our capacity can be multiplied yet again when we package the chunks into still bigger chunks, such as the story "The MD and the PHD RSVP'd to the CEO of IHOP," which can occupy just one slot, with three or four left over for other stories.

Too many visual elements cannot reasonably compete for attention at once. If you overwhelm the reader, then they may disengage. Instead, use gestalt effects, such as enclosure and grouping, to arrange elements into visual chunks. Colin Ware showed how visual search can be enhanced if "smaller objects of search can predictably be associated with larger visual objects." The use of multiscale design chunks information into visual hierarchies that match conceptual meaning.

Overlap   Sameness   Hierarchy   Connection   Enclosure

The inverted pyramid of information puts the critical information first, and elaborative detail after in descending order of importance. It is attributed to Edwin Stanton, Abraham Lincoln's secretary of war, who needed to make sure critical parts of messages were transmitted over telegraphs that were prone to cut out.

A category pulls together many phenomena in a manner that benefits the creature in whose mind it resides. It allows invisible aspects of objects, actions, and situations to be "seen."
HOFSTADTER AND SANDER, 2013

Gestalt psychology emerged out of the Berlin School of experimental psychology in the early 1900s. It attempted to understand how, in the words of Kurt Koffka, "the whole is other than the sum of the parts." Despite some erroneous conclusions, it has inspired a century of psychological inquiry into how we perceive the world.

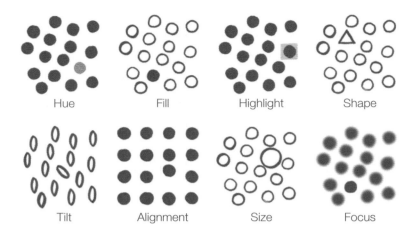

| Hue | Fill | Highlight | Shape |

| Tilt | Alignment | Size | Focus |

Visual pop-out occurs when a distinct item stands out from the rest of the field. It is the opposite effect of grouping. Pop-out is a pre-attentive effect, an automatic process that occurs before the act of attention. In nature, it occurs when we are instantly alerted to the presence of a snake after only spotting a portion of its distinctive scales. Like grouping, pop-out can be achieved with different visual channels. Depending on the data, some techniques will be more effective than others. Pop-out and gestalt grouping can be used to match content to its importance, creating a sequenced appreciation for the reader that first attracts, and then holds their attention as they visually unpack individual chunks.

Threat detection quickly identifies potentially dangerous stimuli such as snakes, spiders, and angry faces in a crowd.

Across graphic design, many trade-offs are considered in pursuit of information harmony. As I warned, it threatens to distract us on a dazzling journey deep into the history of two-dimensional

art. The methodical geometric abstraction of *De Stijl* paintings closely resembles the style of modern data visualization, but lessons can be learned from any aesthetic movement. If we pulled the string long enough we would travel all the way back through Egyptian hieroglyphics and Mesopotamian reliefs, perhaps finally resting in Lascaux to marvel at its cave paintings and wonder what was created before and has since been lost to time.

De Stijl, Dutch for "the style," was an artistic movement that emerged out of WWI Netherlands. It advocated abstraction and universality through reduction to essential form. Piet Mondrian and Bart van der Leck were two of its proponents, known for their rectangular designs in black, white, and primary colors.

Graphic design augments pictures with text to create powerful messages, in a way that fine art painting rarely attempts. Image and words are each better for presenting different information. The two were perhaps first paired by an ancestor pointing to an object and calling out its name. As information-makers, we are still doing the same: showing new pictures and labeling them with words.

Images exists across a spectrum of abstraction, from photographs to cartoons. They present complex patterns for our eye to recognize and investigate. Polymath Leonard Shlain detailed in 1998 how images approximate the real world: "they are concrete. The brain simultaneously perceives all parts of the whole integrating the parts *synthetically* into a *gestalt*. The majority of images are perceived in an *all-at-once* manner." Compared to how we see images, the linear sequence of consuming alphabet writing is a different cognitive process. Its abstract symbols offer other benefits. The A, B, C squiggles we call letters have murky origins. Today, they have lost their connection to the world of experience. Reading abstract symbols lets us explore and communicate the worlds of logic, reason, philosophy, science, and mathematics with amazing efficiency and precision.

Data images are clarified with text. A title introduces the reader to the setting. Annotations help navigate and highlight details. Direct labels offer high precision when specific values need to be conveyed. But visual patterns suffer if text commands too much attention. Words are very efficient at providing information, but only in small amounts. They are not good at describing complex patterns.

Steven Pinker observed that good writers "write as if they have something important to *show*." Great analytic thinkers know that language and vision together helps the mind soar. As data storytellers, we do not have to choose between the two. We get both.

Graphic design is a natural lens to view data storytelling through, but once you turn the page, you will see there is one more two-dimensional craft to observe. It does an even better job of telling stories by integrating the power of pictures and words.

There are numerous origin stories about how we got alphabet symbols. One links the wavy Cretan pictograph for water, MĒM, to the Greek letter mu, and eventually to the sound of our M.

The Hangul Korean alphabet consonant symbols are based on how the mouth shapes different sounds. Its *M* consonant is ㅁ.

Image is, text is always about.
NICK SOUSANIS, 2015

Language can convey complex logical relationships between abstract ideas and support conditional actions. Visual media can support the perception of almost instantaneous scene gist, rapid explorations of spatial structure and relationships between objects, as well as emotions and motivations. Both can maintain and hold the thread of audience attention, which is the essence of narrative.
COLIN WARE, 2008

How do we integrate figures and text? The goal should be to have the two intermingled so that they form a single perceptual unit.
HOWARD WAINER, 1997

CHAPTER

14

CONNECT

How images make you feel matters. Aesthetic qualities like color palette and line texture arouse responses in us all. They do not convey any particular message content, yet sometimes they excite more meaning than a detailed body of text. A striking flash attracts attention, certainly. But the *emotion* of great work can also help us transcend the everyday by causing us to reconsider what the experience of life itself can be.

Some disparage ornamental qualities as frivolous. To them, style is merely superficial. The arts are called soft in contrast to science and technology; those are hard. We do not analyze and decompose aesthetics in the same way as we do the world of machines, and that somehow makes emotional design less intellectual. *How* artists accomplish their effect eludes us, and so their effort is trivialized.

Emotions are real. Chemical hormones excite and calm us. Like a step function or phase change, an emotional impulse that lasts for only moments can permanently alter how we feel and see the world.

Yet we cannot program a computer to spit out perfect emotional design as we can automatically lay out a scatter plot. As I mature as a creator, I have understood that this is cause for celebration. Emotional communication is a fascinating frontier because we humans are the ones uniquely equipped to explore it.

I find myself thinking about emotional perspective shifts more and more. To be honest, they cannot be cataloged in a neat framework, like other topics in this book. But that is even more reason to look, and get you thinking about feeling too.

Loud design demands to be noticed. Shiny objects catch our eye, perhaps because we are wired to recognize shimmering fresh water sources. Novelty attracts the attention of our curiosity. Despite this, we almost immediately close flashy Internet ads and quickly forget recent pop music sounds. Something more is needed if we are to investigate and become invested in the next new thing.

We need emotions. Pleasing experiences make us feel good, causing us to linger and desire more similar enjoyment. In contrast, we naturally distance ourselves from what turns us off. We know that the world assaults our senses with too much to process. Emotional intensity helps us determine what to pay attention to, and ultimately, what to remember. Recall how the patient S., who did not have the power of forgetting, was lost inside a maze of equally salient memories. Emotions move us. They guide us to what is important, in the moment and across time.

Color is perhaps most powerful as an indicator of emotional tone, often invoking the feel of a sunny day, rainy storm, or mysterious night. Movies are emotion manipulators, and their color palettes are a primary ingredient in setting a scene's mood. Across the eight Harry Potter films, the color palette darkens as Harry grows up and adventures through more threatening stories.

How lines and shapes are drawn can tell you a lot. Their expressive potential should be explored. A fuzzy curve could be perceived as warm and gentle. A crisp corner might be rational and conservative. Irregular points are unwelcoming, scary, and severe, like piercing thorns. Heavier lines attract attention because they are bigger, unless of course all of the lines are heavy. Then, a single thin thread might become most salient. The emotions of shape and character are both obviously powerful and also challengingly mercurial, always subject to context.

The clean perfection of the machine is nice, but not always preferable. Our senses often favor a certain roughness, which might be intuited by contrasting the raw authenticity of Nina Simone's jazz with the latest algorithmically manufactured, precisely in-tune pop music. One sound is legendary while the other is fleeting. Or consider the multisensory experience of exploring the winding streets and varying architecture of a Renaissance city center. A cobblestone stroll is more appealing to me than traipsing through a centrally planned metropolitan grid. There, every block is the same and every edifice makes you feel insignificant. Only numbered street signs tell you where you are. And those numbers are pure concept, only weakly associated with any feeling. Perfectly rectangular, a modern grid gives no chance for connection or belonging. Because real life is not perfect, perfection can feel dead.

On the page, hand-drawn illustrations are familiar analogs to the spirit of the jazz singer or the crooked mesh of narrow streets. We could be tempted to dismiss the appeal of human-wrought creations with superficial explanations. Roughness connects us to the unique individuality of the creator, appealing to us as social creatures. It also pops out from an increasingly mechanical environment. But the real power of embracing the imperfections of roughness lies somewhere deeper.

Many small decisions over an extended period of time, most not according to any master plan, lead to imperfections. Let us illuminate this by returning to the city walk. The old city arrived slowly. Streets were formalized over time and buildings were constructed for specific needs. More people, more small decisions, and ultimately more information—all tuned to the experience of individuals—are embedded in the old city. In contrast, the centrally planned metropolis grid was laid out by a small number of similar people across a narrow window of time, often in service to distant stakeholders like real estate developers and tax collectors. Its plan is information poor and has weak relationships with the people who live there now.

The seemingly rough solution—which seems superficially inaccurate—is in fact more precise, not less so, because it comes about as a result of paying attention to what matters most, and letting go of what matters less.
CHRISTOPHER ALEXANDER, 2002

Emotional design evolves with technology and fashion, pinning certain looks to specific decades. I have found the more context I have for a particular period in time, especially for how its people saw the world, the more its visual design resonates with me. Some design elements hit an emotional escape velocity and become timeless.

The superficial aesthetics of roughness can be mimicked. New housing developments imitate old villages and smartphone apps turn digital photos into pencil sketches. Somehow, these approaches are all still stuck in an uncanny valley, but not because we lack the computing power. Perhaps what such superficial styling misses is the time creators put into handmade production. This time can be spent meditating on the subject matter, which leads to better understanding and intuition. It is also time during which emphasis naturally varies across the creation, giving rise to the roughness. This emphasis may vary, often intuitively, in accordance with the values the creator, who is striving to convey the very essence of the thing, places with the information.

I do not mean to suggest we always crowdsource design, or advocate that you draw your final products by hand. Rather, as creators we should give attention and time in order to make space for intuition and variation to naturally appear. I believe that an audience can appreciate when these have been done. When more life goes into making something, it *feels* more alive.

Texture is another way of thinking about the character of a visual. Imperfections and variation are not the only way to create texture, of course. Decorative patterns also change how surfaces make us feel. Gradients, in color and form, create smoother transitions that soften edges and help build connections across elements. If we look past cosmetic qualities, we can see how structure and design relationships change how we feel. Consider the two simple portals below. Which one is more appealing to you? Which one has more life?

In 2002, architect Christopher Alexander advocated a design perspective that focuses on the relationships between centers and wholes. A spatial center is some identifiable, marked coherence.

Your eyes, nose, and mouth are all centers. Wholeness is a global structure that rises from the interaction, interdependence, and relationships between centers. And so your nose is also a whole, including named centers like the bridge, tip, and nostrils. Yet these parts are not enough to make a nose, just like the named parts of the face are not enough to make a face. It is the subtle relationships between these parts that gives rise to a greater whole.

Christopher Alexander showed how a single dot can change the way we experience a piece of paper. We subconsciously perceive a complex system of spatial relationships, and this can change how a design makes us feel. The dot creates zones of perceptual segmentation including a halo around the dot, rectangular divisions, which in turn create even more divided spaces.

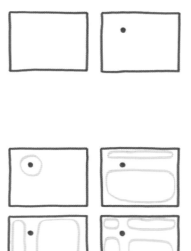

The two portals are also an example adapted from Alexander. We can begin to understand why the arch feels different if we examine the set of salient centers within each design. The arch creates a system of different-sized centers that overlap. The swooping path from the largest center above the portal to the point of the vertex creates dynamic harmony. In contrast, the centers created by the rectangle are more similar in scale. Their separateness makes them less coherent than the arch's centers. Coherence and connection help the arch feel more alive.

Emotional design fills us with wonder, awe, and the joy (and terror) of being alive. When an image arouses emotions in us we feel connected to the art, to the artist, to the great tradition of human experience, and even to existence itself. In the moment of heightened emotion, everything we are, a tangled history spanning failures and success, is recognized.

When I think of them as centers, I become more aware of their relatedness; I see them as focal points in a larger unbroken whole and I see the world as whole. ... The flower is not made from petals. The petals are made from their role and position in the flower. This is an entirely different vision of reality from the one we have become used to. In this new vision, it is always the whole, the wholeness as a structure, which comes first.
CHRISTOPHER ALEXANDER, 2002

A beautiful thing is something that would make us happy if it were ours, but remains beautiful even if it belongs to someone else. Naturally, here we are not dealing with the attitude of those who, when they come across a beautiful thing like a painting made by a great artist, desire to possess it out of a certain pride of enormous economic value. These forms of passion, jealousy, lust for possession, envy, or greed have nothing to do with the sentiment of Beauty.
UMBERTO ECO, 2004

This connection affirms our own identity, simultaneously telling us that we are not alone and who we are matters. This connection can give you confidence, a feeling of inspiration, and energy to flourish.

Some visual experiences reach into our depths and grab the soul. Mark Rothko painted thin layer over thin layer to create archetypal fields of color. He invited us to stand inches from his huge canvases and be overwhelmed by the richness of the total visual experience.

It is not always about personal identity. The ego desires what is next, it wants more consumption, it wants to be advanced. Great emotion can quiet this voice. Intense feeling can stop time. A work that overpowers you emotionally creates space for you to lose yourself and be fully present with the experience, to feel totally alive.

I will not pretend that designing for feeling and emotion is as straightforward as positioning a dot along the number line. But we cannot deny that the form changes how we feel, and that impacts how we perceive. I believe it is a joy to strive toward building more meaningful connections between objective reality "out there" and the personal reality "in here." Perhaps this softer side of design is the hardest opportunity we can embrace.

MAKE

Engineers are passionate about making things. We want to make new objects and we want to make new understandings. Most of all, we want to make new realities. Taking a look at some of the ways engineers use pictures to build can point us to how we can all create diagrams to understand, explain, and make better worlds.

Mechanical designers have to think in ranges of numbers Not just 100, but 100 plus or minus two. They have to because the real world is not perfect. Have you ever measured the length of a wall? You likely found a value that suited your purpose, but how precise was it? Perhaps you measured the wall to the nearest quarter-inch. Yet, many of the objects that enrich our lives, including computer chips and Lego bricks, are manufactured with delicate precision too fine for us to fathom. The creation of any physical object from raw materials is subject to all kinds of variation. The cross-section here shows two parts that a designer wishes to fit together. It is not enough to merely specify the desired dimensions, a one-inch metal peg to fit a one-inch hole. If the hole is drilled a little too narrow, and the peg left a little too thick, then these manufacturing errors may compound to make the fit impossible. In addition to the one-inch dimensions, the designer must also specify a tolerable amount of variation. This variation is indicated here as the darkly lined region of each part's cross-section. As long as both parts are created within their ranges, the desired fit will be achieved. By defining the acceptable range of variation for

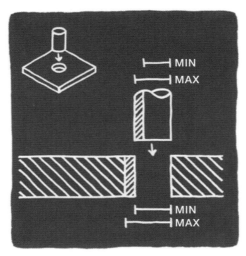

each dimension, the designer can build a trusting relationship with the machinist who creates the parts. They both know the world is messy and have agreed upon how messy these parts can get.

This dialog is necessary because more exact precision, which engineers call tighter tolerance, is more expensive. Finer precision is more expensive because it may require more expensive equipment, higher-quality material, a more experienced machinist, more thorough quality inspection, and ultimately more time for each step of the part's production. Tolerance offers a particular embodied understanding of uncertainty. Manufacture the same one-inch hole a thousand times and the actual diameters of all the holes should be expected to vary. The distribution probably looks like a normal curve centered on the desired value. Object dimensions vary in the real world just like data varies in statistical samples. We can dictate finer precision, with tighter tolerances or by sampling more data, but the costs of these efforts must be considered.

The engineer's problem-solving method is similar across many domains. The first step is to make a sketch of the problem and label its parts. Below is the illustration and starting formulas from a classic beam problem. Making a drawing orients you to what is going on. It also creates a legend for all of the elements that are relevant to the problem, such as dimensions and material properties. Then, determine which elements are given and what variables are still unknown. Once the knowns and unknowns are identified, the work proceeds a little like solving a puzzle. Using what you know, step forward to find each unknown by using physical laws, methods, and lots of math. Along the way, colorful notation can help keep track of variables.

Engineering is from Latin ingenium (cleverness) and ingeniare (to devise). Originally used to refer to the engine'er who operated military siege engines like the trebuchet, and later extended to the steam engine.

The ability of geometric representations to rapidly convey to a problem-solver some of the crucial aspects defining a particular problem, and hence, to suggest possible solutions.
MANUEL DE LANDA, 2000

Beam cross-section

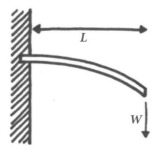

$$I = \frac{bd^3}{12}$$

$$deflection_{MAX} = \frac{1}{3}\frac{WL^3}{EI}$$

Engineering is classified as an applied science. Like medicine, it transfers formal scientific knowledge to the real world. Its practical emphasis is on problem-solving and making things work. In this regard, engineering's focus is similar to business or politics—influenced by theory but ruled by application. As an engineer, I enjoy entertaining philosophical debate, but my preference will always be for seeing what happens when ideas smash into the real world.

Engineers are intensely curious about how things work. Their problem-solving ability depends upon their ability to *see* how things work. They are specifically trained to create visual knowledge to diagnose and solve problems.

Engineers make drawings for many tasks. As we have seen, they include communicating design and guiding problem-solving processes. They also use pictures to coordinate teams, navigate complex systems, record observations, and explore creative design, similar to how artists sketch. Across all of these is a similar through-line: Engineers use pictures to understand reality and to help realize new realities from their imaginations. And here we have come to the heart of what engineering and data storytelling share, diagrams.

In *Structures, or why things don't fall down*, J.E. Gordon uses diagrams to explain an important concept of structural engineering, the thrust line, an invisible force that can wreak very visible disaster:

Engineering also helps me straddle virtual and physical worlds. I will never forget the first time a box full of machined parts that I designed landed in my cubicle. I unwrapped each one from its brown paper to find they were all brilliantly polished. The 3-D virtual model that had previously only lived in a program on my computer had stepped off the screen and onto my desk. I hurriedly assembled my contraption and put it into service on a manufacturing line. My idea became real. This experience always reminds me to remember the gap between the computer world and the real world.

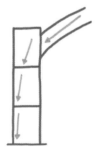

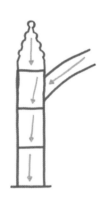

A *thrust line* shows the center of a load force. Here, it passes down the center of a stone wall's stack of blocks.

If the thrust line acts outside the boundary edge of the wall, a stone could hinge, causing the block to topple.

If a wall supports the oblique load of a roof, its thrust line will shift, perhaps dangerously close to the wall's boundary edge.

This shift can be controlled by adding a top weight to the wall, a correction which may be decorated with a pinnacle statue.

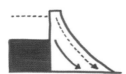

Once you understand how thrust lines work, you can begin to see all sorts of familiar things in new ways. For example, Gothic cathedrals, with their big vaulted ceilings and stained-glass windows, need horizontal support. You can also see how a dam's supporting curve holds back the massive sideways force of its water. I think you could understand thrust lines without the diagrams, but only with lengthy descriptive text that would recreate the same pictures in your mind. Diagrams are certainly not exclusive to engineering. They help a variety of fields make new understandings, new explanations, and new realities.

Consider satellite photos. A satellite photo is a very close representation of what things actually look like from above. But they are only useful for specific purposes. What we generally prefer is the abstract map, like paper road atlases and the web maps that give us directions today. Compared to satellite photos, web maps do not closely resemble how the world actually looks, but instead align with how we think about the world. In the realistic photo, a road

is thin and faint. On the map, the same road is easily discernible because it has been widened and given a color that pops out.

Maps distort and omit in order to direct our attention to what features we care about most. They reduce realism. Exaggerating and diminishing different parts of a scene help diagrams inform. One way to think about diagram transformations is that they take a realistic scene and translate its visible and invisible components into a visual form that mimics how the brain already stores information. In *Understanding Comics*, Scott McCloud describes a continuum between the physical appearance of realism and the meaningful ideas of concepts, a spectrum that is as relevant to information design as it is to cartooning.

When we abstract an image through cartooning, we're not so much eliminating details as we are focusing on specific details. By stripping down an image to its essential "meaning," an artist can amplify that meaning in a way that realistic art can't.
SCOTT McCLOUD,
1993

We encounter diagrams that transform reality all the time. A set of directions tells you to turn with a right-angled arrow, even if the actual turn is not precisely 90°. A safety placard contains humanoid forms, not realistically dressed people. An architectural blueprint tells the builder only what he needs to know, like the mechanical drawing we began this chapter with. Each of these strengthen the signal of their message by abandoning realism and playing with the salience of their elements.

A key component of many diagrams is the arrow. It is an abstract symbol used to show what cannot be seen in the real world. Depending on the context of how it is used, arrows convey different information. Across all uses, the arrowhead provides some kind of meaningful asymmetry that a normal line cannot. The arrow's earliest origins are probably in pointing, the activity of indicating something in the environment with your finger or gaze. Later, an arrow shot from a bow gave us a striking visual of direction and motion toward a target. Today, arrows label, represent motion, reveal invisible forces, indicate direction, and show uneven relations.

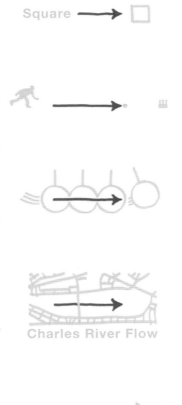

Charles River Flow

Diagrams use visuals to focus our attention on ideas and meaning. We have seen how they can distort elements in a scene and how arrows show the invisible, but diagrams are capable of even more. Diagrams eclipse other communication media when they use the freedom of drawing to transcend space and transport reality through time.

Diagrams have been described in many ways. Diagrams are simplified drawings, schematic representations, visualized thoughts, knowledge aids, relationships seen, cognitive tools, and concepts distilled. Diagram content ranges from resembling realistic specificity, to becoming abstract representations of universal ideals.

Geographic maps are a kind of diagram. They are a simplified view of physical reality. Diagrams are also all maps, as they map some aspect of our experience to pictorial representation.

All the things we experience in life can be separated into two realms, the realm of the concept—and the realm of the senses. ... in emphasizing the concepts of objects over their physical appearance, much has to be omitted.
SCOTT McCLOUD, 1993

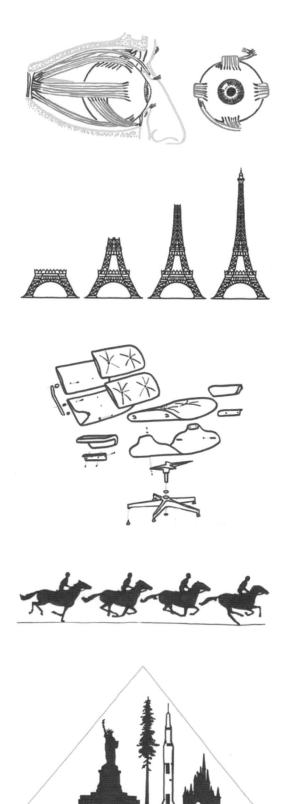

Spatial constraints have no control over diagrams. By thwarting the rules that govern where physical matter exists, we can gain new views about all sorts of phenomena. Layers can be cut-away from a single scene to show what is inside. Buildings on opposite sides of the world can be placed side-by-side for entertaining comparison. Spatial scales can be adjusted to give new appreciation for the miniature or gargantuan. Disparate items of the same group can be collected and rearranged in a tidy grid. Some of these scenes are conceivable in real life—medical students actually do dissect cadavers to better understand how the body works. In these cases, diagrams help bring exclusive vantages to the masses.

Time can similarly be manipulated. Processes that occur over moments or millennia may be sliced into frames and juxtaposed, letting us understand the horse in motion, how a dinosaur fossilizes, or how a structure rises.

Diagrams transport, transform, and rearrange physical reality. They pile on layers of context and invisible concepts. What results is a tighter correspondence between how we see the world, and how we understand the world. Many of these diagrams feature small multiples, juxtaposed items arranged for comparison, and maybe even pattern-spotting. Clever diagrams sequence their temporal slices within the same scene, translating the subject in space to show a

translation in time, all within a single cohesive environment: An athlete's movement is sliced over the playing field, a product is created over an assembly line, or soldiers move over a battlefield.

Sometimes, diagrams show pure concepts. These types have no relationships to physical reality. The sentence diagram is one example. At this extreme, diagrams present total abstraction.

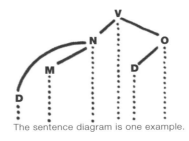

The sentence diagram is one example.

But not all abstract concepts must be displayed with abstract lines and boxes. Just as we began our look at diagrams by removing resemblance to strengthen signals, visual-thinking author Dan Roam shows how we can go in the opposite direction too. To strengthen abstract ideas, add resemblance. In *Draw to Win*, he highlights how two of the most powerful speeches of history use language to paint visual pictures in listener heads. John F. Kennedy inspired American optimism and boldness by declaring "We choose to go to the moon." Martin Luther King, Jr. told us about his dream using visual metaphors everyone can picture, including cashing a check at the bank of justice. Like JFK, MLK painted a vision of the future, one where freedom can ring across America.

From a certain perspective, most statistical charts are also abstract diagrams. We have tried hard to strengthen the correspondence between bar charts and stacks of stuff, but the resemblance is weak compared to a typical pictorial diagram. We have one more picture to examine in this chapter, an abstract diagram I have been waiting to reveal to you ever since we embarked on this journey together.

A diagram of things is derived from depictions, by distillation and rearrangement. Intriguingly, the distillations and rearrangements mirror both the ways people think about the world and the ways they design and arrange things in the world.
BARBARA TVERSKY, 2014

[A diagram is] particularly useful because it suppresses a quantity of details, and so allows the mind more easily to think of the important features.
CHARLES SANDERS PEIRCE, 1839–1914

Now is the time to rise from the dark and desolate valley of segregation to the sunlit path of racial justice. … We cannot walk alone. And as we walk we must make the pledge that we shall always march ahead. …I have a dream that one day every valley shall be exalted, every hill and mountain shall be made low. The rough places will be made plain, and the crooked places will be made straight.
MARTIN LUTHER KING, JR., 1963

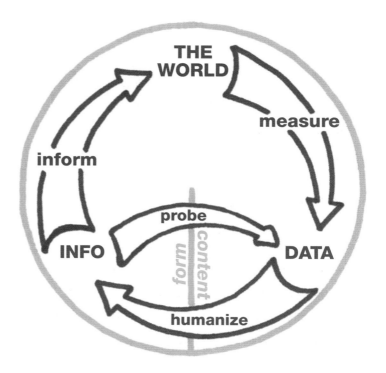

I first drew this diagram to help organize this book, before writing or illustrating anything else. From the beginning, I wanted the sequential flow of this book to mirror the process of working with data. You need data before you can understand it, and you must understand it before you can show it to others. I was very interested in distinguishing just what data is, relevant to the product of our craft, information. One of the first sketches I created was a simple triangle that connected the world, data, and information. But I also knew that I wanted a human, metaphorical framework too. This consideration motivated me to curve the process into a circle.

The larger circle acknowledges that we take data from the world in order to inform that same world. The process loops because there is a cyclical, never-ending nature to understanding reality. The world is not separated from the process, rather, the entire process occurs within the world. We are not isolated, unbiased actors.

The circle helped me to connect the process of working with data to Joseph Campbell's monomyth and to conceptualize data storytellers as heroes who confront data, pure content, in order to produce information. These connections encouraged me to embrace the "data as chaos" and "information as order" metaphors, which inspired the dividing yellow vertical line and mythic perspective. The heart of the first half of the book, the transformation of data into information, is represented by probe-humanize cycles that straddle content and form.

Early on, I found that this conceptual diagram resonated with how I create data stories, both from a process perspective, but also emotionally as a person who must traverse these activities. Perhaps you find it useful, too.

Across the last five chapters we paused our journey around this diagram to look at information from different points of view. I hope you realize by now that we have not actually strayed very far. Each chapter allowed us to examine an aspect of data storytelling in a sensational manner. We could keep going of course. Mathematical mosques, home gardening, and musical lyrics all have something to teach the data storyteller. But we have not yet completed our circumnavigation of the diagram, and we only have a few chapters left to do so. Now, with a better appreciation for what it means to inform, it is time to press on.

INSPIRE

TRUST

*Mankind are not held together by lies. Trust is the foundation
of society. Where there is no truth, there can be no trust, and
where there is no trust, there can be no society.*

FREDERICK DOUGLASS, 1869

I am a junkie for data stories that instantly impact how I see the world. I still cling to a vivid childhood memory of this kind of experience. I was sprawled over the red carpet of my bedroom floor, lost in a *Zoobooks* magazine about pachyderms. One striking spread illustrated an Indian elephant with all the food it consumes in a single year. Towers of hay and alfalfa surrounded the animal. Tanker trucks of water stretched to the horizon. The visual still resonates.

Today, creating this kind of *ah-ha* magic is what I live for. But now I appreciate that inspiring is not a momentary endeavor. Many people have been slow to accept scientific realities, such as the age of the Earth and the evolution of the species. Evidence still competes with strong traditional convictions about where everything comes from. We hope that data shown well will convince audiences to sprint to the side of reason. Any practiced data storyteller knows that it is more complicated than that. Our best efforts sometimes fail to persuade. People are often numb to evidence, and this creates quite a challenge to the data storyteller.

The moral I guess is this: Truth is terrific, reality is even better, but believability is best of all. Because without it, truth and reality go right out the window.
WILLIAM GOLDMAN, 1983

Our Need to Believe

Consider lunch. Hungry and new to the neighborhood, you see that there is a sandwich shop around the corner and walk over. I am sorry this story does not have a delicious ending, but the sandwich you ordered is lousy. The roll is stale, the lettuce is soggy, and the turkey tastes like it was sliced in another time zone. You will never make the mistake of eating here again.

But wait one moment, you only tried that place once. Making decisions based on a sample size of just a single event is not a rational way to live. *Or is it?* There is a gap between the evidence we demand from scientific inquiry and our own everyday life. A single life does not experience a statistically significant number of events. The quantity we witness is rather limited. Yet, we make decisions with absolute confidence all the time. What is going on?

Our mind is able to operate with scant input experience because it already holds a wealth of information. We each cultivate a rich

As people invented new tools for new ways of living, they simultaneously created new realms of ignorance; if everyone had insisted on, say, mastering the principles of metalworking before picking up a knife, the Bronze Age wouldn't have amounted to much. When it comes to new technologies, incomplete understanding is empowering.
ELIZABETH KOLBERT, 2017

conceptual framework for how the world works. Take the sandwich shop as an example. Only one meal can tell me a lot if I believe there is little variation across this shop's sandwiches. How can I assume this? The same food supplier delivers the same ingredients for the same kitchen staff to assemble using the same recipes. What is the likelihood of the same process producing a delicious sandwich, after producing a lousy sandwich? Nil.

We all make similar fast assumptions and assertions. Our existing cognitive structures help us categorize observations. Once you have a model, even a single experience can be put in its place. Simple models of how things work help us navigate the world with efficiency. They have served us well across our development. But like many adaptations, simple models have downsides. A reckless jump to conclusion may result in error. If you never go to the sandwich shop again, you can never know if you are wrong.

Individual models derive from a personal experience. But it is not always *our own* personal experience. We learn how to see the world from others. Everyone inherits models from strangers whose personal context is lost to deep history. Cultural models combine with the unique snippets of reality we each actually experience. As a result, everybody has a unique perspective. Except in extreme cases, people are not crazy, stupid, evil, or incoherent. Perspectives are well-reasoned and in coherence—with one's beliefs. To correct a seemingly trivial error by someone else can pit your way of thinking against the structures they use to understand. To correct a small error may necessitate correcting the entire structure. And changing the entire way someone sees the world is not a trivial matter.

We invest years developing perspectives. It is easy to incorporate new information into our preexisting categories. We become dedicated to these viewpoints. We do not naturally criticize ideas that support our view, but do we attack others that dissent. We relish in confirmation as we dismiss contradiction. Our cognitive coherence becomes part of our identity. To abandon a way of looking at the world stings, as if we are deleting a piece of our self.

When it comes to perceiving the physical world, we appear to mostly see things the same way. When confronted with trees, shoes, and gummy bears, our brains construct these things for us in similar enough ways that we can agree on which to climb, which to wear, and which to eat. But when we move to the social domain of understanding people and their interactions, our "seeing" is driven less by external input and more by expectation and motivation. ...
If I am seeing reality for what it is and you see it differently, then one of us has a broken reality detector and I know mine isn't broken. If you can't see reality as it is, or worse yet, can see it but refuse to acknowledge it, you must be crazy, stupid, biased, lazy, or deceitful.
MATTHEW D. LIEBERMAN, 2017

We rarely expend the time and energy to sort out something unfamiliar, let alone something that creates dissonance with what we already "know."
ABBY SMITH RUMSEY, 2016

The cost of adopting a new view and integrating it with everything else you know is real. But it is not always possible to swap one model for another. In some cases, a simplistic black-and-white way of looking must be abandoned for nuanced shades of grey. *Mostly, there are no good guys or bad guys, just a lot of complicated people.* This kind of orientation steps us closer to the complexity of reality. Suddenly, something that used to be simple is now hard. We feel pushed toward chaos. There is a loss of confidence as we sense a weaker agency to figure things out and get things done. Facing the facts sometimes means feeling less assured about your place in the world.

To influence, evidence must interface with belief systems. Facts compete against long-rooted ways of thinking about the world. As we saw with storytelling, the brain is built for survival, not truth. If we are to be truth-dealers, we need to negotiate survival-seeking brains. And our brains are not built to survive on their own. We are built to thrive in groups. We become dedicated to alliances with others who see like us. Sometimes in life, *tribes beat facts.*

We reject certain facts because we want to belong. Consider "Young Earth" creationism. Its literal reading of the Bible has deduced that Earth was created less than 10,000 years ago. But what practical good can the scientific truth about the actual age of the Earth (about 4.5 billion years) offer a creationist? What benefit is that knowledge, if it costs that person their church community? Belief in a "Young Earth" in the face of so much science seems irrational. It is irrational! That is the point. Groups *demand* belief in the irrational as a committed signal of membership. Belief in the practically useful cannot express group identity. Everyone agrees on the practically useful. If everyone agrees, then everyone can belong, and then you have no tribe.

We can just as easily criticize political tribalism. Think of any divisive social policy issue that plagues a country. Now, realize that the way it is characterized on both sides of the aisle has little to do with solving a problem. The way we sensationalize hot-button issues has a lot to do with maintaining party coherence. In politics, this is called stirring up the base. If we did not demand dedication to extremes, how would we know who was devout? If we did not sensationalize, we might not have any opponents to mobilize against. If we do not have any enemies, how would we know who we are?

Cognitive and social coherence both help us understand why we cling to irrational beliefs. Rejecting the evidence is perfectly rational, if it helps boost our standing in the world. This perspective may not explain everything, but it begins to guard us against casting others out as stupid or crazy. That is a sloppy way of categorizing humanity. It can also toughen us for the long game. Pulling back the curtain on reality, one dataset at a time, is not a casual endeavor. It is a game whose work will outlast us all. Now, with a generous attitude in mind, how should we design for a belief-hungry audience?

Design for Trust

Trust, this book's title quality, holds practical lessons for data stories. Trust is the essence underpinning relationships. It is the reasoned faith that allows us to proceed, despite a lack of specific evidence. Before we jump into its visual design, consider trust through the lens of a transaction.

Say you want to buy my rare painting. If we trust one another, we can schedule payment and delivery based on a handshake deal. It will be quick and easy. But what if we do not trust one another? Now we will have to appeal to a mediator to watch over the exchange, just in case one of us is a crook. Regulations, oversight, and security precautions that protect us will also add costs and slow things down.

Trust is as much a function of character as of competence. We would not trust a family member, who may love us very much, to operate on us. Unless they are a surgeon, they are not competent for the task. And we also would not trust a psychopathic surgeon. He has all the necessary technical skills, but his intentions are dubious.

The key to trust is time, especially the future. The longer we know someone, the more opportunities we have to observe their behavior. We can see if they keep commitments, deliver on

Comeuppance:
To give us an incentive to monitor and ensure cooperation, nature endows us with a pleasing sense of outrage at defection and a concomitant sympathy for the victims of deception
WILLIAM FLESCH, 2007

Trust does not reside in integrated circuits or fiber optic cables.
FRANCIS FUKUYAMA, 1995

expectations, and reciprocate our own altruism. You trust me, the art dealer, because you bought several valuable paintings from me before. We expect our relationship to continue into the future. You want to keep buying and I want to keep selling. For me to cheat you today risks more than today's sale. A bad deal today risks all of the paintings I might sell you in the future. A bad deal today could also ruin my reputation, making it impossible to sell paintings to *anyone* in the future. Relationships that stretch into the future build trust.

Too much trust, blind trust, makes you a gullible fool. Too little trust, distrust, destroys possibility. The right amount of trust makes all kinds of exchanges better: collaboration, execution, partnerships, relationships, and communication. You want your reader to trust the information you serve them. So how do we make trust?

The storyteller does not get to dictate trust. Only the audience determines trust, just as it is the audience who determines what is meaningful. Trust is not something you can serve directly. All you can do is create something that deserves the audience's trust, and then do your best to convey that the work is *trustworthy*.

The first half of encouraging trust is to create something worthy of trust. Do a good job. The second half is to convey that your work is worthy of trust. *To be clear*, the following principles do not supersede competent, quality work.

Trustworthy design makes a positive first impression. Superficial, quickly-observed attributes matter. In any relationship, first impressions stick and are difficult to reverse. Work should be visually appealing, or at least, not off-putting. Aesthetic quality signals that the creator put care into the creation.

Trustworthy design is correct and accurate. Errors and bugs threaten to undermine trust. A typo in a book is embarrasing, but a single misplaced data mark can be devastating. It invites the reader to fixate on the error and question the validity of the entire visual.

Trustworthy design is accessible. It engages audience's capabilities and ready knowledge about the topic. Complexity is O.K., but clutter creates chaos. Creativity gets noticed, but novelty can also build barriers to understanding. Give easy access to what a data story is about and why it is worth a reader's attention. An upfront insight inspires continued engagement.

Trustworthy design is direct. It employs familiar protocols where they are expected. Direct design highlights unique departures from conventions to the reader's attention. Do not burden the reader with unnecessary work.

Trustworthy design is transparent. It elevates its data sources to the reader's attention. It is specific in detailing what it can and cannot do. It qualifies its findings. It acknowledges editorial decisions. It anticipates and addresses criticism before it has to be voiced.

Trustworthy design is vulnerable. Stand by your work. Put your name on it. Include your contact information and then engage in feedback and questions. Align your own reputation with the work. Remain accountable to it. In lieu of a personal relationship with the audience, the creator must convey their real, long-term commitment to the work itself. An audience will have more trust in the work when they see the creator believes in it.

Few things can help an individual more than to place responsibility on him, and to let him know that you trust him.
BOOKER T. WASHINGTON, 1901

Trustworthy design trusts the audience. Readers are intelligent, but they have not yet experienced what you have to show. Do not talk down to them as you help them see something new.

People are curious. We want to understand the world. We want things explained. But we also desperately want to be reassured about our place in the world. We fear being insufficient. We fear not belonging. Presenting an antagonistic view of the world to a reader, no matter how factually correct, is a poor way to convey information. It might make us feel good to be right by telling someone they are wrong, but this is a small accomplishment. We can sometimes avoid rejecting someone's belief by helping them place it in a richer context. In science, this happens when a proposed "theory of everything" is knocked down to the special circumstances where it applies. In the same way, we can help one another qualify when, how, and why certain beliefs apply.

Synthesis occurs when a contradiction between two ideas, a dialectic, is resolved by a higher-order third idea which can account for their differences.

To inspire is to infuse,
animate, or actuate a
person with a feeling,
idea, or impulse.
From Latin *inspirare*
for "breathe into" —
the inspiration that a
muse breathes into a
person.

Other times, there is no substitute for telling someone that their beliefs are misplaced. Engineering school taught me to depersonalize design ideas. It is not *my* idea or *your* idea; it is just *an* idea. If we talk about an idea being mine, then I get hurt when you criticize the idea. Build distance between ideas and identities when you critique. I hope that when we do confront people about what they believe, we remember that it is not a wrong person but a person who believes the wrong thing. Accusing and shouting does not convince minds. The way to convince minds is to persist in offering a clearer worldview and to be patient.

Once a data story is published, it is hard to measure its impact. Content has a long tail. It may influence some immediately. Others may not discover it for years. Some will be ready to graft new information into their way of seeing the world. Others need to hear a lot more, and take a lot more time, before seeing things differently. All at once, or over time with other information, you can never fully know how a data story inspires. Of all the uncertainties that the creator straddles, this might be the most exciting. When I was a child an illustration of an elephant and all the food it ate captured my attention. Its creators could never predict its impact, decades later. Visual stories are so powerful, you cannot know what response they will spark. New information fuels new ideas and changes how people see the world.

As creators, our goal is to inform an audience. As we move forward, and concentrate on serving the reader, let us remember that we are all creatures who want to believe in something. We also all need to trust. Along the way, as much as you can, be kind, encouraging, and persistent. Inspiring the world to new understanding takes time.

CHAPTER

17

IMAGINATION TO IMAGE

*It is when we do not have to believe, but come
into actual contact with Truth, and are related to
her in the most direct and intimate way. …
This world is but canvas to our imaginations.*
HENRY DAVID THOREAU, 1849

This and the next chapter go together. Think of them like a pair of optical lenses. Metaphorical magnifying glasses are often employed by authors to peer at things. But here we will not employ lenses to look through. Instead, we will use them to expand and focus, as prisms transform light.

Exploratory analysis, which we detailed in the first half of the book, expands your personal knowledge. Probing generates insights. It also produces visual artifacts that document what the data has to show. The more time you spend, the wider the field spreads. This expanding process casts a broad spectrum of ways to look at the data. As you begin to understand the data, a new sense of what is emerges. You note that certain views might also help others see what you have learned. This creative expansion and awareness is what this chapter is about. The second lens catches these products and focuses them to the reader so that they receive a meaningful data story. That

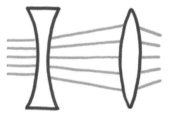

is what the next chapter is about. To take a practical view of each of these broad actions, I want to step through the development of a new data story.

Median Gothic

I recently heard something at a reception that spiked my curiosity: *Gothic cathedrals point toward Jerusalem*. It startled me. Here is what that statement suggests. An arrow that begins at the main doors of a church, continues up the aisle, and through the altar would point, like a compass needle, toward Jerusalem. It claims that not just one Gothic cathedral points like this. *All of them* point toward Jerusalem. Does medieval architecture face worshipers toward the same city, thousands of miles away? It seemed impossible. I had to know.

Cathedrals are deeply symbolic. From above, shorter *transepts* cross a long *nave* to make a Latin cross, what's known as a *cruciform* plan. The nave's name comes from the word for ship (like *navy*).

Its ribbed vault is like an upside-down boat, symbolically bearing its people through the storms of life. Three front portals represent the Trinity doctrine, *one god in three divine persons*. We could go on, but the point is that a lot of thought went into layering meaning into these buildings. Maybe it is possible that their orientation was symbolic too.

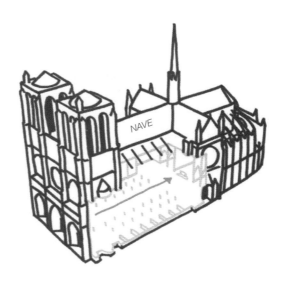

I always associated religious directionality with Islam, not Christianity. But maybe "cathedral compasses" are real. Did every European city clear enough space in their center to make room for a properly angled cathedral? Then, I realize: The cities were planned around their churches, not the other way around. To sort it all out, we need data.

There are a lot of cathedrals in Europe. We are immediately faced with a deluge of possible data points. Constraints are needed to make this inquiry manageable. Gothic architecture emerged in France, where iconic cathedrals are still mobbed by tourists. Looking at the earliest French cathedrals, a few dozen sites, might be enough to satisfy curiosity. The first step is to build a list of early and high Gothic French cathedrals. A list of their names and parent cities is a good start. Right away we can locate them on a map.

Then we can start adding a little context to each point. It seems natural to append a date to each cathedral. They each took a while to build. Many are still symbolically not completed. The year

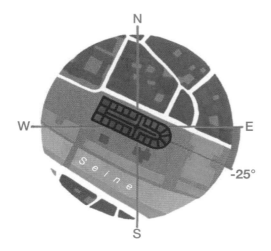

construction began, not the year construction stopped, is the moment orientation was set. So we look for the year of each cathedral's groundbreaking. Different sources provide different years for the same cathedral. Hmm. Maybe we can investigate this discrepancy further. For now, we can filter to cathedrals associated with the 1100s and 1200s.

Next, we need to determine each cathedral's orientation. I visit them on *OpenStreetMap* and layer a compass over each nave's axis. You can see, for example, that Notre-Dame de Paris points 25° south of east, a value I log as -25°. I continue measuring the angle of orientation for the rest of the buildings. Seeing each additional site, I begin to sense interesting repetition and variation. An hour or two later, we have name, city, coordinates, date, and orientation for 38 French cathedrals. The data table is ready to play.

Right away, I scatter the cathedrals according to their groundbreaking dates and angle. Each cathedral gets an orange dot. Time goes to the right. Angle data is anchored on a *due-east* baseline in the middle of the plot. This takes advantage of the *north goes up/south goes down* convention. You can see Paris at 1163, the year its cornerstone was laid, and -25°.

Two things jump out at me from this scatter plot. First, across a possible 360°, there is a definite clustering of orientation.

They all point eastward, staying away from north (+90°) and south (-90°). Not a single one points westward. This encourages me to think there might be something to this orientation idea. Second, there does not seem to be any particular pattern through time. For now, we can abandon the temporal x-axis. I also want to depart the specificity of the scatter plot to see what some grouping might reveal.

If we bin the angles in five-degree increments then we can make a profile. The cathedral orientation histogram represents each cathedral with a blue bar. I placed it next to the scatter plot so you can see the correspondence between the plotted and binned data points.

Now we seem to have something. Even with these few-dozen data points, a rough unimodal distribution appears, peaking around 20° south of east. Before we get too excited, we need to understand one more thing about that original statement. What does *toward Jerusalem* mean? Because the Earth is round and France covers a sizable amount of land, we actually need to consider *directions* toward Jerusalem. The angle, or bearing, changes depending on where you are in France. Could those directions be what we are seeing in the distribution?

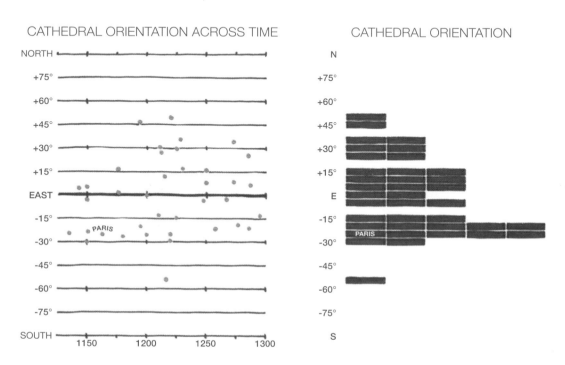

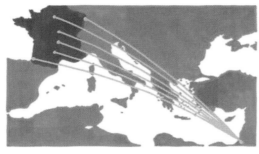

FROM FRANCE TO JERUSALEM

Here is what the direction toward Jerusalem looks like from six of our locations. Flattened on a map, the straight lines across the globe look like arcs.

I calculate the individual bearing from each city to Jerusalem. Then, I find the difference between cathedral orientation and true bearing to Jerusalem. The result is disappointing. Factoring in the unique directions toward Jerusalem seems to refute the Jerusalem hypothesis. This is something we can really appreciate by plotting each cathedral's orientation on a map, in orange. A few of the cathedrals seem roughly aligned with the yellow bearings toward Jerusalem. Many more are not. I feel a little deflated. Cathedrals do not point toward Jerusalem after all. Undeterred, I remember my earlier confusion with groundbreaking dates and return to learn more about when these orientations were set. Maybe looking deeper into the architecture of the buildings can help. I begin looking at top-view plans and entrance facades. Perhaps an aesthetic grouping could help explain what is going on? Maybe based on size or style? I start making a pictorial

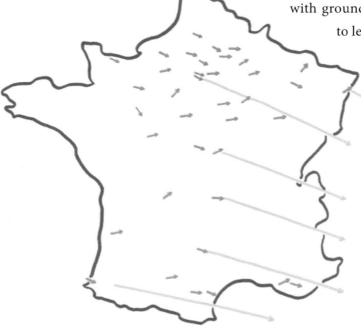

multiple to compare cathedral height, length, and architectural style. Once again, it seems like a dead end. Size was a function of the wealth bishops could muster. Style changed across hundreds of years of construction, famously producing mismatched spires in some cathedrals. Neither size nor style is useful for making any more sense of cathedral orientation.

You might notice that I did not illustrate all the cathedrals before pulling the plug on this path. Knowing when to quit a certain investigation can sometimes be a fuzzy choice. You do not have to carry every idea to its conclusion to know it is the wrong way. Sometimes going partially down a path tells you all it has to offer. And even if it is not what you expect, it might still be interesting.

While reading up on cathedral plans I learned a little about their groundbreaking dates. Many medieval churches have deep roots. Some were built on religious sites that go back to the 400s. Some may even be on the sites of older pagan temples. It would require a bigger effort than I am capable of mounting to say exactly when the angles of these buildings were set. Perhaps dates are another dead end? That is O.K. Rejecting certain paths can help us focus on others.

Reading about cathedral history yields one more discovery. While researching history and design I stumble into a research paper that somehow eluded my initial search. Its title, "The Solar Orientation of the Gothic Cathedrals of France," is full of promise. Its author, Amelia Sparavigna, seems to provide an answer. Cathedrals do not point towards Jerusalem. *Cathedrals point toward the sun!* And not just any location of the sun, but sunrise on a day important to the cathedral. Examples include feast days that honor the saint the cathedral is dedicated to.

S.DENIS   SENS   LANGRES   NOYON   LAON   SENLIS   PARIS

I return to the original histogram and add in a band of yellow to represent the range of sunrise locations across the year in France. The sun, of course, rises at a different point on the horizon every day. Almost all of the cathedrals fit into this solar arc. Metz, Chartres, and Le Mans all lay outside of the sun's band. They can be explained by history: All three are known to be built on the site of an ancient church. Their orientation was set hundreds of years before it became fashionable to face worship towards sunrise.

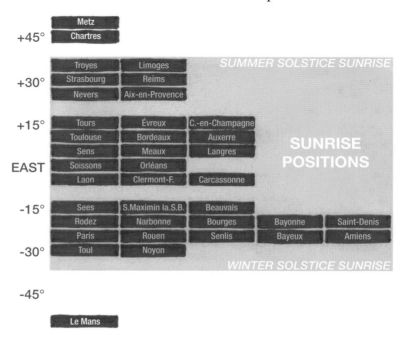

As I look back across this visual investigation, I am satisfied with the maps, diagrams, and charts that helped me see. My initial disappointment, about Jerusalem, has already faded. I savor the knowledge that bogus statement led me to. What is more incredible: that all of these monuments face eastward, or that you could never figure it out if you were standing right in front of one? Looking at the data gives an insight impossible to gain from being there in real life.

The deeper I got into the question, the more I thought about how I might share this insight with others. What is particularly interesting about this? How can I make it resonate in an unforgettable way that you cannot ignore?

Content and Form

Content is the heart of story. Content is the actual events that happened. Form is the way that those events are retold. If numbers are content, how you arrange them on a number line is the form. The fact that something happened is the content; the way a film portrays that event is the form. It is the form that makes the content engaging. Our data is the core of our content. But remember, the raw data is no way to inform anyone. The content has to be arranged into a form so that others may appreciate it.

If you spend time with data, and are a little lucky, you discover something worth sharing. Perhaps it is a specific piece of content, like a surprising correlation or interesting outlier data point. Maybe it is a new form, such as a better way to orient a comparison. Sometimes, the thing you want to share is a map that gives people the context and tools necessary to find their own meaning. Before you consider why other people are going to appreciate the content you have to offer, consider why you care. Why are you ready to put in all the work necessary to craft a data story?

The cathedral-orientation story could be summarized with a terse cocktail party opener. *Did you know that all Gothic cathedrals face the sun? Oh really,* I hear you respond, *that's nice.* This exchange does not get at why my new understanding is so spellbinding to me.

When I was 14 years old I stood before Notre-Dame in Paris. I remember looking up in wonder at its facade of stone and glass, squinting to see the famous gargoyles. Two decades later, I now know that someone had designed the direction of my gaze. And that realization came about from an exciting experience of actually seeing it in a new way. I was amazed as I loaded each individual city map, unable to find a single cathedral that faced west. It was almost dreamlike, as if France's greatest medieval monuments lined-up, one-by-one, in neat rows before me. I now imagine bishops and builders, a thousand years ago, waiting in the cold of night for first dawn so they could determine where to begin building a monument they knew they would never see completed. What an epic story.

Once again, I am awestruck by the same old building. But this time, it is not because I looked deeper into Notre-Dame de Paris. Only by seeing the other orientations did she become more interesting. Each individual cathedral orientation is unexciting. But together, new meaning emerges. Together, they reveal a reality unseen across daily life.

Not all data reaches into your childhood. I do not want to exaggerate the personal resonance (or importance) of this particular vision. But I am sure of one thing: Your own experience examining data makes any insights gained personally meaningful. Figuring out how to share that experience can help the content become more meaningful to others too. I do not want you to take my one-liner about cathedrals at face value. I want you to see the pattern, on your own, so you can create meaning for yourself.

Sometimes, even after you have the data insight, another flurry of creative data sketching is necessary to find the right form. Expansion continues as you search for the right ways to evoke what is meaningful. As we saw with the cathedrals, different visual forms evoke different aspects. Some will highlight the content you want to deliver better than others. This book does not offer any chart-choosing decision-tree flow-map. Instead, pay attention to how well different charts illuminate your data. Depending on the content you wish to elevate, certain charts will create stronger visual metaphors. The same visual meanings of position (*up is good*), size (*big is important*), color, and everything else we have covered apply across all forms.

There are hundreds of statistical chart types we use to visualize data. But, they are only one flavor of visual storytelling available to us. Geographic maps and pictorial diagrams also reveal. They can give us new ways to think about statistical exploration. Those curved yellow lines toward Jerusalem gave me the idea to calculate each cathedral's orientation-bearing difference. Furthermore, maps and diagrams help anchor abstract data back to the real world from which it came.

Once you have the story content, look down. See that you now hold it atop a tower of abstraction and specialized context. For the cathedrals, we climbed and manipulated a stack of abstract ideas. We learned about archaic architecture, geographic bearing, and solar angles. Now, you must guide your audience through the same tangle of concepts, hopefully making the tower easier for them to scale.

We use form to develop more sophisticated understanding of abstract content. And then we must take that knowledge and make it more accessible. We have to make our invisible understanding, visible. From imagination to image.

FOCUS ATTENTION

Vision without execution is hallucination.
WALTER ISAACSON, 2014

The previous chapter began with a visual metaphor about two lenses. The first diverging lens expanded creative exploration. It set loose a search for insights, and better forms for conveying those insights. The second lens is a converging lens. It catches the products of our

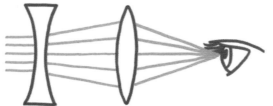

creative exploration and focuses them to the audience. That is what this chapter is about.

Workshopping

There are two ways to draw a dragon. In one approach, first block out the general shapes with light lines so it is easy to correct errors. As you become satisfied with the form, begin adding detail. Gradually, darken lines. The dragon emerges through a conversation between the productive hand and the critical eye.

The other way starts from the head of the dragon and includes every detail in one continuous flow toward its tail. Some master artists are able to draw like this. They may claim that the creative planning occurs in their mind's eye before pen hits the page. I cannot draw anything by making only a single detailed attack. I also do not know how to produce a successful data story without many cycles of creative iteration. Editing is one way of thinking about creative iteration. Its association with deletion can cast a negative connotation. *Throw out the bad and keep the good.* This attitude portrays editing as a purely subtractive process, like carving a statue from stone. Editing is more like working with clay, which allows you to add as you remove. As you critique existing forms, new forms may emerge. You might call editing re*vision*, the work of seeing something anew.

As the designer quickly creates a conceptual design sketch an ongoing perceptual critique is occurring. This can be thought of as a form of meta-seeing in that it is critical and analytic ... It involves the interpretation and visual analysis of the marks on the paper that have just been put down.
COLIN WARE, 2008

Editing is not taking out, it's putting together. It's taking a story, which has been photographed from many different angles and, very often, in many different takes, and making it play in the best possible way that it can.
DEDE ALLEN,
1923–2010

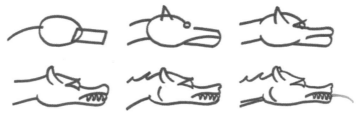

Instead of editing, I call the process of revision *workshopping*. When we workshop a project, we scrutinize it in pursuit of making it better, just as a musical is refined through its rehearsals. Here is the cast of characters who help the creator workshop a project.

The creator is the most important editor. While you are creating, you are the most ruthless critic. During creation, the mind is always considering and rejecting ideas. Some make it to the page. Everything else gets destroyed. Once on the page, you determine what to save and what new directions to try. To inhabit both creator and destroyer personas is to straddle a tension known as the creative process.

The next most important critic is also you. Future you. Allow some time to pass between creation and evaluation. The chain of thoughts that were present in production will fade. Your mind will internalize other thoughts. After a night's rest, or longer, you can re-attack the work with fresh eyes.

Beyond you, the creator, the most valuable critic is anyone else willing to engage with the work. They bring a lot to the table simply by not being you. You suffer from the curse of knowledge. Your critique is clouded by your expertise and familiarity with the story. Things that are still abstract to everyone else have grown familiar to you. Any random reviewer may not be able to tell you how to fix your story. But everyone can help you identify where the story is going off the rails. Do not trust a large focus group's positive reception as a guarantee of future success. Instead, pay attention to where others get lost or bored, or misunderstand what is going on.

Other data storytellers can give some of the most valuable feedback. They understand the process you are waging. You are freer to show a fellow creator an unfinished story. Creators are able to differentiate between aspects that are rough because they are merely unfinished, and aspects that are rough because you are struggling. These colleagues and mentors have the power to not only identify issues, but can also advise how to fix them. Nurture these relationships; they are most valuable.

Whenever you feel an impulse to perpetrate a piece of exceptionally fine writing, obey it—whole-heartedly—and delete it before sending your manuscript to press. Murder your darlings.
ARTHUR QUILLER-COUCH, 1914

An artist at work upon a painting must be two people, not one. ... On one hand, the artist is the imaginer and the producer. But he is also the critic, and ... the critic within the artist is a ruthless destroyer.
BEN SHAHN, 1957

A lot of the questions I ask, a lot of my attack on a property, is to tear it apart and see if it can stand up under really rigorous assault. Because you're going to be attacked later on, you might as well be your own attackee.
GEORGE ROY HILL, 1921–2002

It's time to kill. And it's time to enjoy the killing. Because by killing you will make something else even better live.
IRA GLASS, 2009

The most successful stories, the legends and myths that have survived the centuries and endured the end of several languages, are products of many dozens of generations of creative cultivation.

But what exactly do we mean by improved? How do we know that we are editing our stories toward something better? What are we looking for while we workshop? Advice beyond what we have already explored threatens to get us lost. We will try to navigate between the detail of the weeds and the poetry of the clouds. Here is a smattering of practical perspectives to keep in mind as you workshop a data story.

Mitigate abstraction. Identify conceptual jargon that bars access to the uninitiated. The cathedral story requires some context and explanation. Before you can appreciate cathedral orientation, you have to know what "cathedral orientation" is. I expect many people to have heard of Notre-Dame de Paris, but do not expect anyone to know how many Gothic cathedrals still survive in France. The changing location of the sunrise might be familiar to general audiences. But few think about sunrise in angled degrees. The audience must scale conceptual barriers to appreciate the core insight of the story. A story-first attitude tries to simplify a story. An audience-first attitude builds from its ready level of understanding.

Choose your actors. The unit of analysis determines which data elements receive a mark. Here, the individual cathedrals are the actors. They are *the nouns*. Like a mythological hero or grammatical subject, actors do things. Each cathedral faces a certain direction; that is the action. But there were alternatives to our cast of characters. During my analysis, I considered the difference between actual orientation and bearing to Jerusalem. This difference advanced our exploration, but would be a difficult way to introduce someone to the story. We could also choose to tell the story using an aggregate value. Instead of individual cathedrals, countries could be the actors. A set of French cathedrals could be compared to sets of German and English cathedrals. Or we could aggregate across time, comparing early Gothic to high Gothic periods. Aggregation is sometimes needed to see what is interesting. But making the actor a familiar noun, something you can see in real life, makes the story more accessible.

Spotlight the action. We see physical objects, like cathedrals, but life is not about things. Life is about what things do and how they relate to one another. If actors are nouns, then a change in actor state or the relationship between actors is *the verb*. The verb makes the story interesting. Arrange actors so the audience can see the action for themselves. Meaning builds in the mind of the reader who can detect comparisons and patterns, the action. In a bar chart, the bars are the nouns and the gap between two bars is the action.

Layer context. Reveal the guts of aggregated data. Display a layer of information more detailed than a story's actors. You trust and understand a summary value more when you see its contributing factors. But how do we layer context into non-aggregate values? There are no sub-units for individual cathedrals, but there is a lot of *subcontext*.

The final cathedral histogram highlights sunrise locations with a yellow band. Here, each blue rectangle is a cathedral positioned at its angle of orientation. This representation proves the find-ing to me, but might strain the

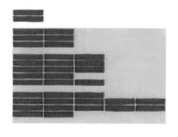

audience. They do not know what these angles are. They do not know how these angles were measured. They do not have any reason to trust that these angles were measured correctly. As the creator, I do not suf-fer these barriers because I actually did the measuring. An audience that only looks at the abstract histogram is totally detached from my personal journey of understanding. They miss out on the trust build-ing of the creative experience. Is there a way to show the subcontext surrounding each measured angle?

De-clutter, but that does not always mean delete. As you develop a story, its many elements and nuances swell. It would be lazy to hand a platter of competing details to the audience and expect them to figure it out. Sure, some extraneous facets might have to go. However, tidy stories are not necessarily simple stories. If a story

Everything is always changing, nothing is constant. The finest physical particles are jiggling. Every mountain is slowly flowing into a new form. Perceiving these actions is just a matter of tempo.

What if we represented the action directly? Representing the difference between two values as a bar focuses attention on the verb, elevating the original action to actor. It provides the opportunity for another layer of abstraction: the ability to see acceleration, the change in action. But burying the original value risks isolating the audience from meaning. We can feel acceleration on a highway, but we do not intuitively see it.

Any graphic which does not enlighten the subject is condemned: this is the supreme rule, which is none other than that of clarity.
PIERRE E. LEVASSEUR, 1885

How can we maintain clarity but add impact?
HOWARD WAINER, 1997

requires many features and complications, then it should have them. Keep them from becoming cluttered by grouping elements into a visual hierarchy. Elevate or diminish each element's salience according to its importance. Audiences can only absorb so much at once. Instead of swamping them with details, chunk information into layers of meaning.

Wrangle information energy. The content's form should fit its importance. We must think about what parts of the data story deserve the most attention. Good data stories quickly inform the audience what they are about and that they have something to say. You do not have to wallop the audience with the big insight immediately. They may not have the context yet to appreciate what you want to show. But you do have to give them a reason to stay engaged. Whatever the audience notices first should be something that encourages them to want to see more.

In 1967, Jacques Bertin used the word *energy* to describe the total salience of how data appears to us. Energy is the visual quality that can distinguish a graphic element from the rest of its field. The energy of a data story is powered by both data-driven and design-driven decisions. Bertin's *retinal variables* each have the ability to change how the value of a data point hits the sensors of the eye's retina. They include position, size, darkness, hue, texture, shape, and orientation. Others have since reshuffled and relabeled Bertin's stack of data-driven retinal variables. Important non-data design decisions include composition, emotional aesthetics, and what details receive annotation.

Both data and design-driven decisions should be creatively explored. Together, they can build information chunks, each with the right amount of energy. Use graphic redundancy to infuse an element with more meaning. It is fine to emphasize a single data value with unique position *and* circle size *and* fill color *and* texture *and* label. The purpose of a data story is to inform. We care about people being informed efficiently, not about graphic efficiency. Minimal design is risky design because it assumes perfect decoding by the audience.

To workshop a data story is to become obsessed with conveying context, insights, and meaning. Provide quick access to what is going on. Create perceptual groupings and match each one's energy to the attention it deserves. Make it easy to discriminate between elements. Annotations should guide understanding and provide additional context. Incorporate them at multiple levels of salience.

Keep Watch

Owning a timepiece used to be a big deal. Experts crafted them from precious metals and jewels. Watches were physical signals of wealth and sophistication. They represented the age of enlightenment, which sought an ever-finer model of the world. Over time, watches became more and more complicated. Features crept in. Outstanding showmanship of ingenuity took command. Super-wealthy collectors pushed makers to the limit of what

a watch could do. Designs inflated past practicality to include dozens of functions. Watches could tell you the day, phase of moon, time of sunset, temperature, and help keep track of passing time with chime and stopwatch functions. These features were called *complications*.

It was not enough to just have these features. Owners wanted to display the micro-mechanical marvels, behind the face, that made the complications tic. Transparent backs became fashionable. Now, others could admire the craftsmanship of the watchmaker, and the wealth of the owner. Telling the time became a second thought.

We have to ask ourselves what side of the clock we want to present to the audience of our data stories. On one end of the spectrum is intricate encoding so original that it is a marvel to behold.

How do you know it works? How do you argue that one design is better or worse than another for the intended users? For one thing, what does better mean? Do users get something done faster? Do they have more fun doing it? Can they work more effectively? What does effectively mean? How do you measure insight or engagement? What is the design better than? Is it better than another vis system? Is it better than doing the same things completely automatically? And what sort of thing does it do better? That is, how do you decide what sort of task the users should do when testing the system? And who is this user?
TAMARA MUNZER, 2014

It must be stressed that a center does not get more life merely according to the number of its subsidiary centers. Such an idea would only lead to the fallacy of baroque architecture which piles on detail, but which never reaches a very intense kind of life.
CHRISTOPHER ALEXANDER, 2002

On the other end is a simple bar chart. It rests quietly on a dashboard, waiting to alert us when an indicator is off-target.

Do we wish to dazzle our audience with our complications or help them tell the time? The watchmaker, the data storyteller, will delight in the complexity of their creation. Technical creators must exercise some awareness. We love the back of the watch. We are obsessed with pushing data story forms into the future. New chart types and new ways of implementing data stories across a vast array of technologies is part of our craft.

To be a good storyteller, though, you must fall in love with the front of the watch. Sometimes that means employing well-proven forms to push new content into the world. Sometimes that means a new invention under the hood. In either case, the storyteller transcends the celebration of the artifact for its own complications. The storyteller focuses on delivering to the audience. Whatever kind of data storytelling you engage in, I hope you are able to pause and consider: *What side of the watch am I showing to the audience?*

Ad Orientem

Many views of the cathedral story appeared on the way to arriving to the central insight: *Gothic cathedrals face worshipers toward sunrise.* We can revisit them by placing our map, diagram, and chart on the corners of the triangle below. These pure forms were also blended for new views, shown on the sides of the triangle. Each one reveals something interesting—but showing an audience the whole platter would not help illuminate anything. We must workshop all of our findings into a coherent story. Perhaps there is a final form that mixes useful views from charts, diagrams, and maps. Considering the essence of this particular data: what form belongs in the center of the triangle?

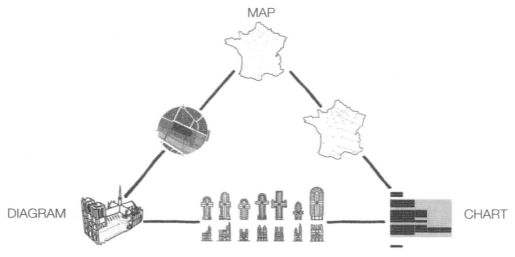

MAP

DIAGRAM

CHART

The chart, a histogram of cathedral angles with the yellow sun band, most clearly tells me the story. But it is not accessible. How can we make it more relatable? The pure diagram, with the guts of Notre-Dame de Paris revealed, explains how a cathedral faces worship. It is impossible to appreciate the project without this understanding. The maps of France advanced the search by helping refute the Jerusalem hypothesis. As explorers, we now know that Jerusalem was a mistaken recipient of the cathedrals' orientation. As storytellers, we need not burden the audience with this futile pursuit. Seeing the distribution of cathedrals across France is nice, but no longer critical. The country map offers no real insight other than showing that we are in France. The map-diagram was created to explain how to measure cathedral angle. It best reflects the most meaningful part of my own investigation, where I visited each city on a web map and recorded each angle.

I return to consider the yellow-banded histogram. The thing that bugs me is that angles are circular, not rectangular like the chart on the triangle. It should really be represented in polar coordinates, as redrawn here. It may not be as natural to analyze distributions in this form as with Cartesian coordinates, but it helps in other ways. The radial histogram is less abstract. It reflects how the angles were measured, and how we think about angles generally. It also looks like a compass.

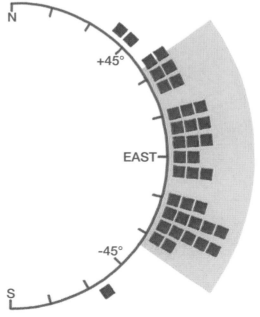

Thinking about compasses gives me an idea for a visual metaphor I could use to arrange the whole story. I begin workshopping a new form that takes into account this idea and everything I have learned from the other views. Workshopping is a messy process. There is no satisfactory way to show you all the erasures and tweaks I made between thinking of compasses and putting together a coherent story. For now, I invite you to turn the page, and engage with the finished cathedral story by rotating this book.

Praying Toward the Sun

French Gothic cathedrals face worshipers toward sunrise.

To-scale maps detail French Gothic cathedrals associated with the 1100s and 1200s. Each is positioned according to the long axis of its cathedral. For example, see how Notre-Dame de Paris faces worship 25° south of east. A pattern is revealed: All cathedrals are *oriented*, or face eastward. Most face worship toward the location of sunrise, seen in yellow, on a certain day of the year.

Before building began, cathedral orientation was chosen by marking the location of sunrise from the construction site, often on a feast day associated with the cathedral. Three outliers do not face a sunrise. Each was built on the foundation of an ancient church whose orientation was set long before it became fashionable to orient worshiper prayers toward the sun.

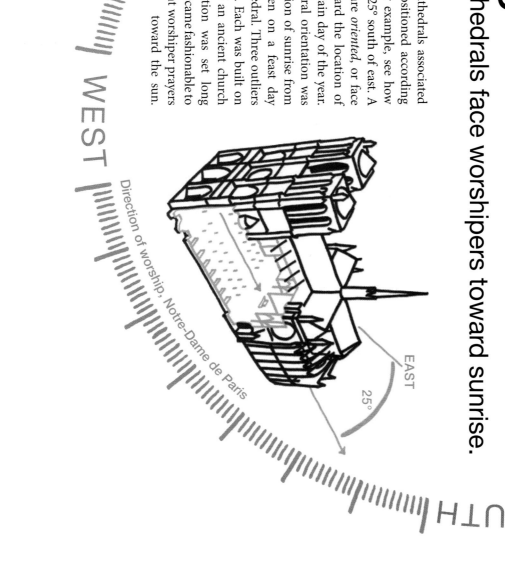

NORTH

EAST

25°

Direction of worship, Notre-Dame de Paris

SOUTH

WEST

Cathedral angles were measured using OpenStreetMap.

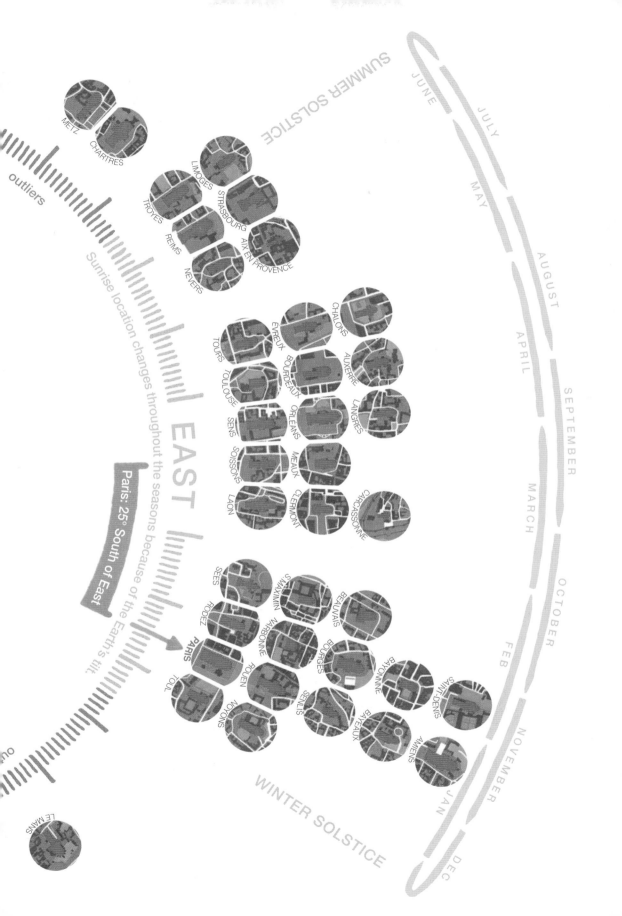

SUMMER SOLSTICE

JUNE
JULY
MAY
AUGUST
APRIL
SEPTEMBER
MARCH
OCTOBER
FEB
NOVEMBER
JAN
DEC

WINTER SOLSTICE

EAST

outliers

Sunrise location changes throughout the seasons because of the Earth's tilt.

Paris: 25° South of East

METZ
CHARTRES

LIMOGES
STRASBOURG
TROYES
REIMS
AIX EN PROVENCE
NEVERS

CHALONS
EVREUX
TOURS
AUXERRE
BOURDEAUX
TOULOUSE
LANGRES
SENS
ORLÉANS
SOISSONS
MEAUX
LAON
CLERMONT
CARCASSONNE

SÉES
S MAXIMIN
RODEZ
BEAUVAIS
PARIS
NARBONNE
BOURGES
TOUL
ROUEN
BAYONNE
SAINT-DENIS
SENLIS
NOYON
BAYEUX
AMIENS

LE MANS

The cathedral story came together across many weeks, during which it benefited from input by several friends. Now that you have seen it too, I can further detail the thinking behind its design.

The familiar convention to put north on top is honored, but the story is all about facing east. So, the text is oriented eastward. This requires you to interact with the story by turning the book, as if you were turning a compass or map, and face east, too. The turning action also reflects how a cathedral faces its worshipers. This gimmick takes advantage of the special properties of the printed book. It also creates a unique experience for you to associate with the story.

The tiny cathedral maps cumulate into larger coherent structures, producing a story that contains many micro and macro readings: Comparisons between cathedral sizes, cruciform plans, and surroundings with the tiny maps. A distribution of cathedrals inside the yellow band of sunrises. A cluster of cathedrals on only one side of the compass.

The sign is always less than the concept it represents, while a symbol always stands for something more than its obvious and immediate meaning.
CARL JUNG,
1875–1961

Showing the actual building outlines, instead of representing each cathedral with a labeled abstract circle, assures that they are in the right spot. You do not need to trust that their orientation was measured correctly because the order is apparent. Any cathedral out of line would pop out as an error. Including the buildings, parks, and streets that surround each cathedral pushes the limit of how much room is available on the page. If the graphic was any smaller we might lose the cathedral. The discs give even salience to a group of cathedrals of varying size. They also remind us that each church is one piece of a bigger world. Most of the story is desaturated to spotlight the distribution of cathedrals. Yellow highlights the sun. Orange connects the inset Paris diagram to the broader story. The piece is heavily annotated. Text is rotated, arced, colored, and sized—lavishing more context wherever possible.

Confections stand or fall on how deeply they illuminate ideas and the relations among those ideas
EDWARD TUFTE, 1997

Is this information a success? That is for you to determine. I expect everyone might want to shape this form a little differently and I hope you have enjoyed seeing how I thought about telling this story.

CREATIVE ROUTINES

When I write, I must convince myself that it's going to be wonderful. ... I'm going to write it and this time, this time, it won't be crap. When I don't have that confidence. I'm in big trouble.
WILLIAM GOLDMAN, 1983

The shore of our destination is in sight. Before our voyage lands and we share a triumphant close, here is a handful of observations, tips, and quirks learned through my own work. Of course, my experience as a data storyteller has shaped this entire book. But we have not yet seen the practical daily experience of what it is like, something—in the spirit of tethering lessons to reality—we can do now.

Day-to-Day

The first pages of this book showed Mozart's creative routine. That project surprised me. It revealed no similar patterns of activity between different creatives. Some people worked in the early morning while others melted late-night candles. Some exercised every day while others burned out their bodies with chemical cocktails. The only commonality between them was the inclusion criteria: All these creatives had a routine. There is no best way, but to make it on the list, you must have had a routine. No one can tell you when to eat. No one can tell you the best time to be creative. It is your job to hone a daily practice that works for you.

A routine helps by automating certain activities so that you do not have to burn cognitive calories on questions like *what's for breakfast?* every morning. Your time and energy are finite. Do all you can to direct them toward what is important to you. Creativity is a product of showing up every day and doing the work. Magical *aha!* moments are lovely when they arrive. But real creative production is about steady discipline, not waiting around for inspiration. You must create the time and space for the work to happen.

If you are able to maintain a variety of projects and activities, you can always engage your energy with what is most interesting in the moment. However, efficiency is not the goal. Play is a critical part of the process. Others might call this experimentation, learning, or exploration. Make room to play inside your routine, and with the routine itself. Allow your curiosity to get the upper hand.

Enthusiasm and curiosity carry me through each day. When I tackle a new project I am full of ravenous zeal for its potential. I am hungry to figure out what it might reveal to others. *Maybe this project will be the one to make a big difference.* At the outset, my energy appears crazy, as if I am delusional or hallucinating. Well, in a way, I am. In the beginning, the creative is the only one who can see the potential. It takes loads of hard work to realize this vision to show it to others.

Positive hopefulness is balanced by looking back at prior work with heavy self-criticism. All of my past work could be overhauled with what I know now. The duality of future-facing optimism and backward-looking criticism reflects a belief in momentum. With each new data story, my craft is getting better. I am still learning, and there is still lots to learn.

The data storyteller's success comes from straddling many different fields. To operate in all of them, you must learn from many different kinds of experts. One consequence of this is that you will unfairly compare yourself to specialists. That can lead to feeling like an impostor. Do not be too hard on yourself. Remember, you are straddling worlds to create new visions, and that takes time. Figure out how to sustain your creative process for the long haul.

Wild enthusiasm comes naturally to me. It is tamed by a humble curiosity that I have had to develop. I had to learn to recognize and stay mindful that I mostly do not understand what is going on. I realized that it was easy, natural, to just nod and go along. Accepting things without inquiry is a trap that I still fall into, every day in some way. It is an essential adaptation for navigating our chaotic world. But sometimes I have the awareness to acknowledge that I do not understand. Then I can choose when to follow that admission with the enthusiasm necessary to figure things out.

To understand the unknown requires a real hunger for learning. That desire sparks a search for the information you desire. Often, what you need in order to understand can only be found with the help of others. Social intelligence is essential to the seeker of understanding. Closing my curiosity gaps requires convincing others to explain and re-explain until I can understand. You have to admit *I still don't get it* and press others on until you do.

There must be a complete belief in any work of art—belief in what one is doing.
BEN SHAHN, 1957

The child in me is delighted. The adult in me is skeptical.
SAUL BELLOW, 1976, after winning the Nobel Prize for Literature

Pack and Breathe

Creativity is all about making new mappings between previously unconnected things. For these intersections to occur, you first need a warehouse of material that is worth connecting. Then, you must give the time and space for the mental fireworks.

To be creative, first, fill up your mental hopper with concepts. I joke that this activity can feel like you are becoming an "overnight expert" because of the exhilaration you get while plunging into a new topic. We have access to the most incredible body of knowledge ever assembled. Most of it is free and nearly instant. You can enjoy YouTube, podcasts, Wikipedia, research papers, and digitized archives from the comfort of an armchair. Many subject matter experts are only a tweet or email away. Public libraries will let you check out stacks of book at a time. Gorge yourself.

When is it time to swing out of homework mode? A switch occurs where your mind turns over from being curious to being so excited about an idea that you have to charge forward into making. Screenwriter William Goldman wrote about the switch from research to the flurry of creation, "Once you start writing, go like hell—but don't fire until you're ready." But how exactly do these ideas, the *aha!* moments, arrive?

As you fill up your mental warehouse with material you need to carve out time and space for creative intersections to fire. This period is popularly imagined as the mental wanderings during a hot shower. Newly learned concepts bounce off one another. They collide with everything else you know, settling with or challenging preconceived notions. Physical activities like running and swimming are also marinating empty time for me. While part of my brain moves my meat vehicle around, the rest catalogs and connects concepts. There are moments when creative solutions rush in. The narrative structure of the museum chapter, for example, laid itself out while I was on a run.

Sleep is essential for health, but it is also a productive creative tool. Taking a nap or sleeping on it overnight creates a natural space

Do your homework. The more you know about it, the more likely you are to come up with a big idea. ... Big ideas come from the unconscious. This is true in art, in science, and in advertising. But your unconscious has to be well informed, or your idea will be irrelevant. Stuff your conscious mind with information, then unhook your rational thought process. You can help this process by going for a long walk, or taking a hot bath, or drinking half a pint of claret.
DAVID OGILVY, 1985

Those first months are as full of research as I can make them… All this, of course, is building up to the moment of actual writing. I am getting myself as full of the material as I possibly can. When I can't stand it any more. I try and write. If the writing goes well X weeks later, I have a first draft.
WILLIAM GOLDMAN, 1983

for the brain to ingest new information. The brain filters thoughts for keeping in long-term memory. Sleep also gives you more energy to re-attack a problem. I try to sleep between loading new data and getting to know it with exploratory analysis. Why? Loading data and guaranteeing that it is ready for your workflow is a messy and draining experience. Have as much energy and enthusiasm as possible when you greet data for the first time. When possible, load data the night before.

You cannot always be energetic. Learn how to recognize and aim your most spirited time to where it is needed most. Be intentional about when you attack the biggest and thorniest challenges. When your mind is tired, it is sometimes better to rest than continue, inefficient and making errors. But also, a tired mind can give you a new critical view on a design. Sleepy eyes see differently than caffeinated focus.

Whenever possible, prototype. If you disappear for months to work on a masterpiece, you risk falling victim to faulty assumptions. Instead, identify design risks early and attack those first. Before making a data-rich interactive I might first test a static map. What did we learn? What can be gained with more data and interactivity?

This whole book is oriented to the perspective of a solitary creative. It is easier to describe the process as an independent journey to the individual reader. But lots of creative data work happens across teams. The same guiding principles for individual creative routines applies to teams. Be mindful of what rhythms work and seek to improve your collective practice. Engage with enthusiasm, but remember that collaborators need space to learn, and space to breathe. Seek ways to play well together.

Throughout this book, I have not addressed any specific technology tools. File types, software, programming languages, and libraries... I use many and there are too many that I do not use. My approach to digital tools is the same as my approach to search: *anticipate*. In search, I expect that the thing I need exists. It is my job to find it. With tools, I assume the tool can do what I want and

Scientific theories are not 'derived' from anything. We do not read them in nature, nor does nature write them into us. They are guesses— bold conjectures. Human minds create them by rearranging, combining, altering and adding to existing ideas with the intention of improving upon them.
DAVID DEUTSCH, 2011

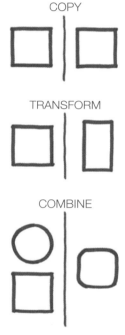

COPY

TRANSFORM

COMBINE

Remixing is a folk art, anybody can do it. Yet these techniques, copying materials, transforming them, combining them, are the same ones used at any level of creation. You might even say everything is a remix.
KIRBY FERGUSON, 2010

I just need to figure out how to make it happen. Once you become familiar with the metaphors used to organize a handful of digital tools, you can begin making good guesses about what a new tool can do. Then it becomes about figuring out how to do it. The crash between my expectations and the reality of the tool is a fertile plain for all kinds of new creative intersections.

At a project's outset, try to avoid design by defaults. It helps to have a vision for what you are pursuing before figuring out how to implement. Exploring data and presenting a data story with two different tools can help differentiate these modes.

Of course, being a technology omnivore comes at a real cost. You cannot spend all your time learning how to pull new levers, but tools change so quickly that you have to figure out some healthy rhythm of continuous learning. For me, this happens within projects. Intentionally learn how to do something new today that might be useful tomorrow.

The final daily practice I will mention might be obvious. To be a good data storyteller, you must consume many data stories. Allow yourself to become an obsessive enthusiast for the craft. This does not require you stay absolutely current with everything published every week. That would be a full-time job.

Be in touch with what gets published today, and explore how the craft got here. Use survival bias to your advantage. Most of what has come down to us from hundreds of years of development survived for a reason. Delight in the charts, diagrams, maps, and full-blown data stories from past generations. Study the masters of the past. They all negotiated a unique blend of data, tools, and problems to serve the same audience we serve: people in search of understanding. Deconstruct past work to reveal your own unique blend of technical and temporal biases.

Data stories help us understand and behave in an uncertain world, but for me they do even more. The experience of creating and consuming makes my brain feel happy.

BEAUTIFUL
TOMORROW

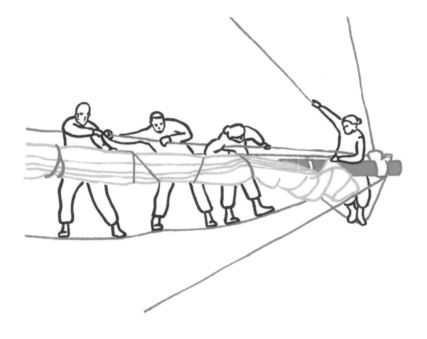

Press on with the work beyond fear.
JOSEPH CAMPBELL, 1961

Today's information age invites us to do great things with data. We are lucky to live in a time rich with such possibility. I hope we set our eyes toward embracing this potential. Together we can augment one another's intelligence and capabilities. Together we can strive to not only better understand the world, but also to better know each other.

In 2014, MIT researchers Erik Brynjolfsson and Andrew McAfee characterized this spirit as racing *with* machines, not against them. External aids—information—are the tools that make this possible. Just as the left and right sides of our brain are spanned by the corpus callosum, information links data and humans. In doing so, information expands our knowledge, know-how, and imagination. Information expands what is humanly possible.

To expand human imagination is to create doors to new worlds. Many scientists have echoed this enthusiasm across the last hundred years. I am particularly struck by how Marie Curie, the only person to win a Nobel Prize in two different sciences, put it:

> *I am among those who think that science has great beauty. A scientist in his laboratory is not only a technician: he is also a child placed before natural phenomena which impress him like a fairy tale. We should not allow it to be believed that all scientific progress can be reduced to mechanisms, machines, gearings, even though such machinery also has its beauty. Neither do I believe that the spirit of adventure runs any risk of disappearing in our world. If I see anything vital around me, it is precisely that spirit of adventure, which seems indestructible and is akin to curiosity.*

But it is not just science, not just data, that shares in this adventure. One of my favorite storytellers, Charlie Chaplin, also talked about racing with machines. Chaplin wrote, directed, produced, scored, and starred in the *The Great Dictator*. The climax of his 1940 political satire is pure Hollywood magic. Chaplin begins his monologue by characterizing technology in a way that still rings true:

We have developed speed, but have shut ourselves in.
Machinery that gives abundance has left us in want. …
We think too much, and feel too little.

I am inspired by his optimism for technological humanism. The scene swells as Chaplin stares into the camera, gushing:

In the 17th Chapter of St Luke it is written: "the Kingdom of God is within man"—not one man nor a group of men, but in all men! In you! You, the people have the power—the power to create machines. The power to create happiness! You, the people, have the power to make this life free and beautiful, to make this life a wonderful adventure.

We must strive for a decent world. We must strive for a world of reason. We must strive for a world of science and progress toward a way of life that is free and beautiful for all people.

The hero's journey helped anchor this book's narrative. But it is just a narrative model, a useful approximation, of how it really works. Science fiction author Ursula Le Guin made that clear in an essay titled "The Carrier Bag Theory of Fiction." She distinguished the heroic myth as a masculine hunting narrative: An anointed hero penetrates the mystery of the unknown with his weapon, evolves as an individual, and comes home to boast.

In contrast, Le Guin offered the feminine gathering narrative: A community collects whispers, secrets, and gossip. Context swirls and the truth emerges, but not because of the daring of an individual, but because of the evolving relationships of all. Instead of the hunting weapon, the tool is the gathering bag that helps forage for food. A *narrative* bag aggregates stories from all. Just like a community of gatherers, we collect facts and arrange them in pursuit of emergent truths. And so, in the last pages of this book, I hope we can see by Le Guin's counterpoint that the hero's journey into the unknown is just one way of seeing, one model of data storytelling.

Art after all, is about rearranging us, creating surprising juxtapositions, emotional openings, startling presences, flight paths to the eternal.
ZANDER AND ZANDER, 2000

The design of charts and diagrams, representing, as it does, a synthesis of art and science, has the potential for carrying the glory of each.
HOWARD WAINER, 1997

The reason we strive: To enhance the spread of ideas, to exemplify attention to detail, and to add to the beauty of the world.
STEVEN PINKER, 2014

It is a strange realism, but it is a strange reality. …trying to describe what is in fact going on, what people actually do and feel, how people relate to everything else in this vast sack, this belly of the universe, this womb of things to be and tomb of things that were, this unending story.
URSULA LE GUIN, 1986

Every good dialectic deserves its synthesis. Writer Venkatesh Rao bridged hunter and gatherer narratives with the *boat story*. A boat story is about a community that goes on an adventure together. Rao described:

A boat is at once a motif of containment and journeying. The mode of sustenance it enables—fishing, especially with a net, a bag full of holes—is somewhere between gathering and hunting ways of feeding; somewhere between female and male ways of being.

No single narrative model can fully capture the exhilaration of our craft. Sometimes we are on an individual quest. Sometimes we are part of something bigger than we could ever perceive. Sometimes we band with others to sail over the waves. Data is like water. It can be put to good use or it can drown. To harness data, the world needs information: more information, better information, more complex and nuanced understanding, and better narratives that can show ways for all to flourish. Data storytellers have a vital role to play in this endeavor. We are not the only informers, but we do have a very special responsibility to construct new ways for humanity to engage with data. To be a data storyteller is to be a creator, a maker, a constructor. We do not just make information, but new and enthusiastic visions of how things are and how they might be.

Today, apathy, irony, and snark are seductive ways to engage with the world. However, these perspectives sap the energy necessary to address the very problems they identify. Criticism will always have a role serving the creative process. But what I believe the world needs more of is what Hans Rosling called *possibilists*. Possiblists have a clear idea about how things are and have a conviction and hope that further progress is possible. Possibilists have a worldview that is constructive and useful.

Data story critics are nothing new. In 1786, William Playfair published the first modern bar chart and line chart. It was the birth of modern data visualization. And guess what? In 1786, William Playfair had critics. That same year, Dr. Gilbert Stuart responded with a seven-page review of Playfair's inventions:

> To each of his charts the author has added observations [that] … in general are just and shrewd; and sometimes profound … Very considerable applause is certainly due to this invention as a new, direct, and easy mode of conveying information to statesmen and to merchants; although we would recommend to the author to do whatever he can, in any future editions, to make his leading ideas as familiar as possible to every imagination, by additional illustrations and directions; for these in some instances, seem to be wanting.

In response to Stuart's review of his 1786 Atlas, William Playfair admitted that the last bit of criticism, "is certainly just; and I have attended to the hint." He took it to heart and he did not stop. Playfair went on to create even more new forms of seeing data: the bubble chart, pie chart, and a proto-Venn diagram.

Today, there is an incredible wave of data storytellers carrying us to new shores of reality. They are the ones who do not just think differently, do not just see differently, but also work to help us all think and see differently. Data storytellers are not going to be stopped and humanity will never be quite the same again because of their efforts. I am so excited to voyage with them to new lands.

And so, as we look forward, I hope to have enrolled you in championing the craft too. I wish all data storytellers joy and…

… may your critics be constructive
and help you improve your craft.
May your stories excite meaning in many.
And may you convey information,
in the words of Dr. Gilbert Stuart,
in a most direct and easy manner.

This book has been a joy to compose. We stretched across time to become adventure companions for a short while. I truly appreciate your attention. Now, I believe it is time to turn ourselves toward the open horizon and sail on, across the water.

RJ

RJ Andrews

HOW THIS BOOK CAME TO BE

I wrote this book in a room so small that we talked about using it as a closet.

One data storytelling tradition is to follow projects with a design essay that documents some lessons learned during the process, so future creatives may benefit. In that spirit, here is a short essay about how this book took form.

A new book is just another problem that can be analyzed and solved with creativity, right? The process I forged (and endured) to make this book flowed from the practices discussed in Chapter 19. I have since learned that some parts of my process were a bit idiosyncratic, and will focus on these more unique aspects of production.

My perspective as a data storyteller was the foundation and reference point throughout this book's composition. I believe what is useful for the analysis of a data story is not always relevant to the creation of a data story. I left out what is useful only to the critic. Instead, I wrote to what I believe is useful to the creator. I also consciously reached beyond technical aspects of the craft, in search of deeper meaning. Beyond these, I included what interested me.

As soon as the book was greenlit, I rushed to learn all I could about writing. Steven King's *On Writing* best motivated my day-to-day rhythms. I learned the importance of daily physical exercise, daily word-count goals, and the beauty of writing to very loud rock 'n roll. Light exercise for cognition gave me space to think and kept my energy and spirits high. I also reduced my consumption of alcohol. Maybe the

write drunk, edit sober quip works for some. Not me. Every day was precious and missing one because I was not sharp was not an option.

I found the whole journey to be a complexity management process. Inhabiting the roles of researcher, writer, illustrator, and book designer meant I always had options for where to direct my energy. A walk with coffee along the San Francisco Bay, looking for sea lions, started many days. As a kind of creative hydra, I spent this time asking myself *what does the book want me to do today?* No matter the task, I aspired to hit two heavy creative periods each day. Mornings were my most productive time. My creative energy slumps in the afternoon, so that's when I would exercise. Sometimes I would take short naps to spring a little energy and get an extra dose of free-association time. If things were humming then I would stay up, sometimes until sunrise.

Word-count goals spurred progress. 2,000 words a day was my goal when I wrote. It was instantly obvious when I had not done the necessary preparation of reading, thinking, sketching, and outlining. It was also obvious at the end of the night when I had run out of steam. When words turned to mush, I said goodnight.

I split my desk into digital and analog workspaces. All research materials relevant to the section I was working on were at arm's length in a bookcase behind me. At the beginning they all fit. By the end, every flat surface I had was covered in stacks of books and papers. I got myself out of more than one haze by rearranging the

ALLEGORY OF THE CAVE
PLATO'S REPUBLIC

DATA

STORY

INFORMATION

piles of books. Colored pens, markers, index cards, book holders, and whatever mix of books I was reading at the time were stored in a small rolling cart. That way, I could wheel essential materials to the kitchen table or comfy chair whenever I got tired of my desk.

I did research by reading books in thematic bundles. For example, I read three books in one day that each explain statistics to the layperson. Across this project, I found myself developing a style of "extractive reading." Reading for purpose, in support of a project or specific inquiry, helps focus attention. This aggression was tempered with caution. I did not read for confirmation, but genuine discovery and learning.

I took a careful approach to reading other books about data visualization. Before writing anything, I read the modern classics (Bertin, Tukey, Tufte, Cleveland, Holmes) written before 1985. This cutoff date is just before interactive computer graphics made a big splash. I read these to discover what still rang true from back then. My hunch was if it was true then and still resonates with my own practice, then it has a good shot at being timeless.

I did not review any recent data visualization books or articles until after my first draft was complete. I wanted to make sure the skeleton of the book came from my own experience and what I had discovered to be timeless. I also did not want to be too influenced by any other contemporary authors. The story had to be told in my own voice. Once the first draft was finished, I was able to turn to my colleagues to help polish and sharpen my perspective.

For books that were not about data visualization, I used a similar but more immediate process. For example, for the chapter "Encounter" I wrote everything I could without doing any research. Then I read six books on museum design, curating, and human-scale urban planning that I already had staged. Then, I returned and revised the chapter.

Here is how I processed material from research to writing. Except in the case of a couple of rare old books, I underlined and made notes directly on the page in red ink. Once the book was read I put it aside, usually for about a day. After this short gap, I re-opened the book to review the redlines. Every book I read got a page (or more) of handwritten notes in a big black Moleskine journal. I copied exact quotes, summaries, and my own reactions in color-coded handwriting into the journal. This process resulted in a hand-lettered notebook chock-full of sketches, quotes, and observations. Condensing research into a single place was useful in many ways. A sequence of different looks at the sources acted as a set of filters. They also gave me and the material time to breathe. Collating everything in one notebook fostered unexpected connections. It expedited writing as I did not have to spend lots of time fumbling between hundreds of sources. As I typed, the journal was open and in view. It is now a neat physical artifact of my experience.

While reading, I also kept a jumbo-sized index card as a book mark. There, I could write random thoughts that came to me as I read. Anything that came to me across any part of the process got written down. I found my memory generally deteriorated to becoming useless across the writing process. Externalizing any idea was essential if it was to prevail. As the book's form took shape, I would note which chapter, and later, which page number, the idea was relevant to. These cards were stacked and later processed into the draft.

I now know what other writers meant about pushing through the first draft so that the real work, editing, can begin. Writing the first draft felt like going into an empty room, my nerd cave, and summoning a wild cave bear. Then, all the work that followed was to go back into that room every day to wrestle with the bear. The more I worked with it, the more I found that it had a spirit of its own. It became my responsibility to focus its spirit so that it could sing. I found that being an author, much like any designer, is not so much about producing something out of thin air, but rather about being the motivating force behind an evolutionary process. For editing style, I devoured Steven Pinker's *The Sense of Style*. His mechanical breakdown of how sentences and paragraphs work was the perfect lens for this engineer-author. I used different search strategies to highlight phrases that might benefit from extra attention. Instead of hedging with fluff words (*almost, apparently, nearly…*), I learned to qualify where necessary. Instead of lifeless nominized verbs (*-tion, -sion, -ing*), I learned to resurrect dynamic

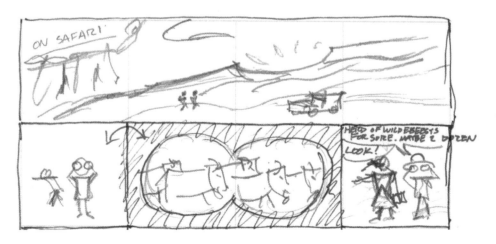

Reality   FACTS   DATA   INFORMATION

verbs. Instead of invisible meta-concepts (*process, level,* ...), I tried to include illustrative examples. I learned that intensifiers (*very, highly,* ...) do not intensify. *Very* turns a true/false statement into a gradated scale. The use of margin notes was directly inspired by Robert Greene's *The 48 Laws of Power*. About half of my marginalia made it into the final draft. There is so much wonder out there left to explore.

After the first draft was written I prototyped a single chapter, which forced me to figure out image style, color palette, layout design, and how all of the visual elements might work together. In addition to giving me a very real design challenge, this prototype gave me something to show others. Early feedback from designers and authors helped me define the entire look of the book.

Across the rest of the process I not only workshopped the words, but also the illustrations and the book layout. Months in, I discovered that it was necessary to do all of this on my own in order to create the composition harmony across each page spread that I desired. Doing

it all was equally challenging and insightful. It gave me more constraints, and more ways, of seeing every aspect of the book.

The primary color palette of Oliver Byrne's 1843 *Elements of Euclid* inspired the colors. The hundreds of illustrations were a joy to produce. They were all hand-drawn with markers and scanned for digital polishing. Many referenced printed digital collages, YouTube video frames, charts made with D3 and Tableau, Google Earth, and 3-D SketchUp renders. I wanted the illustrations rough enough to convey emotion, but not so rough that they distracted.

Most of the historic images I reference are manipulated in some way to better serve the story. For example, the found illustration of the Mad Hatter at a tea party was transformed into the Chapter 6 title image. I repositioned his arms, gave him the teapot, and created the stacks of cups by photographing teacups and mugs in my kitchen.

The following notes have more details about the illustrations. They now reside in a drawer in the same small room.

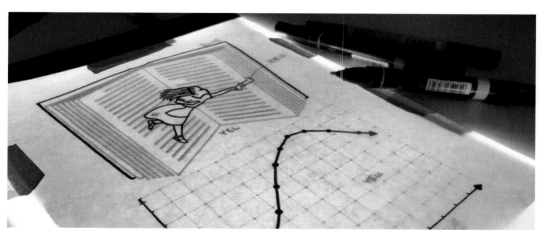

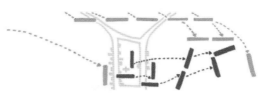

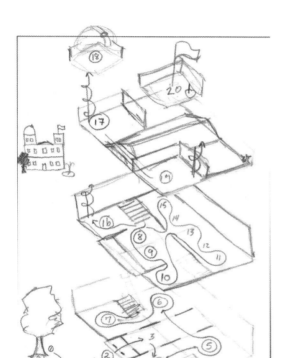

01001000
01000101
01001100
01001100
01001111
01010111
01001111
01010010
01001100
01000100

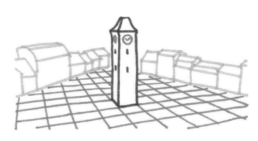

ACKNOWLEDGMENTS

One Greek myth has the giant hunter Orion blinded as punishment for a rowdy night on the island of Chios. Not able to see, Orion stumbled to another island where the servant Cedalion comes to his aid. Cedalion stands on the giant's shoulders and orients him toward the East so that the rays of Helios, the sun, can heal Orion's sight.

Like Cedalion, I too stand on the shoulders of giants. And like Orion, I see better because so many friends have oriented me towards the light. Their unique contributions, mentioned below, mask the overwhelming support they all supplied over many years.

I am indebted to Ben Jones and Cole Nussbaumer Knaflic for their early enthusiasm for this book. You hold it because they believed.

Executive Editor Bill Falloon was a trusted protector and advocate of my creative vision. He worked to coordinate a talented team at Wiley that included Steve Csipke, Michael Freeland, Michael Henton, Steven Kyritz, Amy Laudicano, Jean-Karl Martin, Kimberly Monroe-Hill, Purvi Patel, Paul Reese, and Rebecca Sandercock. Christina Verigan's copyediting animated my words to life.

My sister, Elizabeth Andrews, helped make the illustrations and compositions better. Her beautiful eye was there for me every day. Ron Toelke taught me everything I know about book design. Nick Sousanis encouraged me to reach beyond stiff vector art and draw everything by hand. Catherine Madden helped solidify the look while it was still just a fledging prototype. Dan Roam showed me how much fun you can have playing with a book's storytelling.

I was often blind to the very quest I was on. The following readers, reviewers, and confidants helped me see: Mara Averick, Alice Francis, Lisa Han, Keith Helfrich, Kim Johnston, Susie Lu, Elijah Meeks, Alice Nhu, Peretz Partensky, Matt Plitch, Lisa Charlotte Rost, Leigh Ryan, Rob Simmon, Micah Stubbs, and Shirley Wu. I would especially like to acknowledge Howard Wainer, whose voice rang true across many dimensions. Scott Stern and Amy Abernethy taught me everything I know about data and strategy, I am so grateful for their mentorship. Many supporters of my craft have been with Info We Trust since I first pitched the need for more visual information at MIT's E52, especially Aman Advani, John Aquadro, Sean Bonawitz, Joost Bonsen, Cathy Fazio, Katja and Lukas Gerber, Jorge Guzman, Craig Hosang, Hoolie Tejwani, and Blaize Wallace. Many teachers across my life pushed me forward into new realities. Deirdre Leland, William Hornick, and Hameed Metghalchi: thank you.

My mother, Mary Ellen Andrews, taught me to be filled with awe and wonder at it all. My father, Ray Andrews, taught me how to build. My wife, Kelly Han, inspires life into the whole adventure.

NOTES

Dates used in the main text best reflect the date of original composition. If composition or publication date was not clear, life-span dates were used. Dates in these notes reflect the formal publication date referenced in the following bibliography. In some cases there is a discrepancy between text and bibliography dates. This occurs with lectures, translations, and posthumous publications—all of which were not published until years after original composition.

ii The frontispiece title is a mirrored ambigram. It was inspired by the work of Douglas Hofstadter and refined by studying Langdon (2005). **vii** *Of course the first thing to do...* Carroll (1871) Chapter III: Looking-Glass Insects.

Preface: Ancient Roots

xi Etymology, for the preface and throughout the book, was compiled by referencing the *Oxford English Dictionary*, etymonline.com, wiktionary.org, *Merriam-Webster's Collegiate Dictionary*, and Google Dictionary. **xiii** *nostalgia for paradise* Eliade (1952) p. 55.

Origin: The Goal of Our Craft

1 *This art takes as given...* Plato Book VII, 518d, Bloom trans. (1968) p. 194. **2** "international organization" referred to is the International Union for Conservation of Nature (IUCN). **5** *writhing sea-dragons...* Beowulf lines 1426-1432, 1442-1443, Heaney trans (2008) pp. 97–99. • "The water dragons of chaos represent..." motivated by Peterson (2017). • *The monsters of the abyss...* Eliade (1991) p. 158. • *Our willingness to distinguish good and evil...* Zander and Zander (2000) p. 105. • The heroine illustration is based on the *Libertas Americana* medal, conceived by Benjamin Franklin to celebrate America's Revolutionary War military victories and enhance Franco-American goodwill. The sea monster

she is confronting is based on a map dragon from Olaus Magnus's 1539 *Carta Marina.* **6** *I am interested...* Popper (1959) p. xviii. • *The ways of seeing put forth...* Sousanis (2015) p. 46. **7** *And is there no implied intention...* Campbell (1972) p. 17. • *Explanations establish islands...* Carse (1986) p. 139. • *1 Separation: a hero ventures forth...* Campbell (2008) p. 23. • *All utopias are depressing...* Perec (1982), Bellow trans. (2011) p. 149. **8** *Helmets, Their Kinds and Developments during the Centuries*, educational chart devised by Bashford Dean and drawn by Stanley Rowland, 1915. **9** Bashford Dean biography from Pyhrr (2012) p. 10. • *Each field has its own concept...* Spear (1969) p. 1. **11** *I am looking for someone...* Gandalf to Bilbo Baggins, Tolkien (1937) Chapter I.

Chapter 1: Data Shadows

13 James Brown illustration based on photograph taken by Michael Ochs (New York, 1962). • *Matter and all else...* Eddington (1929) pp. 33, 43. **14** *The value of a fact shrinks...* Wainer (1997) p. 25. **15** "only six percent of workers in the United States are in STEM occupations." STEM Jobs: 2017 Update, U.S. Department of Commerce. • *the truth is nothing other than...* Plato Book VII, 515c-d, Bloom trans. (1968) p. 194. **16** The Inca *quipucamayoc* is inspired by a drawing by Felipe Guaman Poma de Ayala in *El Primer Nueva Crónica Y Buen Gobierno* (1615). **17** Evolution of numerals illustration based on Menninger (1969) pp. 418–419. Like many evolutionary processes, numbers did not develop in any simple linear fashion. A richer exploration would depict Gwalior, Sanskrit (Devanagari), West Arabic, East Arabic, and countless other numeral variations across a complex temporal-network. • *At one time, there was speculation that the figures past 4...* Mazur (2014) p. 35. • Base-10 box tally system: Tukey (1977) p. 16. **18** "The roar of the crowd...." refers to American Joe Louis's historic rematch against German Max Schmeling at Yankee Stadium in 1938. Heavyweights used to fight at less than the 200 pounds modern minimum. • Value type overview motivated by Kirk (2016) pp. 100–105. • *Many codes... exist primarily to...* Norman (2013) pp. 86–87. **19** *Rote learning and drill...* Lakoff and Núñez (2000) p. 49. **20** *It's not the numbers...* Rosling et al. (2018) p. 20. **21** *S. suffered from....* Rumsey (2016) pp. 120–121. • *Storytellers of all stripes...* Austin (2010) p. 34. • *To see why encoding is necessary...* Hofstadter and Sander (2013) pp. 172, 347.

Chapter 2: Information Murmurs

23 *Data! data! data!...* Conan Doyle (1892) p. 618. • Harvest scene illustration inspired by the Tomb of Sennedjem, Deir el-Medina, Egypt. **24** The wheat stack illustration is a tribute to the Statistical Society of London's original logo. Founded in 1834 with the mission to procure, arrange, and publish facts, *Aliis Exterendum* (for others to thresh out, i.e., interpret). It became the Royal Statistical Society in 1887. • *These plants domesticated Homo Sapiens...* Harari (2015) pp. 80–81. • Uruk table illustration adapted from Englund (1998) pp. 50–63. **25** *objective witnesses...* Rumsey (2016) p. 21. • *The application of figures of arithmetic...* Guy (1885) p. 72. • The plague victim being lifted into a cart is inspired by the 1740s print by James Hulett titled *Plague in 1665.* **26** Progress of information technology motivated by Rumsey (2016). • *As knowledge increases and multiplies...* Playfair (1786) p. vii. • *We can no longer rely...* Rumsey (2016) p. 4. **27** "James Webb Space Telescope..." The JWST will be the scientific successor to the Hubble Space Telescope. Its primary mirror, made of 18 hexagonal sections, has a diameter of 6.5 meters. • *more evidence is better...* Stigler (2016) p. 55. • *A river cannot...* Huff (1954) p. 20. • *If, for example, it is a gasoline account...* Ogilvy (1985) p. 34. **28** *We live in an era of social science...* Pinker (2014) p. 24. • *Human centered design [emphasizes]...* Norman (2013) p. 218. • *We are ready to question...*

Lupi (2017). **29** Book-to-shelf story builds on Hidalgo (2015) p. 63. • *Engineers and businesspeople are trained to...* Norman (2013) p. 218. • *The foundation of an edifice is of vast importance...* Brinton (1914) pp. 1–2. • *Facts are incomplete without context...* Wainer (1997) p. 134. • *To see an object in space...* Arnheim (1969) p. 54. **30** "a pile of stones is not a house." references Henri Poincaré's *Hypotheses in Physics,* Tr. George Bruce Halsted (1913): *Science is built up with facts, as a house is with stones. But a collection of facts is no more a science than a heap of stones is a house.* **31** *Round—a lot!* Wainer (2007) p. 97. • *Basic problem: Make data more easily...* Tukey (1977) p. v. • *A table is for communication...* Wainer (2007) p. 95. **32** "John Tukey advised...." Tukey (1977) p. 332. • *As statistical results never can...* Playfair (1801) p. 11. • *to avoid the tedious repetition...* Robert Recorde *The Whetstone of Witte* (1557). **34** *In the course of executing that design...* Playfair (1801) p. 3.

Chapter 3: Embodied Encoding

35 Greek battle illustration inspired by combat between Achilles and Memnon on a volute krater (bowl for mixing wine and water) made in Attica c. 490BC–460BC, British Museum number 1848,0801.1. • *What our eyes behold...* Stevens (1951). **36** *The hero has to go...* Eliade (1952) p. 83. • *The ceaseless activity of making mappings...* Hofstadter and Sander (2013) pp. 126–127, 440. **37** *'You don't know much,'...* Carroll (1865) Chapter VI: Pig and Pepper. • *All that has been learned empirically...* Edward O. Wilson quoted by Austin (2010) p. 133. • *From the experientialist perspective...* Lakoff and Johnson (1980) p. 235. **38** Illustration of intersecting figures is a tribute to Sousanis (2015). • *Imagination lets us exceed...* Ibid. pp. 88–89. • *a form of cognitively induced deprivation...* Loewenstein (1994) p. 75. • *Interesting theories are those which...* Davis (1971) p. 309. **39** *Your claims are indefensible...* Lakoff and Johnson (1980) p. 4. • *For we, on our little pile...* Voltaire

(1752) Chapter I. • *We are at our human best...* Raymo (1998) p. 48. • *Analogy is the fuel...* Hofstadter and Sander (2013) p. 3. • *The essence of metaphor is...* Lakoff and Johnson (1980) p. 5. **40** For more on snake detection see Van Strien and Isbell (2017). • *The sole aim of a metaphor is...* Orwell (1946). • *One's interaction with one's body...* Hofstadter and Sander (2013) p. 288. **41** For more on the study of color concepts see Davidoff (2006). • The imaginative reader illustration references Norman Rockwell's *Boy Reading Adventure Story* (1923) and the *Britain Needs You at Once* WWI propaganda poster (1915). • *The abstract is understood in the context of...* Geary (2011) p. 93. • *Theory-laden: There is no such thing as 'raw' experience...* Deutsch (2011) p. 41. • *Our psychology also limits our perception...* Hofstadter and Sander (2013) p. 171. **42** *You have the power to...* Elizabeth Andrews in conversation with author (2018). • *This "mental cinema" is always at work...* Calvino (2016) p. 102. **43** "Big things are important" is motivated by Lakoff and Núñez (2000) p. 41. • *The essence of graphical display...* Wainer (1997) p. 20. • *The great criterion is the effect produced...* Playfair (1801) p. 16. • *Clever encoding does not always translate...* Cleveland (1985) p. 20. • *Seeing comes before words...* Berger (1972) p. 7. **44** "Big things are important in Zulu, Hawaiian…" see Geary (2011) page 24. • *An appeal to the eye when proportion...* Playfair (1801) pp. 4, 14.

Chapter 4: Counting Time

45 Dorothy and Toto illustration inspired by W.W. Denslow's illustrations for Baum (1900). • *There were several roads near by...* Baum (1900) p. 33. **46** This chapter's chain of mathematical metaphors is inspired by Lakoff and Núñez (2000). • "assembly-number metaphor" Lakoff and Núñez (2000) pp. 65–68. • "Closure is an engine for creating..." motivated by Ibid pp. 81–82. **47** "length-number metaphor" Ibid pp. 68–71. • "The rod, equal to sixteen feet..." inspired by Stigler (2016) p. 31.

• Sixteen feet illustration after Jacob Köbel's original 1522 illustration. **48** "distance-number metaphor" Lakoff and Núñez (2000) pp. 71–72. **49** "Source-path-goal" and "fictive motion" motivated by Ibid. pp. 37–39. • Fictive motion bicycle illustration inspired by work of Nigel Holmes. • *Personification is a general category...* Lakoff and Johnson (1980) p. 34. • *Science interests me...* Calvino (2016) p. 111. • *We use the same language...* Lakoff and Núñez (2000) p. 74. **50** *The depiction of time: The process begins with metaphor...* Lippincott (1999) p. 169. • *Perception of time is not linear...* Wong (2010) p. 100. **51** "Like someone looking out the back window of a car..." this vision of time is inspired by John-Paul Sartre's comments on William Faulkner's *The Sound and the Fury*. *Time travel is only science fiction...* Bierut (2005) p. 203. • "You can be traveling through time..." motivated by Lakoff and Johnson (1980) pp. 41–45. **52** Skeleton with hourglass is inspired by Jolly Roger pirate flags. • Three-headed illustration references Titian's *Allegory of Prudence* (c. 1560–1570). • *Then I reflected that everything happens...* Borges (2003) p. 30. **53** "Time is linear travel over a landscape" metaphor inspired by Lakoff and Johnson (1980) pp. 41–45 and Lakoff and Núñez (2000) pp. 406–407. • Levidrome, the name for a word that spells something else backwards, was coined by six-year-old Levi Budd.• "Linear time on the page moves from left to right..." A curious exception to this rule is financial statement tables which puts the most important accounting period, the most recent, first. • *In all these cases...* Norman (2013) p. 122. **54** Chinese Mandarin contrast motivated by Shlain (1998) p. 183. • "how the Chinese language orients time." see Geary (2011) pp. 98–99. • Zodiac animals illustration inspired by emoji.• *A man who explains...* Hui Tzu quoted in Geary (2011) p. 172. • *While the Indo-Aryans and Semites found...* Shlain (1998) p. 181. • *The cosmic clock: If time was conceived as the precise measure of...* Umberto Eco in Lippincott (1999)

p. 10. **55** *In [South American] Aymaran culture...* Geary (2011) p. 98. • *[Australian Aboriginal] Pormpuraawans arrange time...* Boroditsky and Gaby (2010) p. 1635. **56** "A different visual metaphor for time..." motivated by Lakoff and Johnson (1980) pp. 7–9. • "time is an irreversible performance" motivated by Hidalgo (2015) chapter 3 summary of Prigogine (1984).• *There is no past...* Hidalgo (2015) p. 40.

Chapter 5: World Building

57 *The Grid, a digital frontier...* Daft Punk featuring Jeff Bridges. "The Grid." Tron: Legacy. Walt Disney Records, 2010. **58** *In one dimension...* Sousanis (2015) p. 23. • *One might say that the world...* Valéry (1950) p. 123. • *Imagine a vast sheet of paper...* Abbott (1884) p. 4. **59** "Find your way home..." and other quests motivated by Roam (2016) p. 93. • *What do we make of our contemporary interactive maps'...* Mattern (2015). • *The crowning achievement of memory...* Rumsey (2016) p. 110. **60** Globe-projection illustration is inspired by Albrecht Dürer's "Perspective Machine" (c. 1525). **61** "Descartes cemented the convention of..." see Levins (2014) and Moore (2012). **63** Historic city center illustration is based on Oviedo, Spain c. 1777. • *To look is a territorial activity.* Carse (1986) p. 70. • *None of these things exist...* Harari (2015) p. 28. **64** "Other animals..." see Dell'Amore (2013). • Muhammad Ali illustration is inspired by the famous photograph Neil Leifer shot for *Sports Illustrated* after Ali's first round knockout of Sonny Liston in 1965.

Chapter 6: Infuse Meaning

67 Mad Hatter illustration inspired by John Tenniel's illustration for Carroll (1865). • *That was an instance of the charts meaning...* Neurath and Kinross (2009) p. 26. **68** "Good goes up" motivated by Lakoff and Johnson 1980 pp. 14–21. **69** Opioid chart inspired by *Iraq's Bloody Toll,* Simon Scarr, South China Morning Post, Dec 17, 2011, http://www.scmp.com/infographics/

article/1284683/iraqs-bloody-toll • *The principles...* Bang (2000) pp. 42–44. **70** "ways of showing time..." inspired by Cleveland (1985) pp. 178–186. In tribute to Cleveland the same geomagnetic data series he used has been refreshed to include the last 30 years. The aa index is derived from two approximately antipodal observatories, one in the UK and one in Australia. Collection began in 1868, making it the oldest planetary index time-series. **71** "Dona Wong advocates..." Wong (2010) pp. 50–53. • Alice is being pulled through her own story by the Red Queen's hand, inspired by John Tenniel's illustration for Carroll (1871). • *The dashed line...* Malamed (2012). • *Ratio scales...* Cairo (2016) p. 107. **73** Stack of coins illustration inspired by Holmes (1984) p. 39. • *columns of stacked facts* Levasseur (1885) p. 227. • *Suppose the money received by a man...* Playfair (1786) p. xi. **74** *believed that by wedding...* Wainer (2005) p. 49. **75** *[Euclid] gave his famous...* Dyson (1988) p. 16. **76** "The page lacks natural depth cues..." motivated by Ware (2008) p. 90. and Munzer (2014) pp. 118–120. **77** The maze is modeled after the set used by Stanley Kubrick to shoot THE SHINING horror film (1980). • *Most of us must undertake...* Biderman et al. (1963) p. 6.

Chapter 7: True Colors

79 Colorful birds illustration inspired by "The dream of Nebuchadnezzer" from the *Morgan Beatus,* a medieval illuminated manuscript now in the Pierpont Morgan Library, New York. • *Man lives with what...* Valéry (1950) p. 222. **81** Dorothy and Toto illustration are inspired by W.W. Denslow's illustrations for Baum (1900). • "The sequence from dark to light..." motivated by Stone (2003). **82** "Distinct hues are farthest separated..." motivated by Ware (2008) pp. 69–79. **83** "Basic colors" Berlin and Kay (1969). **84** CMY subtractive color illustration inspired by Stone (2003) p. 164. • Gamut comparison illustration based on CIE 1976 chromaticity diagram by the Commission Internationale de l'Eclairage. • *Take a brightly colored object...* Stone (2003) pp. 36-37. **85** Human cone distribution illustration adapted from by Roorda (1999). • *A color scale should vary...* Simmon (2013) Part 2. • "The 'opponent process' theory of color is..." motivated by Stone (2003) pp. 28–29. **86** For a productive use of rainbow palettes see Munzer (2014) pp. 231–232. • The bathymetric color palette that diverges from sea level is based on an example palette from Cynthia Brewer's ColorBrewer2.org. **87** Binned color illustration inspired by Ware (2008) p. 73. • *Perceptual effects [can] strengthen...* Stone (2003) p. 261. • *Pleasing colors blend...* Cleveland (1985) p. 207. • *To label (color as noun)...* Tufte (1990) p. 81. **88** *Whenever possible, make intuitive palettes...* Simmon (2013) Part 4. • *Recognize that it's hard...* Meeks (2018).

Chapter 8: Explore to Create

89 *And this I believe...* Steinbeck (1952) p. 131. **90** "the man is Michelangelo..." this particular telling of the story is based on the film *The Agony and the Ecstasy* (1965) • The gesture drawing is based on one in pen and brown ink by Michelangelo in 1511. It is now held by Ashmolean Museum, Oxford, https://www.michelangelo-gallery.com/sistine-sketchbook-6.aspx • *The germ of an idea may often come...* Ware (2008) p. 147. **91** "John Tukey introduced" Tukey (1977) p. 1. • *Simple arithmetic and easy-to-draw pictures...* Tukey (1977) p. v. • *Which general-purpose plot...* Wainer (1997) p. 181. • *The term "forensic"...* Rumsey (2016) p. 99. • *A means of orchestrating a conversation...* Sousanis (2015) p. 79. **92** "enough context for the viewer to make sense of a lonely number..." for a more critical take on lonely numbers see Rosling et al. (2018) pp. 130, 142. • *Hypotheses are nets...* Novalis *Schriften II* (1802) cited in Popper (1959) p. xiv. • *There is no logical path to these laws...* Einstein (1918). • *Every discovery contains an irrational element...* Popper (1959) p. 8. • *In my research I have needed...* Rosling

et al. (2018) p. 191. **93** "The language used to describe these differences" Tukey introduced this distinction with *Bill is a head taller than Jim ... George weights twice as much as his brother Jack...* Tukey (1977) p. 110. • "Add and subtract comparisons..." motivated by Lakoff and Núñez (2000) pp. 55–56. • "Multiplication is a conceptual extension of addition..." motivated by Lakoff and Núñez (2000) pp. 60–61. • The astronauts are inspired by ISOTYPE forms. • "Newborns have been studied to count..." see Butterworth (1999) p. 108 cited in Lakoff and Núñez (2000) p. 19. **94** "Jacques Bertin extolled the power..." see Bertin (1983) p. 11. • *pains and labour* full sentence is *As it is not without some pains and labour that the memory is impressed with the proportion between different quantities expressed in words or figures, many persons never take that trouble— and there is even, to those that do so, a fresh effort of memory necessary each time the question occurs.* Playfair(1801) p. 6. • *learn how to make one picture do.* Tukey (1977) p. 109. • "Cleveland distinguished two types..." Cleveland (1985) p. 22. • "Exports and Imports" illustration is a tribute to Playfair (1786). **95** "The mind ingests many" for a detailed look at how 2-D space is structured in the mind see Ware (2008) Chapter 3. • *Trend: Something practically everybody is...* Huff (1954) p. 62. • "Binding" motivated by Ware (2008) p. 47. **96** "Scagnostics" Wilkinson and Wills (2008). • *Theory and experimentation led...* Cleveland and McGill and McGill (1988). **97** *Each of the four data sets...* Anscombe (1973). **98** Average bridge traffic illustration plots San Francisco commuter traffic. • *Drawing with data is...* Lupi (2017). • *The greatest value of a picture is...* Tukey (1977) p. vi. • *The eye cannot look on similar forms...* William Playfair's Statistical Breviary (1801) p. 6 in Playfair (2005).

Chapter 9: Create to Explore

99 *When the human realm seems doomed...* Calvino (2016) p. 8. **100** *Histograms reduce information...* Cleveland (1985) p. 125. See Izenman (1991) for work on "optimal" histogram bin-sizing. **101** Four Grand Canyon sites are marked in blue, from left-to-right: North Rim (North Kaibob Trailhead), Phantom Ranch, Colorado River, and South Rim (Bright Angel Trailhead). • "Hinge diagram" see Tukey (1977) pp. 32–37. Howard Wainer (2018) shared, *Why did Tukey call them Hinges? The first and fourth quartiles are, in German "die fliegenden Viertel", or 'the flying quarters' or 'wings'. But wings flap and so the place where they join the main body of the distribution must be hinges.* **102** *simplifies the images without diminishing...* Bertin (1983) p. 36. • Reordered category illustration cells inspired by Ibid. **103** "Smooth and Rough" see Tukey (1977) p. 205. • Seasonal analysis inspired by Armstrong (2016). • *Not everything is a straight line* Tukey (1977) p. 207. **104** *A changed approach is precisely the goal...* Sousanis (2015) p. 27. • *The entire problem is one of...* Bertin (1983) p. xiv. • *Most of modern statistics is built around...* Wainer (2017) in correspondence with author. **105** "content and form" framing was also made by Bertin (1983) p. 4. • *If the way numbers were gathered...* Tukey (1977) p. 57. **106** *It is an unusual data set indeed that yields...* Wainer (2005) p. 96. • *If we want to learn more we must think more.* Tukey (1977) p. 141. **108** "Tukey's sum-difference graph" Cleveland (1985) pp. 136–138. • *Augment human capabilities rather than...* Munzer (2014) p. 1. **109** Temperature anomaly data from climate.NASA. gov, CO_2 data from NOAA ESRL. Global Mean Sea Level variation data from NASA MEaSUREs program. • *And chaos theory teaches us...* Crichton (1990) p. 171. **110** "In the words of Italian writer Italo Calvino..." see page 99. • *Our brains, wired to detect patterns...* Silver (2012) p. 63. • *For if vision be...* Browne (1646) p. 124. • *certain of the evidence...* Popper (1959) p. 24.

Chapter 10: Uncertain Honesty

111 *Doubt is not a pleasant condition...* Voltaire (1770). **112** *observations can give us...* Popper (1959) p. 79. • *The desire for truth is so prominent...* Eddington (1929) p. 246. • *I say not that it is...* Alyea cited in Wainer (2009) p. 210. **113** *A true story: I, too have turned to lying...* Lucian in Casson (1962) p. 15. • "CIA analyst Sherman Kent..." see Kent (1964). • *Part of our knowledge we obtain direct...* Keynes (1921) pp. 3–4. **114** "But, neither do our minds!..." motivated by Tetlock and Gardner (2015) p. 80. • Die rolls are predictable, see Kapitaniak et al. (2012). • *Stare at the world...* Kling (2017) article. **115** • Wizard and Toto characters are inspired by W.W. Denslow's illustrations for Baum (1900). • *Just as the ability to devise simple but evocative models is the signature of the great scientist...* Box (1976) p. 792. • *If a meteorologist says there is a 70% chance of rain...* Tetlock and Gardner (2015) p. 57. • "prediction horizon" see Gaspard (2005) p. 7. **116** *Science never pursues the illusory aim of...* Popper (1959) p. 281. • *Measurements are only useful for...* Stigler (2016) p. 64. • *We very soon got to...* Carroll (1893) p. 169. **117** *If there is no possible way to determine...* Friedrich Waismann, Erkenntnis 1 (1903) p. 229 cited in Popper (1959) p. 17. • *Science does not rest upon...* Popper (1959) p. 94. • *If I were to suggest that between the Earth and Mars...* Russell (1952) pp. 547–548. **118** *estimate, which presumably does not differ...* Neyman (1937) p. 346. • *No theory that involves just the probabilities...* Howard (1966) p. 22. • "A 95% confidence interval conveys..." motivated by Cox and Hinkley (1974) pp. 49, 209. **119** *The more money...* Huff (1954) p. 91. **120** "Howard Wainer taught..." see Wainer (2009) p. 121. • *Sigma...* Savage (2009) p. 78. • *The truthful art: Truth is unattainable...* Cairo (2016) p. 15. • *If a man will begin...* Bacon (1605) The First Book V.7. • *The only certainty is...* Pliny the Elder's Naturalis Historia (79) Book II Sec. 5 quoted in Savage (2009) p. 1. • *It's time to leave behind any presumption of...* Lupi

(2017). **121** *I am convinced that this is as good as we can do so far.* related to author by Wainer (2018). • *We shall not cease from exploration...* Elliot (1942) Little Gidding V. **123** Alice going through the looking-glass illustration inspired by John Tenniel's illustrations for Carroll (1871).

Chapter 11: Encounter

126 "good management of visitor attention" motivated by Bitgood (2013). • *Objects are where we deposit information...* Hidalgo (2015) p. 178. • *The exhibition-maker's job is to arrange...* Robert Storr, MoMA Painting and Sculpture Curator, quoted in Marincola (2006) p. 24. **127** *One may think of an information forager...* Piroilli and Card (1991) p. 646. • *What information consumes is rather obvious...* Herber Simon's *Designing Organizations For An Information Rich World* in Greeberg (1971) pp. 40–41. **128** *You-are-here-maps...* Levine (1982). • *In a general way, I have come to the conclusion that...* Dean (1915) p. 173. **129** *Space is the medium...* Robert Storr, MoMA Painting and Sculpture Curator, quoted in Marincola (2006) p. 23. **130** *The most important...* Ware (2008) p. 24. • "More distance..." motivated by Ingrid Schaffner (2003) quoted in Marincola (2006) p. 163. **131** *the standard placement...* Ingrid Schaffner (2003) quoted in Marincola (2006) p. 163. An anecdotal look into the galleries of Arabic museums, via Google Arts & Culture's museum gallery explorer, showed that left-reading Arabic labels match Schaffner's convention. They appear to the left of the museum object. • *If the concluding sentences of a label...* Laurence Coleman *Manual for Small Museums* (1927) quoted in Marincola (2006) p. 164. • *never overestimate the...* Virgil Thomson quoted in Marincola (2006) p. 28. • *Appeal to someone who...* Ingrid Schaffner (2003) cited in Marincola (2006) p. 165. • *Just as people can tell a good steak from...* Paola Antonelli, MoMA Curator of Architecture and Design, R&D cited in Marincola (2006) p. 89. • The Atlantean statue illustration is moti-

vated by the pillars (c. 1000) that stand over 4.8 meters tall from the ancient Toltec city of Tula. **132** Cabinet of curiosity illustration adapted from Levinus Vincent's *Het Wondertooneel der Natuure* (1706) Plate III. • *organize and explain...* Obrist (2014) p. 42.

Chapter 12: Listen

134 *I am a storyteller...* Karen Blixen 1957 interview quoted in Arendt (1958). • *If we have our own why...* from Frederich Nietzsche's *Twilight of the Idols, or, How to Philosophize with a Hammer* (1889) Maxims and Arrows 1.12. **135** "The world we are wired for" motivated by Austin (2010) pp. 56, 120–121. • *Modern man is in fact...* Jung (1964) p. 86. • *Useful fictions: We perceive truth and utility to be...* Austin (2010) pp. 136, 137, 99. • *The character of a society...* Shahn (1957) p. 39. **136** "Every story arrives..." motivated by Glass (2009). • "Narrative flow puts content..." motivated by Ware (2008) p. 139. • *Before the word became synonymous with...* Gabler (1998) pp. 16, 21. • *Narrative logic and the visual connection between...* Katz (1991) p. 121. • *I find that most people know...* O'Connor (1969) p. 66. **137** "Story sequence can..." motivated by Pinker (2014) pp. 160–166. • Story structures inspired by CineFix (2016). • *A linear ordering of phrases which...* Pinker (2014) p. 83. • *[The narrated story is always] more than mere...* Paul Ricoeur *Life: A Story in Search of a Narrator* in Doeser and Kraay (1986) p. 122. **138** "Endings satisfy..." motivated by Ware (2008) p. 142. • Question and answer illustrations inspired by Katz (1991) pp. 148–150. • "Even more structures exist..." see Nancy Duarte's TED Talk The Secret Structure Of Great Talks (Feb 2012) https://www.ted.com/talks/nancy_duarte_the_secret_structure_of_great_talks **139** *Endings, frankly, are a...* Goldman (1983) pp. 118–119. • *[A] familiar pattern merely shows...* Katz (1991) p. 151. • *The art of creating suspense...* Truffault (1983) p. 16. • *Comics panels fracture both...* McCloud (1993) p. 67. **140** *The king died and* *then...* Forster (1927) p. 130. • *Our knowledge and impressions of...* Sklar (2005) p. 159. • *The meaning or the significance of...* Paul Ricoeur *Life: A Story in Search of a Narrator* in Doeser and Kraay (1986) p. 122. • *Meaning is derived from context...* Hidalgo (2015) p. xvi. • *We don't see things as they are...* Anaïs Nin referenced these "Talmudic words" in *Seduction of the Minotaur* (1961) p. 124. The quote has a complicated history which can be read at https://quoteinvestigator.com/2014/03/09/as-we-are/ **141** "Symbols imply more than is obvious ..." see Jung (1960) pp. 3–4. • *A text is not an entity closed in...* Paul Ricoeur *Life: A Story in Search of a Narrator* in Doeser and Kraay (1986) pp. 126, 127. • *On myths and mythology: What would we be without the help of...* Valéry (1950) p. 201 **142** *[Archetypes] are pieces of life itself...* Jung (1960) pp. 87, 88. • *It is precisely the colouring...* Tolkien (1964) p. 126. • *The universal is that unique thing which...* Shahn (1957) p. 54. • *Myths, told for their own sake...* Carse (1986) p. 142.• *Special effects are just a tool...* Lucas (1983).

Chapter 13: Freeze

143 "Freeze": An early draft title for this chapter was "Frieze," a pun which references both the stillness of graphic design and the horizontal band of sculpted or painted decoration. • *Narrative art is art that tells...* Lucas Museum of Narrative Art http://lucasmuseum.org/about/what-is-narrative-art **144** "Advertising has always been on the cutting edge of attracting attention..." see Wu (2016). • "David Ogilvy has advice..." Ogilvy (1985). • *Illustrators have to tell a lot in one frame...* Lucas (2013). • *When telling a story with just one image...* Lupton (2015) p. 160. • *I do not regard advertising as...* Ogilvy (1985) p. 7. **145** The surrealist knight illustration is a tribute to Magritte's painting *Le Blanc Seing* (1965). • *If a scene with clearly expressed gist...* Ware (2008) p. 122. • *A superficial feature...* Hofstadter and Sander (2013) p. 340. • *An imitation may be described...* Stevens (1951). **146**

"Glossy magazine pages..." and following illustrations motivated most by Lupton (2015). • The arrow-apple story illustration is inspired by the painting by Thomas Woodruff on the cover of Prigogine (1996). • *What did these old-fashioned advertising men mean by...* Munari (1971) pp. 84–86. **147** "Psychologist George Miller introduced us to the idea that we can only hold seven..." see Miller (1956). • *We can only hold in mind just a few of the letters...* Pinker (2014) p. 351. • *A category pulls together many phenomena...* Hofstadter and Sander (2013) p. 14. **148** "Visual pop-out occurs..." see Healey and Enns (2012). • "Pop-out is a pre-attentive effect..." see Treisman and Gormican (1988). • The De Stijl rider illustration is after Bart van Der Leck's *De Ruiter* (1919). **149** *they are concrete...* Shlain (1998) p. 4. • *write as if they have something important to show.* Pinker (2014) p. 26. • "There are numerous..." see Meggs (2016) p. 20. • "The Hangul Korean..." see Ibid. p. 32. • *Image is, text is always about.* Sousanis (2015) p. 58. • *Language can convey complex logical relationships...* Ware (2008) p. 145. • *How do we integrate figures and text?...* Wainer (1997) p. 144. **150** See McCloud (1993) pp. 152–161 for a tour of how comics combine words and pictures.

Chapter 14: Connect

152 "we are wired to recognize shimmering..." see Meert (2014). • "How lines and shapes are drawn..." motivated by McCloud (1993) p. 125 and Bang (2000) pp. 70–71. • The abstract illustrations are inspired by the bouba/kiki effect, a non-arbitrary mapping between speech sounds and the visual shape of objects, first observed by psychologist Wolfgang Köhler in 1929. • *The healthy brain does not waste space...* Rumsey (2016) p. 118. • *[Emotion] comes from the Latin verb...* Geary (2011) p. 21. • *One of the first things I like to do...* film designer Tony Walton interviewed in Goldman (1983) p. 549. **153** *The seemingly rough solution...* Alexander (2002) p. 211. **154** The portal illustrations are adapted from Alexander (2002) p. 89. • *Data is alive...* Roam (2016) p. 84. • *Austerity may serve certain purposes...* Wainer (2007) p. 150. **155** "a single dot can change..." Alexander (2002) p. 81–82. • *When I think of them as centers...* Alexander (2002) pp. 85–88. • *A beautiful thing is something that would...* Eco (2004) p. 10. **156** Gallery illustration is a tribute to Mark Rothko's Untitled (Yellow on Orange) No. 579 (1957). • *I'm not an abstractionist...* Mark Rothko *Notes from a conversation with Selden Rodman*, 1956 cited in Rodman (1957) p. 93. • *Visual design [has the] power to...* Lupi (2017). • *Not everything that can be counted...* The full quote is *It would be nice if all of the data which sociologists require could be enumerated because then we could run them through IBM machines and draw charts as the economists do. However, not everything that can be counted counts, and not everything that counts can be counted.* Cameron (1963) p. 13.

Chapter 15: Make

158 *The ability of geometric representations to rapidly convey...* De Landa (2000) p. 33. **159** Thrust line illustrations adapted from Gordon (1978) pp. 181–186. **160** *When we abstract...* McCloud (1993) p. 30. • Face illustrations are a tribute to McCloud (1993). **161** "A key component of many diagrams is the arrow..." motivated by Alikhani and Stone (2018). • *All the things we experience in life...* McCloud (1993) pp. 39, 41. **162** The chair is the iconic Eames Lounge Chair • The horse is a tribute to Eadweard Muybridge's *Horse In Motion* (1878). **163** Airplane emergency exit diagram inspired by RYANAIR Boeing 737-200 Safety Information card. • "Dan Roam shows..." Roam (2016) pp. 88–89. • *A diagram of things is derived from depictions...* Tversky (2015) p. 105. • *[A diagram is] particularly useful because...* Peirce (1998) p. 13. • *Now is the time to rise from the dark...* King (1963).

Chapter 16: Inspire Trust

167 Handshake illustration is adapted from the throne base from Fort Shalmaneser, which shows king of Assyria Shalmaneser III (on the left) grasping the hand of Marduk-zakir-šumi, king of Babylonia. It is one of the oldest surviving depictions of a handshake. • *Mankind are not held together by lies...* Douglass (1869). **168** "One striking spread illustrated an elephant..." the spread described was drawn by Mark Hallett and painted by Barbara Hoopes for *Zoobooks: Elephants* (1980). • "Many people have been slow to accept..." 38 percent of U.S. adults believe in the strict creationist view according to Gallup (2017). • "Our mind is able to operate with scant input experience because it already holds a wealth of information..." motivated by Tenenbaum et al. (2011) p. 1279. • *The moral I guess is this...* Goldman (1983) p. 145. • *As people invented new tools...* Kolbert (2017). **169** "Everyone has a unique perspective..." motivated by Kling (2017) book pp. 26, 72. • *When it comes to perceiving the physical world...* Matthew D. Lieberman *Naïve Realism* in Brockman (2018) p. 101. • *We rarely expend the time and energy...* Rumsey (2016) p. 119. **170** *Truth is therefore a function of...* Lakoff and Johnson (1980) p. 179. • *Coalitional instincts: To earn membership in a group you must...* evolutionary psychology founder John Tooby *Coalitional Instincts* in Brockman (2018) p. 498–499. • *Having an enemy is important...* Eco (2011) p. 2. **171** *Comeuppance: To give us an incentive to monitor...* Flesch (2007) p. 50. • *Trust does not reside...* Fukuyama (1995) p. 25. **172** "Too much trust..." motivated by Covey (2006) pp. 19, 287. • *The connection between style and substance...* Fry (2011). **173** "We fear being insufficient. We fear not belonging." motivated by Zander and Zander (2000) pp. 95–97. • *Few things can help an individual more than...* Washington (1901) p. 172. **174** *The evolution of trust: In the short run, the game defines the players...* Case (2017).

Chapter 17: Imagination to Image

175 Opening door illustration was inspired by the opening credits of The Twilight Zone. • *It is when we do not have to believe...* Thoreau (1849) p. 146. **176** "I recently heard..." happened at the Barry Lawrence Ruderman Conference on Cartography at Stanford's sous Rumsey Map Center, October 19–21, 2017. **178** "Different sources provide different years" one of the more comprehensive sources was Eupedia's List of Gothic edifices by year of construction https://www.eupedia.com/europe/gothic_buildings.shtml • The Notre-Dame de Paris map illustration was made referencing *OpenStreetMap* and *Google Maps*. **180** From France to Jerusalem illustration directions were mapped using *SunEarthTools* Distance tool https://www.sunearthtools.com/tools/distance.php **181** "I stumble into a research paper..." Sparavigna (2014). **184** *Form cannot be greater than content...* Shahn (1957) p. 83. • *As we become familiar with something...* Pinker (2014) p. 71.

Chapter 18: Focus Attention

185 *Vision without execution...* Isaacson (2014) p. 481. **186** *As the designer quickly creates...* Ware (2008) p. 160. • *Editing is not taking out...* film editor Dede Allen quoted in Goldman (1983) p. 558. **187** *Whenever you feel an impulse...* Quiller-Couch (1916) XII. On Style. • *An artist at work upon a painting must...* Shahn (1957) pp. 39–50. • *A lot of the questions I ask...* film director George Roy Hill quoted in Goldman (1983) p. 573. • *It's time to kill...* Glass (2009) **188** *From the data given in words and figures...* Neurath and Kinross (2009) pp. 77–78. • *People make the deepest analogies that they can...* Hofstadter and Sander (2013) p. 360. **189** *Any graphic which does not enlighten...* the entire paragraph is *Some statisticians have tried to formulate rules for the construction of graphs and to somehow fix this scientific language, as the chemical notation has been fixed. Without doubt, mathematicians have to determine the geometrical processes which best correspond to the figurative expression of numbers; but they do not have to impose definite types of representation. There is the matter to classify, as we have tried to do, rather than regulate. Any graphic which does not enlighten the subject is condemned: here is the supreme rule, which is none other than that of clarity.* Levasseur (1885) p. 248. • *How can we maintain clarity but add impact?* Wainer (1997) p. 147. **190** "Jacques Bertin used the word energy..." Bertin (1983) pp. 60–61. • "Horror Vacui" motivated by Lidwell et al (2015) p. 70. • *Most of these solutions use icons...* Wainer (2005) p. 116. • *If we're going to make a mark...* Tukey (1972) p. 296. **191** Watch illustrations are based on the Seagull 1963 Airforce Watch, produced by the Tianjin Watch Factory for the Chinese Air Force. • *How do you know it works?...* Munzer (2014) p. 14. • *It must be stressed...* Alexander (2002) p. 128. **192** "Ad orientem" is a Latin phrase for "to the east" and is used to describe the orientation of a priest in Christian liturgy facing the wall behind the altar, with priest and people looking in the same direction. **196** *The sign is always less...* Jung (1964) p. 41. • *Confections stand or fall on how deeply they...* Tufte (1997) p. 141.

Chapter 19: Creative Routines

197 *When I write...* Goldman (1983) p. 255. **198** *Because play is often about breaking rules...* Johnson (2016) p. 15. **199** *There must be a complete belief...* Shahn (1957) p. 52. • *The child in me...* The New York Times (1976). **200** *Once you start writing...* Goldman (1983) p. 124. • *Do your homework...* Ogilvy (1985) p. 11. • *Those first months are as full of research as...* Goldman (1983) p. 576. **201** *Scientific theories are not 'derived'...* Deutsch (1985) p. 4. • Copy-Transform-Combine illustrations inspired by Ferguson (2010). • *Remixing is a folk art...* Ibid. **202** "makes my brain feel happy" is how David Rumsey described his love of maps to me. I immediately recognized we shared the same affliction.

Finale: Beautiful Tomorrow

203 "Beautiful Tomorrow" references the song "There's a Great Big Beautiful Tomorrow" from Walt Disney's Carousel of Progress. • *Press on with the work...* Campbell (1972) p. 20. **204** "racing with machines" Brynjolfsson and McAfee (2014) pp. 188–192. • "information expands our knowledge, know-how, and imagination." motivated by Hidalgo (2015) pp. 51, 71. • *I am among those who think that science has great beauty...* Curie (1937) p. 341. **205** *We have developed speed, but have shut ourselves in...* Chaplin (1940). • "feminine gathering narrative..." see Le Guin (1989) "The Carrier Bag Theory of Fiction." • *Art after all, is about rearranging us...* Zander and Zander (2000) p. 3. • *The design of charts and diagrams...* Wainer (1997) p. 2. • *To enhance the spread of ideas...* Pinker (2014) p. 304. • *It is a strange realism, but it is a strange realism...* Le Guin (1989) "The Carrier Bag Theory of Fiction." **206** *A boat is at once a motif of containment and journeying...* Rao (2018). • "Possiblists have a clear idea..." see Rosling et al. (2018) p. 69. • *We have to find new languages...* Lupi (2017). • *It is not the critic who counts...* Roosevelt (1910). **207** *To each of his charts the author has added...* Stuart (1786) pp. 302, 305. • *is certainly just; and I have attended to the hint.* Playfair (1786) p. viii. • "I wish all data storytellers joy..." this closing is inspired by Goldman (1983) p. 585.

SELECTED
BIBLIOGRAPHY

Color indicates category. Each ● is one book and each ○ is an article or other media.

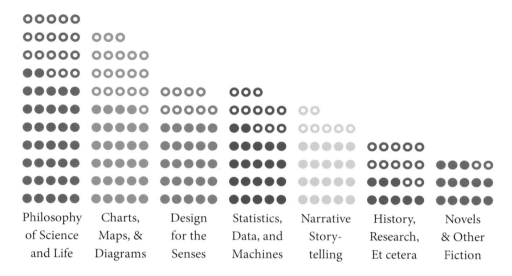

| Philosophy of Science and Life | Charts, Maps, & Diagrams | Design for the Senses | Statistics, Data, and Machines | Narrative Story-telling | History, Research, Et cetera | Novels & Other Fiction |

● Abbott, Edwin. *Flatland: A Romance in Many Dimensions.* London: Seeley & Co, 1884.

● Alexander, Christopher. *The Phenomenon of Life: An Essay on the Art of Building and the Nature of the Universe.* Berkeley, CA: Center for Environmental Structure, 2002.

○ Alikhani, Malihe, and Matthew Stone. "Arrows Are The Verbs Of Diagrams." *Proceedings of the 27th International Conference on Computational Linguistics* (2018): 3552–3563.

○ Andrews, Elizabeth, message to author, Jun, 2018.

○ Anscombe, F.J. "Graphs in Statistical Analysis." *The American Statistician* 27, no. 1 (1973): 17–21.

● Arendt, Hannah. *The Human Condition.* Chicago: University of Chicago Press, 1958.

○ Armstrong, Zan. "Everything is Seasonal." Speech. OpenVis Conf, Apr 25–26, 2016, https://youtu.be/IiF4-g001EQ.

● Arnheim, Rudolf. *Visual Thinking.* Berkeley, CA: University of California Press, 1969.

● Austin, Michael. *Useful Fictions: Evolution, Anxiety, and the Origins of Literature.* Lincoln, NE: University of Nebraska Press, 2010.

● Bacon, Francis. *Of the Proficience and Advancement of Learning, Divine and Human.* Oxford: University of Oxford, 1605.

● Bang, Molly. *Picture This: How Pictures Work.* San Francisco, CA: Chronicle Books, 2000.

● Baum, L. Frank. *The Wonderful Wizard of Oz.* Chicago: Geo. M. Hill Co., 1900.

○ Benedictine Monks of Buckfast Abbey. "The Laying of the Foundation-Stone of a Church." *Homiletic & Pastoral Review* (January 1927): 405–412.

Berger, John. *Ways of Seeing: Based on the BBC Television Series with John Berger.* London: British Broadcasting, 1972.

Berlin, Brent, and Paul Kay. *Basic Color Terms: Their Universality and Evolution.* Berkeley, CA: University of California Press, 1969.

Bernstein, Peter L. *Against the Gods: The Remarkable Story of Risk.* New York: John Wiley & Sons, 1996.

Bertin, Jacques. *Semiology of Graphics: Diagrams Networks Maps.* Translated by William J. Berg. Redlands, CA: ESRI Press, 1983.

Biderman, Albert D., Margot Louria, and Joan Bacchus. "Historical Incidents of Extreme Overcrowding." *Bureau of Social Science Research, Washington DC* (1963).

Bierut, Michael. *Seventy-nine Short Essays on Design.* New York: Princeton Architectural Press, 2007.

Bitgood, Stephen. *Attention and Value: Keys to Understanding Museum Visitors.* Walnut Creek, CA: Left Coast Press, Inc., 2013.

Borges, Jorge Luis. "The Garden of Forking Paths." *The NewMediaReader* 1 (2003): 29–34.

Boroditsky, Lera, and Alice Gaby. "Remembrances of Times East: Absolute Spatial Representations of Time in an Australian Aboriginal Community." *Psychological Science* 21 (2010): 1635–1639.

Box, George E.P. "Science And Statistics." *Journal of the American Statistical Association* 71, no. 356 (1976): 791–799.

Brinton, Willard C. *Graphic Methods For Presenting Facts.* New York: The Engineering Magazine Company, 1914.

Brockman, John. *This Explains Everything: Deep, Beautiful, and Elegant Theories of How the World Works.* New York: Harper, 2013.

Brockman, John. *This Idea Is Brilliant: Lost, Overlooked, and Underappreciated Scientific Concepts Everyone Should Know.* New York: Harper Perennial, 2018.

Browne, Thomas. *Pseudodoxia Epidemica: Or Enquiries Into Very Man Received Tenents and Commonly Presumed Truths.* London: A. Miller, 1646.

Brynjolfsson, Erik, and Andrew McAfee. *The Second Machine Age: Work, Progress, and Prosperity in a Time of Brillant Technologies.* New York: W.W. Norton & Company, 2014.

Butterworth, Brian. *What Counts: How Every Brain is Hardwired for Math.* New York: Free Press, 1999.

Byrne, Lydia, Daniel Angus, and Janet Wiles. "Acquired Codes of Meaning in Data Visualization and Infographics: Beyond Perceptual Primitives." *IEEE Transactions On Visualization and Computer Graphics* 22, no. 1 (2016): 509–518.

Byrne, Oliver. *The First Six Books of The Elements of Euclid.* London: William Pickering, 1847.

Cairo, Alberto. *The Functional Art an Introduction to Information Graphics and Visualization.* Berkeley: New Riders, 2013.

Cairo, Alberto. *The Truthful Art: Data, Charts, and Maps for Communication.* Berkeley: New Riders, 2016.

Caldwell, Sally. *Statistics Unplugged,* 3rd ed. Belmont, CA: Wadsworth, 2010.

Calvino, Italo. *Six Memos for the next Millennium,* Translated by Geoffrey Brock. New York: First Mariner Books, 2016.

- Cameron, William Bruce. *Informal Sociology: A Casual Introduction To Sociological Thinking.* New York: Random House, 1969.
- Campbell, Joseph. *Myths to Live by.* New York: Viking, 1972.
- Campbell, Joseph. *The Hero with a Thousand Faces*, 3rd ed. Novato, CA: New World Library, 2008.
- Carroll, Lewis. *Alice's Adventures in Wonderland.* London: Macmillan and Co., 1865.
- Carroll, Lewis. *Through the Looking-Glass, and What Alice Found There.* London: Macmillan and Co., 1871.
- Carroll, Lewis. *Sylvie and Bruno Concluded.* London: Macmillan and Co., 1893.
- Carse, James P. *Finite And Infinite Games: A Vision of Life as Play and Possibility.* New York: Free Press, 1986.
- Case, Nicky. *The Evolution of Trust.* Web game. 2017, https://ncase.me/trust/.
- Casson, Lionel, trans. *Selected Satires of Lucian.* New York: W.W. Norton & Company, 1962.
- Chaplin, Charles. *The Great Dictator.* Film. Distributed by United Artists. 1940.
- CineFix. *10 Best Structured Movies of All Time.* Documentary Film. 2016, https://youtu.be/mgk6e8gWDbk.
- Cleveland, William S. *The Elements of Graphing Data.* Monterey, CA: Wadsworth, 1985.
- Cleveland, William S., Marylen E. McGill, and Robert McGill. "The Shape Parameter of a Two-Variable Graph." *Journal of the American Statistical Association,* 83, no. 402 (1988): 289–300.
- Conan Doyle, Arthur. "The Adventure of the Copper Beeches: Adventures of Sherlock Holmes." *The Strand Magazine,* June 1892.
- Couclelis, Helen. "Worlds of Information: The Geographic Metaphor In The Visualization of Complex Information." *Cartography and Geographic Information Systems* 25, no. 4 (1998): 209–220.
- Covey, Stephen M. R. *The Speed of Trust.* New York: Free Press, 2006.
- Cox, D.R., and D.V. Hinkley. *Theoretical Statistics.* Boca Raton, FL: Chapman & Hall/CRC, 1973.
- Curie, Eva. *Madame Curie: A Biography*, Translated by Vincent Sheean. Garden City, NY: Doubleday, Doran & Company, 1937.
- Crichton, Michael. *Jurassic Park.* New York: Knopf, 1990.
- Cybulski, Jacob, Susan Keller, and Dilal Saundage. "Interactive Exploration of Data with Visual Metaphors." *International Journal of Software Engineering* 25, no. 2 (2015): 231–252.
- Davidoff, Jules. "Color terms and color concepts." *Journal of Experimental Child Psychology* 94 (2006): 334–338.
- Davis, Murray S. "That's Interesting!: Towards a Phenomenology of Sociology and a Sociology of Phenomenology." *Philosophy of the Social Sciences* 1, no. 4 (1971): 309–344.
- De Landa, Manuel. "Deleuze, Diagrams, and the Genesis of Form." *Amerikastudien / American Studies* 45, no. 1 Chaos/Control: Complexity (2000): 33–41.
- Dean, Bashford. "An Explanatory Label For Helmets." *Bulletin Of The Metropolitan Museum of Art* 10, no. 8 (1915): 173–177.
- Dell'Amore, Christine. "5 Amazing Animal Navigators." National Geographic News. Jan 26, 2013, https://news.nationalgeographic.com/news/2013/130125-5-amazing-animal-navigators/.

Deutsch, David. *The Beginning of Infinity: Explanations That Transform the World*. New York: Viking, 2011.

Doeser, M.C., and J.N. Kraay, ed. *Facts and Values: Philosophical Reflections from Western and Non-Western Perspectives*. Dordrecht: Martinus Nijhoff Publishers, 1986.

Douglass, Frederick. "Our Composite Nationality." Speech. Boston, MA, Dec 7, 1869, http://teachingamericanhistory.org/library/document/our-composite-nationality/.

Dyson, Freeman J. *Infinite In All Directions*. New York: Harper & Row, 1998.

Eco, Umberto, ed. *History of Beauty*, Translated by Alastair McEwen. New York: Rizzoli, 2004.

Eco, Umberto. *Inventing the Enemy: and Other Occasional Writings*, Translated by Richard Dixon. Boston: Houghton Mifflin Harcourt, 2011.

Eddington, Arthur. *Science and the Unseen World*. New York: The Macmillan Company, 1929.

Eddington, Arthur. *Space Time and Gravitation: An Outline of the General Relativity Theory*. Cambirdge: Cambridge University Press, 1920.

Einstein, Albert. *Principles of Research*. Speech. Physical Society, Berlin, Apr 23, 1918, http://www.site.uottawa.ca/~yymao/misc/Einstein_PlanckBirthday.html.

Eliade, Mircea. *Images and Symbols: Studies in Religious Symbolism*. Princeton, NJ: Princeton University Press, 1991.

Elliot, T.S. *Four Quartets*. New York: Harcourt, Brace and Co., 1943.

Englund, Robert K. "Texts From the Late Uruk Period." In *Mesopotamien: Späturuk-Zeit und frühdynastische Zeit*. Freiburg, Schweiz: Göttingen, 1998.

Ferguson, Eugene S. *Engineering and the Minds Eye*. Cambridge, MA: MIT Press, 1992.

Ferguson, Kirby. *Everything Is A Remix*. Documentary Film. Produced by Kirby Ferguson. 2010. https://www.everythingisaremix.info/.

Flesch, William. *Comeuppance: Costly Signaling, Altruistic Punishment, and Other Components of Fiction*. Cambridge, MA: Harvard University Press, 2007.

Forster, E.M. *Aspects Of The Novel*. New York: Harcourt, Brace and Co., 1927.

Fukuyama, Francis. *Trust: The Social Virtues and the Creation of Prosperity*. New York: Free Press Paperbacks, 1995.

Fry, Stephen. "Christopher Hitchens Is Hailed by Stephen Fry as a Man of Style and Wit." The Daily Beast. Dec 16, 2011.

Gabler, Neal. *Life The Movie: How Entertainment Conquered Reality*. New York: Knopf, 1998.

Gadda, Carlo Emilio. *That Awful Mess on the Via Merulana*, Translated by William Weaver. New York: New York Review Books, 1957.

Gallup. "In U.S., Belief in Creationist View of Humans at New Low." Gallup News. May 22, 2017, https://news.gallup.com/poll/210956/belief-creationist-view-humans-new-low.aspx.

Gaspard, Pierre. *Chaos, Scattering and Statistical Mechanics*. Cambridge: Cambridge University Press, 2005.

Geary, James. *I Is An Other: The Secret Life of Metaphor and How It Shapes the Way We See the World*. New York: Harper Perennial, 2011.

Glass, Ira. *Ira Glass On Storytelling*. Interview. Produced by Current TV. Jul 2, 2009. https://youtu.be/5pFI9UuC_fc

Goldman, William. *Adventures in the Screen Trade*. New York: Hachette, 1983.

Gonick, Larry, and Woollcott Smith. *The Cartoon Guide to Statistics*. New York: HarperResource, 1993.

Gonyea, Mark. *A Book about Design: Complicated Doesn't Make It Good.* New York: Henry Holt and, 2005.

Gonyea, Mark. *Another Book about Design: Complicated Doesn't Make It Bad.* New York: H. Holt, 2007.

Gordon, J.E. *Structures: Or Why Things Don't Fall down.* London: Da Capo Press, 1978.

Greenberger, Martin, ed. *Computers, Communications, and the Public Interest.* Baltimore, MD: Johns Hopkins Press, 1971.

Greene, Robert, and Joost Elffers. *The 48 Laws of Power.* New York: Viking, 1998.

Guy, William A. "Statistical Development, With a Special Reference to Statistics as a Science." In *Jubilee Volume of the Statistical Society* (1885). London: Harrison and Sons, 1885.

Harari, Yuval Noah. "Brains, Bodies, Minds … and Techno-Religions." a16z Podcast. Feb 23, 2017, https://a16z.com/2017/02/23/yuval-harari-from-homo-sapiens-to-homo-deus/.

Harari, Yuval Noah. *Sapiens: A Brief History of Humankind.* New York: Harper, 2015.

Healey, Christopher, and James Enns. "Attention and Visual Memory in Visualization and Computer Graphics." *IEEE Transactions On Visualization And Copmuter Graphics* 18, no. 7 (2012): 1170–1188.

Heaney, Seamus, trans. *Beowulf: An Illustrated Edition.* New York: W.W. Norton & Company, 2008.

Hemingway, Ernest. *Green Hills of Africa.* New York: Charles Scribner's Sons, 1935.

Hidalgo, César. *Why Information Grows: The Evolution of Order, from Atoms to Economies.* New York: Basic Books, 2015.

Hofstadter, Douglas R., and Emmanuel Sander. *Surfaces and Essences: Analogy as the Fuel and Fire of Thinking.* New York: Basic Books, 2013.

Holmes, Nigel. *Designer's Guide to Creating Charts & Diagrams.* New York: Watson-Guptill Publications, 1984.

Holmes, Nigel. *The Best in Diagrammatic Graphics.* London: Quarto Publishing, 1993.

Howard, Ronald A. "Information Value Theory." *IEEE Transactions On Systems Science and Cybernetics* 2, no. 1 (1966): 22–34.

Huff, Darrell. *How to Lie with Statistics.* New York: W.W. Norton & Company, 1954.

Isaacson, Walter. *The Innovators: How a Group of Hackers, Geniuses, and Geeks Created the Digital Revolution.* London: Simon & Schuster, 2014.

Izenman, Alan Julian. "Recent Developments in Nonparametric Density Estimation." *Journal of the American Statistical Association* 86, no. 413 (1991): 205–224.

Johansson, Frans. *The Medici Effect: What Elephants and Epidemics Can Teach Us about Innovation.* Boston: Harvard Business Review Press, 2006.

Johnson, Steven. *Wonderland: How Play Made The Modern World.* New York: Riverhead Books, 2016.

Jung, Carl G., ed. *Man and His Symbols.* London: Aldus Books, 1964.

Kapitaniak, M., J. Strzalko, J. Grabski, and T. Kapitaniak. "The Three-Dimensional Dynamics of the Die Throw." *Chaos* 22, no. 047504 (2012).

Katz, Steven D. *Film Directing Shot by Shot: Visualizing from Concept to Screen.* Studio City, CA: Michael Wiese Productions, 1991.

Kent, Sherman. "Words of Estimative Probability." *CIA Studies In Intelligence*, Fall 1964.

Keynes, John Maynard. *A Treatise on Probability.* London: Macmillan and Co., 1921.

King, Martin L. "I Have a Dream." Speech presented at the March on Washington for Jobs and Freedom, Washington, D.C., August 1963.

King, Stephen. *On Writing: A Memoir of the Craft*. New York: Scribner, 2000.

Kirk, Andy. *Data Visualisation: A Handbook for Data Driven Design*. Los Angeles, CA: Sage Publications, 2016.

Kling, Arnold S. "The Practitioner's Challenge." The Library of Economics and Liberty. Jul 3, 2017, http://www.econlib.org/library/Columns/y2017/KlingBookstaber.html.

Kling, Arnold S. *The Three Languages of Politics*. Washington, DC: Cato Institute, 2017.

Knaflic, Cole Nussbaumer. *Storytelling with Data: A Data Visualization Guide for Business Professionals*. Hoboken, NJ: Wiley, 2015.

Kolbert, Elizabeth. "Why Facts Don't Change Our Minds." The New Yorker Magazine. Feb 27, 2017, https://www.newyorker.com/magazine/2017/02/27/why-facts-dont-change-our-minds.

Lakoff, George, and Mark Johnson. *Metaphors We Live by*. Chicago: University of Chicago Press, 1980.

Lakoff, George, and Rafael E. Núñez. *Where Mathematics Comes From: How the Embodied Mind Brings Mathematics into Being*. New York: Basic Books, 2000.

Langdon, John. *Wordplay*. New York: Broadway Books, 2005.

Le Guin, Ursula. *Dancing At The Edge Of The World: Thoughts on Words, Women, Places*. New York: Grove Press, 1989.

Levasseur, Pierre Émile. "La Statistique Graphique." In *Jubilee Volume of the Statistical Society* (1885), translated by RJ Andrews. London: Harrison and Sons, 1885.

Levine, Marvin. "You-Are-Here-Maps: Psychological Considerations." *Environment And Behavior* 14, no. 2 (1982): 221–237.

Levins, Melissa. "The Origins of the Mathematical Convention of Using "X" as the Unknown." Today I Found Out. Nov 11, 2014, http://www.todayifoundout.com/index.php/2014/11/origins-mathematical-convenTION-usING-x-unknown/.

Lidwell, William, Kritina Holden, and Jill Butler. *The Pocket Universal Principles of Design*. Beverly, MA: Rockport Publishers, 2015.

Lippincott, Kristen, ed. *The Story of Time*. London: Merrell Holberton, 1999.

Loewenstein, George. "The Psychology of Curiosity: A Review and Reinterpretation." *Psychological Bulletin* 116, no. 1 (1994): 75–98.

Lucas, George. Interview. CBS This Morning, Jul 3, 2013, https://youtu.be/vacSFe7DhC8.

Lucas, George. *Star Wars to Jedi: The Making of a Saga*. Documentary Film. Written by Richard Schickel. Lucasfilm, 1983.

Lupi, Giorgia. "Data Humanism: The Revolutionary Future of Data Visualization." Print Magazine. Jan 30, 2017, http://www.printmag.com/information-design/data-humanism-future-of-data-visualization/.

Lupton, Ellen. *How Posters Work*. New York: Cooper Hewitt, Smithsonian Design Museum, 2015.

Lupton, Ellen. *Design Is Storytelling*. New York: Cooper Hewitt, Smithsonian Design Museum, 2017.

Malamed, Connie. "The Visual Language of Dashed Lines." Understanding Graphics. 2012, http://understandinggraphics.com/brainy/the-visual-language-of-dashed-lines/.

Malamed, Connie. *Visual Language for Designers: Principles for Creating Graphics That People Understand*. Beverly, MA: Rockport Publishers, 2009.

Marey, Étienne-Jules. *La Méthode Graphique Dans Les Sciences Expérimentales: Et Principalement en Physiologie et en Médecine,* edited by G. Masson. Paris: Libraire de l'Académie de Médecine, 1885.

Marincola, Paula, ed. *What Makes a Great Exhibition?* London: Reaktion Books, 2006.

Mattern, Shannon. "Gaps In The Map: Why We're Mapping Everything, And Why Not Everything Can, Or Should, Be Mapped." Words In Space. Sep 18, 2015, http://wordsinspace.net/shannon/2015/09/18/gaps-in-the-map-why-were-mappING-everythING-and-why-not-everythING-can-or-should-be-mapped/.

Mazur, Joseph. *Enlightening Symbols: A Short History of Mathematical Notation and Its Hidden Powers*. Princeton, NJ:: Princeton University Press, 2014.

McCloud, Scott. *Making Comics: Storytelling Secrets of Comics, Manga and Graphic Novels*. New York: Harper, 2006.

McCloud, Scott. *Understanding Comics: The Invisible Art*. New York: William Morrow, 1993.

McPhee, John. *Draft No. 4*. New York: Farrar, Straus and Giroux, 2017.

Meeks, Elijah. "Viz Palette for Data Visualization Color." Towards Data Science. Apr 20, 2018, https://towardsdatascience.com/viz-palette-for-data-visualization-color-8e678d996077.

Meert, Katrien, Mario Pandelaere, and Vanessa Patrick. "Taking A Shine To It: How the Preference For Glossy Stems From An Innate Need For Water." *Journal of Consumer Psychology* 24, no. 2 (2014): 195–206.

Meggs, Philip B., and Alston W. Purvis. *Meggs' History of Graphic Design*, 6th Edition. Hoboken, NJ: Wiley, 2016.

Meirelles, Isabel. *Design For Information: An Introduction to the Histories, Theories, and Best Practices Behind Effective Information Visualizations*. Beverle, MA: Rockport Publishers, 2013.

Menninger, Karl. *Number Words and Number Symbols: A Cultural History of Numbers*, Translated by Paul Broneer. Cambridge, MA: MIT Press, 1969.

Miller, George. "The Magical Number Seven, Plus or Minus Two: Some Limits on our Capacity for Processing Information." *Psychological Review* 63 (1956): 81–97.

Moore, Terry. "Why Is 'X' the Unknown?" Speech. TED2012, Feb 2012, https://www.ted.com/talks/terry_moore_why_is_x_the_unknown.

Munari, Bruno. *Design As Art*, Translated by Patrick Creagh. London: Pelican Books, 1971.

Munzer, Tamara. *Visualization Analysis & Design*. Boca Raton: CRC Press, 2014.

Murphy, James T. "Building Trust In Economic Space." *Progress in Human Geography* 30, no. 4 (2006): 427–450.

Neurath, Marie, and Robin Kinross. *The Transformer: Principles of Making Isotype Charts*. London: Hyphen Press, 2009.

Neyman, Jerzy. "Outline of a Theory of Statistical Estimation Based on the Classical Theory of Probability." *Philosophical Transactions of the Royal Society of London. Series A, Mathematical and Physical Sciences* 236, no. 767 (1937): 333-380."

Norman, Don. *The Design of Everyday Things: Revised and Expanded Edition*. New York: Basic Books, 2013.

O'Connor, Flannery. *Mystery And Manners: Occasional Prose*, edited by Sally Fitzgerald and Robert Fitzgerald. New York: Farrar, Straus and Giroux, 1969.

Obrist, Hans Ulrich. *Ways Of Curating*. New York: Farrar, Straus and Giroux, 2014.

Ogilvy, David. *Ogilvy on Advertising*. New York: Random House, 1985.

Orwell, George. "Politics and the English Language." *Horizon* 13, no. 76 (1946): 252–265.

Peirce, Charles Sander. *The Essential Peirce: Selected Philosophical Writings Volume 2 (1893–1913)*. Bloomington, IN: Indiana University Press, 1998.

Perec, Georges. *Thoughts of Sorts*, Translated by David Bellos. London: Notting Hill, 2011.

Peterson, Jordan. "The Psychology of the Flood." Lecture. Isabel Bader Theatre, Toronto, performed June 27, 2017, https://youtu.be/wNjbasba-Qw.

Pinker, Steven. *The Sense of Style*. New York: Penguin, 2014.

Pirolli, Peter, and Stuart Card. "Information Foraging." *Psychological Review* 106, no. 4 (1999): 643–675.

Plato. *The Republic of Plato*, Translated by Allan Bloom. New York: Basic Books, 1968.

Playfair, William. "The Commercial and Political Atlas (1786)." In *The Commercial and Political Atlas and Statistical Breviary*, edited and introduced by Howard Wainer and Ian Spence. Cambridge: Cambridge University Press, 2005.

Playfair, William. "The Statistical Breviary (1801)." In *The Commercial and Political Atlas and Statistical Breviary*, edited and introduced by Howard Wainer and Ian Spence. Cambridge: Cambridge University Press, 2005.

Popper, Karl R. *The Logic of Scientific Discovery*. London: Hutchinson & Co., 1959.

Prigogine, Ilya. *Order out of Chaos: Man's New Dialogue with Nature*. London: Bantam, 1984.

Prigogine, Ilya. *Art Meets Science and Spirituality, The Chaotic Universe*. Documentary Film. Directected by Maxine Harris. 1990, https://www.youtube.com/watch?v=y4AnTsB-OsQ.

Prigogine, Ilya. *The End of Certainty: Time, Chaos, and the New Laws of Nature*. New York: Free Press, 1996.

Pyhrr, Stuart W. *Of Arms and Men: Arms and Armor at the Metropolitan 1912–2012*. New York: The Metropolitan Museum of Art Bulletin, 2012.

Quiller-Couch, Arthur. *On The Art Of Writing: Lectures delivered in the University of Cambridge, 1913–1914*. Cambridge: Cambridge University Press, 1916.

Rao, Venkatesh. "Boat Stories." Ribbon Farm. Jan 9, 2018, https://www.ribbonfarm.com/2018/01/09/boat-stories/.

Raymo, Chet. *Skeptics and True Believers: The Exhilarating Connection between Science and Religion*. New York: MJF Books, 1998.

Roam, Dan. *Draw to Win: A Crash Course on How to Lead, Sell, and Innovate with Your Visual Mind*. New York: Portfolio/Penguin, 2016.

Rodman, Selden. *Conversations With Artists*. New York: Devin-Adair Co., 1957.

Rogers, Simon. *Facts Are Sacred: The Power of Data*. London: Faber and Faber Limited, 2013.

Roorda, Austin, and David R. Williams. "The Arrangement of the Three Cone Classes in the Living Human Eye." *Nature* 397, no. 6719 (1999): 520-522.

Roosevelt, Theodore. "Citizenship In A Republic." Speech. Sorbonne, Paris, April 23, 1910.

Rosling, Hans. *Factfulness: Ten Reasons We're Wrong About The World—And Why Things Are Better Than You Think*, with Ola Rosling and Anna Rosling Rönnlund. New York: Flatiron Books, 2018.

Rumsey, Abby Smith. *When We Are No More: How Digital Memory Is Shaping Our Future*. New York: Bloomsbury Press, 2016.

Russell, Bertrand. "Is There a God? (1952)." In *The Collected Papers of Bertrand Russell, Vol. 11: Last Philosophical Testament, 1943–68*, edited by John Slater and Peter Köllner, 542–548. London: Routledge, 1997.

Savage, Sam L. *The Flaw of Averages: Why We Underestimate Risk in the Face of Uncertainty.* Hoboken, NJ: John Wiley & Sons, Inc., 2009.

Shahn, Ben. *The Shape of Content.* Cambridge, MA: Harvard University Press, 1957.

Shlain, Leonard. *The Alphabet versus the Goddess: The Conflict between Word and Image.* New York: Viking, 1998.

Silver, Nate. *The Signal and the Noise: The Art and Science of Prediction.* London: Penguin, 2013.

Simmon, Rob. "Subtleties of Color." NASA Earth Observatory: Elegant Figures. Aug 5, 2013, https://earthobservatory.nasa.gov/blogs/elegantfigures/2013/08/05/subtleties-of-color-part-1-of-6/.

Sklar, Howard. "Believable Fictions: The Moral Implications of Story-Based Emotions." In *Cognition and Literary Interpretation in Practice,* edited by Harri Veivo, Bo Pettersson, and Merja Polvinen, 157–182. Helsinki: Yliopistopaino, 2005.

Sousanis, Nick. *Unflattening.* Cambridge, MA: Harvard University Press, 2015.

Sparavigna, Amelia Carolina. "The Solar Orientation Of The Gothic Cathedrals Of France." *International Journal of Sciences* 3, no. 4 (2014): 6–11.

Spear, Mary Eleanor. *Practical Charting Techniques.* New York: McGraw-Hill, 1969.

Steinbeck, John. *East of Eden.* New York: Viking, 1952.

Stevens, Wallace. "Three Academic Pieces: I." In *The Necessary Angel,* by Wallace Stevens, 71–82. New York: Alfred A. Knopf, 1951.

Stigler, Stephen M. *The Seven Pillars of Statistical Wisdom.* Cambridge, MA: Harvard University Press, 2016.

Stone, Maureen C. *A Field Guide to Digital Color.* Natick, MA: AK Peters, 2003.

Stuart, Gilbert. "The Commercial and Political Atlas." *The Political Herald* 3, (1786): 299–306.

Tenenbaum, Joshua B., C. Kemp, T. Griffiths, and N. Goodman. "How To Grow A Mind: Statistics, Structure, and Abstraction." *Science* 331 (2011): 1279–1285.

Tetlock, Philip E., and Dan Gardner. *Superforecasting: The Art and Science of Prediction.* New York: Crown Publishers, 2015.

The New York Times. "Award Brings U.S. A Sweep Of Honors." Oct 22, 1976.

Thoreau, Henry David. *A Week On The Concord And Merrimack Rivers.* Boston: James Munroe and Company, 1849.

Tolkien, J.R.R. *The Hobbit.* London: George Allen & Unwin, 1937.

Tolkien, J.R.R. *Tree and Leaf: Including Mythopoeia.* London: George Allen & Unwin, 1964.

Treisman, Anne, and Stephen Gormican. "Feature Analysis in Early Vision: Evidence From Search Asymmetries." *Psychological Review* 95, no. 1 (1988): 15–48.

Truffault, François. *Hitchcock*, Revised Edition. New York: Simon & Schuster, Inc, 1983.

Tufte, Edward R. *Envisioning Information.* Cheshire, CT: Graphics Press, 1990.

Tufte, Edward R. *Visual Explanations.* Cheshire, CT: Graphics Press, 1997.

Tufte, Edward R. *The Visual Display of Quantitative Information: Second Edition.* Cheshire, CT: Graphics Press, 2001.

Tukey, John. "Some Graphic and Semigraphic Displays." In *Statistical Papers in Honor of George W. Snedecor*, edited by T.A. Bancroft, 293–316. Ames, IA: Iowa State University Press, 1972.

Tukey, John. *Exploratory Data Analysis*. Reading, MA: Addison-Wesley, 1977.

Tversky, Barbara. "The Cognitive Design Of Tools Of Thought." *Review of Philosophy and Psychology* 6, no. 1 (2015): 99–116.

Valéry, Paul. *Selected Writings*, Translated by Malcolm Cowley et al. New York: New Directions Publishing Corporation, 1950.

Van Strien, J. W., and L.A. Isbell. "Snake scales, partial exposure, and the Snake Detection Theory: A human event-related potentials study." *Scientific Reports* 7, Article number: 46331 (2017).

Voltaire. "Letter to Frederick William, Prince of Prussia, Nov 28, 1770." In *Voltaire in His Letters*, edited by S.G. Tallentyre. New York: G.P. Putnam's Sons, 1919.

Voltaire. *Micromegas*, Translated by Peter Phalen. Paris: A. Firmin Didot, 1829.

Wainer, Howard. *Visual Revelations: Graphical Tales of Fate and Deception from Napoleon Bonaparte to Ross Perot*. Mahwah, NJ: Lawrence Erlbaum Associates, 1997.

Wainer, Howard. *Graphic Discovery: A Trout in the Milk and Other Visual Adventures*. Princeton, NJ: Princeton University Press, 2005.

Wainer, Howard. *Picturing the Uncertain World: How to Understand, Communicate, and Control Uncertainty through Graphical Display*. Princeton, NJ: Princeton University Press, 2009.

Wainer, Howard, email messages to author, Apr, 2017–August, 2018.

Ware, Colin. *Visual Thinking for Design*. Burlington, MA: Elsevier Morgan Kaufmann Publishers, 2008.

Washington, Booker T. *Up From Slavery: An Autobiography*. New York: A.L. Burt Company, 1901.

Wexler, Steve, Jeffrey Shaffer, and Andy Cotgreave. *The Big Book of Dashboards: Visualizing Your Data Using Real-World Business Scenarios*. Hoboken, NJ: John Wiley & Sons, Inc., 2017.

Wilkinson, Leland. *The Grammar of Graphics*, Second Edition. New York: Springer, 2005.

Wilkinson, Leland, and Graham Wills. "Scagnostics Distributions." *Journal of Computational and Graphical Statistics* 17, no. 2 (2008): 473–491.

Wilson, E.O. *Consilience: The Unity of Knowledge*. New York: Knopf, 1998.

Wong, Dona M. *The Wall Street Journal Guide to Information Graphics: The Do's and Don'ts of Presenting Data, Facts, and Figures*. New York: W.W. Norton & Company, 2010.

Wu, Tim. *The Attention Merchants: The Epic Scramble to Get Inside Our Heads*. New York: Alfred A. Knopf, 2016.

Yau, Nathan. *Visualize This: The FlowingData Guide to Design, Visualization, and Statistics*. Indianapolis: Wiley Publishing, Inc., 2011.

Yau, Nathan. *Data Points: Visualization That Means Something*. Indianapolis: John Wiley & Sons, Inc., 2013.

Zander, Rosamund Stone, and Benjamin Zander. *The Art of Possibility*. Boston: Harvard Business School Press, 2000.

Ziemkiewicz, Caroline. "Understanding The Structure of Information Visualization Through Visual Metaphors." PhD diss., The University of North Carolina at Charlotte, 2010.

INDEX

Blue page numbers indicate terms in marginal notes.

Buddha, xii
Buddhist philosophy, 42

C

distance-number metaphor in, 48–49

fractions in, 46, 48

length measurements and, 47, 47

length-number metaphor in, 47–48

newborns and, 93

object-number metaphor in, 46

systems for, 16–18

timelines and, 52–53

Courage, 10

Creationism, 170

Creation myths, 4, 52

Creative Routines (poster), 3

Creativity, 173, 198, 200–201

Credible interval, 118

Cruciform plans, 176–177, 196

Curie, Marie, 204

Curiosity

data exploration and, 104

design thinking and, 29–30

human nature with, 138, 173

information gap theory of, 38

as motivated search for answers, 15, 37

museum layouts and labels and, 127, 131, 132

novelty in design and, 152

storytelling and, 138–140

variety of projects maintained with, 198–199

visuals arousing, 145

Currey, Mason, 3

D

Daily Rituals (Currey), 3

Dashboard design, 10

Data

context and material origins of, 14, 22

daily rituals of creative people and, 3

digital production of, 26–27

effective presentation of facts in, 29

encoding in a visual form, 42–44

endangered species and, 2

energy of, 190

hero's journey as metaphor for encounters with, 7, 7, 9, 36, 121, 205

importance of learning human side and origins of, 28–29

information differentiated from, 30

meaningful information made with, 4

metaphors for visualizing, 19, 58, 68

polar and rectangular mental maps and, 64

reality as flow of, 56

relationships and nodes in portraying, 65

superficial contradiction between *story* and, 6–7

tabular arrangement of. *See* Tables

Unicode encoding of, 30

value creation and new sources of, 27

Databases, 19–20

Data exploration, 89–110, 176

changed approach for finding new ways of seeing in, 104

comparisons for, 92–94

data sketches for, 90–91, 98

mean (average) in, 97

median in, 98, 98

patterns for, 95–98

profiles of data in, 100–101

reordering data in, 102–104

transforming data in, 104–108

Data sketches

climate example of, 109

methods used in, 90–92, 91, 98

trust in, 110

Data storage

evolution of, 26

location and types in, 19–20, 19

mental models in, 20

tables for, 20, 31, 34

value types in, 18, 18, 19

Data stories, 4–10

context needed for, 14, 20–21

conveying information using, 4, 6, 207

critics of, 206–207

design of, 133–142

exploring and studying, 202

fictive motion in, 49

helmets illustration as example of, 8–9

hero's struggles and, 5–6, 5

interdisciplinary nature of, 9–10

mind's eye in, 42

narrative model for, 205–206

superficial contradiction between *data* and *story* in, 6–7

ways of packaging, 186

Data storytellers

as heroes, 9, 10, 11, 164–165

individual perspectives and context of, 15

trust and, 172

Forster, E.M., 140, 141

Fractions, 17, 46

France, cathedrals in, 177–178, 188, 194

Freedom From Fear (Rockwell), 144

French language, 95, 198

Frequentism, 114

Fry, Stephen, 172

Fukuyama, Francis, 171

Future time, perception of, 50, 51, 55

G

Gabler, Neal, 136

Gaby, Alice, 55

Gantt, Henry, 56

Gantt charts, 56

Gardner, Dan, 115

Gautama Buddha, xii

Geary, James, 41, 55, 152

Gemini program (NASA), 92, 93

Gemowe lines, 32

Genesis (Bible book), xii–xiii, 52

Geographic maps, 74, 161, 184

Geometric representations, conveying information using, 158

Géométrie, La (Descartes), 61

Gesamtkunstwerk, 132

Gestalt, 149

Gestalt effects, 147, 148

Gestalt psychology, 147

Gesture drawings, 90

Gettysburg Address (Lincoln), 16

Glass, Ira, 187

Globes, maps and curved surface of, 60, 63, 180

Goldman, William, 139, 168, 197, 200, 200

Gordon, J.E., 159

Graphicacy, 43, 43

Graphic design, 143–150. *See also* Visual design

    advertisements and, 144–145, 144, 145

    characters in, 144

    chunking information in, 147–148, 190

    grids in, 145

    guidelines for, 146–147

    power of story and, 143

    superficial decoration versus, 145, 145

    trade-offs in, 148

    World War II poster example of, 143

Graphical information. *See also* Charts

    helmets illustration as example of, 8–9

horizontal dimension and, 68, 69, 69

importance related to size in, 43–44, 72

individual fields with concept of and standards for, 9

proportion and, 44

shapes used in, 74–78

skill in using, 43

smaller shapes assembled into bigger patterns in, 77–78

three-dimensional volume on, 76–77

up direction and vertical dimension and, 68–69, 68, 69

Graphs

    dashed line on, 71

    metaphor of display in, 43

    node-link networks on, 65–66

    scales used in, 71, 71

    time shown on, 70–71

Graunt, John, 25–26, 27, 31

Greece, Ancient, xi, 17, 26, 61, 104, 127, 128

Greek language, xi, 33, 40, 41, 61, 107, 120, 149

Gregorian calendar, 52

Grids, in graphic design, 145

Guy, William A., 25

H

Hammett, Dashiell, 20

Hangul Korean alphabet, 149

Harari, Yuval Noah, 24, 56, 63

Harmonograf, 56

Hawaiian language, 44

Helmets, illustration on evolution of, 8–9

Heroes

    collective body of knowledge expanded by, 6

    data storytellers as, 9, 10, 11, 164–165

    dragons and monsters of abyss confronted by, 5–6, 5

    journey of, as metaphor for encounters with data, 7, 7, 9, 36, 121, 205

    narrative model for, 205

    time-series progression of, 70

Hidalgo, César, 56, 126, 140

Highlighting

    color for, 81, 83, 86

    line weight in charts for, 32

    navigation using, 130, 149

    spans of time with, 56

Hill, George Roy, 187

Hindu-Arabic numeral system, 16, 17

Visual design. *See also* Graphic design
    austerity in, 154
    creating effortless experiences for viewer in, 44
    emotional design and, 151–152, 153, 155–156
    perception of numbers and, 46
    perceptual effects and, 87
    readability of data in tables and, 31
    relationships between centers and wholes in, 154–155, 155
    roughness preference in, 153–154, 153
    rules and conventions in, 42, 43
    spacing in, 31
    spatial biases in, 69
    texture in, 154
    trade-offs in, 42–43
    trust and, 171–174
Visual cognition, color categories in, 41, 82, 83, 88, 147
Visualization, 9, 10, 42
    creating effortless experiences for viewer in, 44
    mind's eye in, 42
    reading using, 41–42
Visual metaphors
    graphical display and, 43
    importance related to size in, 43–44
    meaning conveyed by, 68
    power relationships shown with, 64
    shared common set of, 43
    similarity and physical closeness in, 44
    visualizing data using, 19, 58, 68
Visual world, 57–66
    children and, 43
    common set of visual metaphors in, 43
    conveying information within, 68
    correlation between body's physical experience and perception in, 44
    decoding (interpreting) data in, 43, 44
    encoding data for, 42–44
    importance related to size in, 43–44
    maps as, 61
    mental cinema and, 42
    mind's eye and, 42
    proportion and, 44
    similarity related to physical closeness in, 44
    spatial diagrams in, 58–61
    stimulus strength and perception in, 42–43, 42
Voltaire, 39, 111

W

Wagner, Richard, 5, 132
Wainer, Howard, 14, 29, 31, 31, 43, 74, 91, 104, 106, 120, 149, 154, 189, 190, 205
Waismann, Friedrich, 117
Walton, Tony, 152
Ware, Colin, 90, 130, 145, 147, 149, 186
Washington, Booker T., 173
Wheat, symbolism of, 24
When We Are No More (Rumsey), 21
Wilson, E.O., 37
Wong, Dona, 50, 71

X Y Z

x, in mathematics, 61

"Young Earth" creationism, 170

Zander, Benjamin, 5, 205
Zander, Rosamund Stone, 5, 205
Zero
    baseline in charts with, 71, 73
    distance-number metaphor and, 49–50
    length measurements and, 48
    object-number metaphor in, 46
Zulu language, 44

©Elizabeth Andrews

RJ Andrews is a data storyteller. He wrote, illustrated, and designed this book in San Francisco. See more at InfoWeTrust.com.